Communication Ethics, Media, & Popular Culture

D1519697

Toby Miller
General Editor

Vol. 9

PETER LANG
New York • Washington, D.C./Baltimore • Bern
Frankfurt am Main • Berlin • Brussels • Vienna • Oxford

Communication Ethics, Media, & Popular Culture

Phyllis M. Japp, Mark Meister,
& Debra K. Japp, Editors

PETER LANG
New York • Washington, D.C./Baltimore • Bern
Frankfurt am Main • Berlin • Brussels • Vienna • Oxford

Library of Congress Cataloging-in-Publication Data
Communication ethics, media, and popular culture /
edited by Phyllis M. Japp, Mark Meister, Debra K. Japp.
p. cm. — (Popular culture and everyday life; v. 9)
Includes bibliographical references and index.
1. Mass media—Moral and ethical aspects. 2. Popular culture.
I. Japp, Phyllis M. II. Meister, Mark. III. Japp, Debra K.
IV. Series: Popular culture & everyday life; v. 9.
P94.C5725   175—dc22   2004027922
ISBN 0-8204-7119-4
ISSN 1529-2428

Bibliographic information published by **Die Deutsche Bibliothek.**
Die Deutsche Bibliothek lists this publication in the "Deutsche
Nationalbibliografie"; detailed bibliographic data is available
on the Internet at http://dnb.ddb.de/.

Cover design by Joni Holst

© 2005 Peter Lang Publishing, Inc., New York
275 Seventh Avenue, 28th Floor, New York, NY 10001
www.peterlangusa.com

CONTENTS

Communication Ethics, Media, and Popular Culture: An Introduction

Phyllis M. Japp, Mark Meister, and Debra K. Japp

A sports celebrity makes a racist comment, a government official decides to tell the "truth" (that truth being that what he or she said earlier was untrue), news organizations debate whether or not to show images of the brutality of war, and on national television the "F" word slips past an entertainer's lips and a female breast pops free of its restraints. Few would deny that these examples raise issues of ethical communication. What is right or wrong, should or should not be communicated, approved, or censured? Yet for every instance that raises conscious awareness of ethical issues, multitudes of communicative messages slip below our ethical radar. If we invoke communication ethics only in cases of flagrant violations of social norms, we miss an important point—the fact that the ethical dimension is an inherent, necessary, and inescapable dimension of all communication behavior. Communication scholars are fond of saying that we cannot *not* communicate, a cryptic phrase that, translated, means that all our behaviors, even those of which we may be unconscious, hold the potential for imputation of meaning. What we say or don't say, engage or ignore, the words and images we choose, our preferences and disinclinations, can be "read" as communicative messages by others, without our permission or even without our knowledge. Moreover, these readings are evaluative; that is, they embody perceptions of character, attributions of the rightness or wrongness of our actions. This book is an invitation to engage the ethical dimensions of mediated popular culture. Our introductory chapter defines the major concepts, "communication ethics" and "popular culture," explains the theoretical orientation of the authors, and previews the range of ideas and applications that follow.

Although definitions of both *communication* and *ethics* abound, there are few concise definitions of what the term *communication ethics* means and what it includes. Obviously the term suggests that ethics is an aspect of the practice of communication but leaves open for discussion when and where that ethical element may be operative. And although there are shelves of books on the nature, scope, and source of ethics, what is the role of ethics in the process of communication? To cut through the complexity, a simple definition seems best. Richard Johannesen (2001) writes, "Matters of ethics, of degrees of rightness and wrongness, virtue and vice, and moral obligation, I believe, are inherent in the human communication process" (p. 202). By this definition it would seem that all instances of communication, from interpersonal to mediated, are subject to ethical inquiry. Johannesen continues, "It seems to me that the human communication process is a paradigm of human behavior that inherently involves matters of ethics, no matter how we resolve them or even whether we face them" (p. 202). And perhaps even if we may be unaware of them.

As Johannesen asserts, all forms, contexts, and instances of communication are infused with ethical dimensions. Certainly some communicative behaviors seem more loaded with ethical implications than others, especially if undertaken intentionally. Deliberately lying in a public statement is more potently unethical by most standards than unintentionally glossing over aspects of truth in the attempt to win acceptance or approval. Yet both are open to assessment of ethical responsibility, although the first may involve a conscious intent to deceive and the second "merely" an unconscious editing of information to serve one's own ends. The ethical impact of the former may be immediate; the impact of the multitudes who practice the latter on a daily basis may be less easy to assess but perhaps greater in the long run.

Johannesen's definition asserts that concern with the ethical requires judgments about the moral implications of communication.
Judgments, however, imply the presence of criteria by which we
can evaluate the worth or quality of what we see and hear. Failure
to recognize the standards by which we are evaluating does not
mean we have none; we all constantly make implicit or explicit attributions of value based on our internalized criteria, however well
or poorly articulated these may be. In some cases ethical standards
are consciously foregrounded and grow from our philosophical,
religious, or group orientations. In other cases, they may be based
on unconscious adherence to social norms or even on individual
emotion and desires. "Thou shalt not steal" is a religious ethical imperative, while "Take what you can get away with" is an accepted
social norm in some circles. Yet both are standards used to justify
the rightness or wrongness, vice or virtue, of our own and others'
actions. Acknowledging the range and variety of standards does not
mean that ethics reduces to whatever an individual determines to
be ethical; rather that as human actors we necessarily invoke standards when we make judgments of ourselves and others. It should
go without saying that some standards are better than others;
that is, they are more conducive to the development of high-quality
personal and communal life. A standard that respects others' property is likely to create better relationships, families, and communities than one that allows taking whatever hasn't been explicitly
forbidden.

Thus, inquiry into what it means to communicate ethically
invites consideration of all communicative behaviors. The essays
in this book are based on the following assumptions about the relationship of communication and ethics. First, ethical dimensions
are present in all instances of communication. All communication,
verbal and nonverbal, any actions or situations where meaning
can be constructed and shared, possesses the potential to affect self
and other and therefore is open to ethical reflection on the means,
manner, and outcomes of that communication for good or ill. Even
if communication is not intentional or consciously strategic, it requires consideration of the ethical. Conscious and deliberative
ethical choices may determine the amount of responsibility we can

assign to a communicator, but even unintentional behaviors can impact others and therefore can be assessed for the ethical components of that communication.

Second, the ethical dimensions of communicative behaviors are constructed dialogically, negotiated in the communication process. Communicators bring their explicit or implicit, conscious or unconscious, standards and values to every communication situation. There they engage the standards and values of others. Thus, ethical meanings are determined in the situated dialogic interactions among communicators. Certainly this does not suggest that agreement equals rightness. A pact to deceive, however firmly agreed upon, cannot be called ethical. But we all know that one can be truthful and yet be perceived as lying; one can be deceitful and be perceived as truthful because what is accepted as true is so because of tacit agreement among the communicators. A "successful" liar requires those who accept the lie, co-define its meaning, and support its justification.

Finally, if we pay attention only to those communication situations that overtly address ethical issues, we miss the import of the subtle, incremental, cumulative messages that surround us in our daily lives. It is, in fact, the meta-messages internalized by constant exposure to ideas, values, and ways of life that construct for most of us the "everyday ethic" we use as a standard to determine what we find acceptable and unacceptable.

What Is Popular Culture?

The focus on everyday ethics makes popular culture an ideal arena for consideration of communication ethics, as they are enacted in daily life and displayed in everyday knowledge. *Popular culture* proves as difficult to define as *communication ethics* for the opposite reason—definitions abound and are quite different depending on the theoretical orientation within which they are generated. Again a simple definition suffices. Barry Brummett (1994) defines popular culture as the "systems of meaning and/or artifacts that most people share and that most people know about," part of the "everyday knowledge and experiences of most people" (p. 21). Certainly "popular" suggests materials and practices accessible to and circulating among a people, while the concept of "culture" denotes the connections formed by a common core of shared meanings. Thus, popular culture provides us with our everyday knowledge about things around us and what they mean; it is the vast context of communicative messages within which people understand themselves and others, enact what they believe to be important, and embody their ethic of living.

Brummett's definition allows for varying degrees of knowledge, attachment, involvement, and attitudes. As Mark Meister and Phyllis M. Japp (2002) note:

> Whether one loves rap music or hates it, few are totally unaware of its existence.... Most people shop at least occasionally in shopping malls, purchase greeting cards, decorate homes on holidays, and participate in other common cultural practices. They read popular advice literature, listen to music, engage in celebrations, play games, and view advertising. This vast domain of popular culture, then, includes what we read, watch, wear, use, play with, talk about, argue about over time and with enough consistency to form conscious and unconscious impressions of various aspects of life. (pp. 4–5)

From this informal knowledge, we absorb the values and ideas that seem to be emphasized in our culture, learn what is generally understood to be acceptable or unacceptable. Although communication ethics are invoked in all such practices and activities, most of the analyses that follow address some form of mediated popular culture (for example, television, sports, popular news, film, the Internet); thus the following discussion focuses primarily on popular culture as shaped and communicated via media.

Ethical Engagement of Mediated Popular Culture

Many observers charge that mediated popular culture, especially television, is an ethical void, shallow, market-driven, and formulaic. Given the pressures of the marketplace and the conventions of entertainment media—time constraints, need for drama, action, sexual titillation, demand for quick resolution, fear of offending sponsors, investors, and others—popular news and entertainment exhibit little moral complexity, and thus cannot be a sufficient arena for ethical exploration. Programming allows insufficient time or space for moral reflection; all problems must be resolved within the parameters of the program, film, or page limit. Given these constraints mediated popular culture seems ethically challenged at best, actively immoral at worst.

So why turn to this venue rather than, for example, classic literature to explore ethical communication? There are two compelling reasons that mandate attention to mediated popular culture, the first of which is familiarity. Popular media, for good or ill, has become our cultural thesaurus of everyday life, often the only common frame of reference across race, gender, class, and other social divides. Popular culture appears to have replaced religious texts, literary classics, history, ritual, and oral tradition as the source for immediately recognizable examples. Because we understand new life situations by their connections to old ones, plots, analogies, phrases, proverbs, and metaphors from familiar sources provide a "shorthand" that allows us to fill in the particulars and quickly categorize immediate happenings. Those of us who teach have discovered that classroom references to classic literature or history are met with blank stares—we must either recite the whole plot of a novel or provide a description of a past event or fail utterly to make the desired point. But a line from *Seinfeld*, a slogan from advertising, a plot from a sitcom, or reference to a character from a popular film are instantly understood by many.

The second mandate for working with mediated popular culture is contemporaneity. Popular mediated culture mirrors the world in which we live, demonstrates the difficulties of discovering and maintaining ethical standards in a postmodern, mediated, commercialized culture. If ethics seems a lacuna in much of popular media, so it often seems in contemporary life. Few of us lead epic lives, hold to unvarying moral dictates, or even spend much time in moral reflection. Instead we lurch from idea to idea, place to place, occupation to occupation, each move requiring some readjustment of our identities and identifications, revisions of our expectations and assumptions. Yet in our fast-paced world, we seldom take adequate time to make those adjustments. More so than we may want to admit, our lives resemble Jerry Seinfeld's rather than Hamlet's, and are filled with a multitude of small ethical problems rather than the profound moral dilemmas of literary kings or gods.

In our lives, as in the worlds of popular media, everything is simultaneously oversimplified and complexified. On the one hand, we are awash in simplifications—"Just do it," or "Just say no"— that reduce complex moral issues to clichés and advertising slogans and promise quick and easy moral decisions absent reflection or soul searching. On the other hand, everything in the contemporary world as refracted by popular media is becoming more and more complex. The fragile balance of global economies in multicultural worlds, the conflicting claims on limited environmental resources, the seemingly unlimited choices of services and products, images and ideas, can quickly create moral paralysis. We seem often to be choosing what we hope is the least damaging alternative, because every action or inaction can potentially hurt someone, sometime, somewhere. Few of our beloved classic literary heroes wandered through such bewildering thickets on their way to locating moral positions.

Unfortunately, mediated popular culture seldom stops to reflect on its moral dimensions. One seldom sees explicit struggles with ethical principles—"Shall I lie to this person?" or "What is fair in this situation?" This is especially true in visual media, where the moral soliloquy is not dramatic enough to hold audiences. (If talking heads are unacceptable, we can hardly expect to see a single head talking to itself!) Yet in popular media as in life, every action is imbued with moral significance. For example, a sitcom deception, where characters' lies to each other are played for laughs, may be unremarked upon in the script, yet the behavior is enacted for viewers' consumption. The moral integrity (or lack thereof) of a character in a favorite television drama or film invites consideration of what integrity means and how it is enacted. As popular media dramatizes what people say or do, it implicitly supports some actions over others, and constructs moral universes for our evaluation.

Admittedly, in popular media texts we lose much of the depth, richness, and clear focus on ethical issues provided by classic literature, history, or philosophy. What we gain is a life context closer to our own and moral dilemmas that more closely resemble the situations in which we find ourselves. By virtue of its familiar packaging and compulsion for closure, popular media is powerfully oriented toward the production of unreflective acceptance, yet used by critically aware consumers who are able to extricate the implicit ethical issues undergirding action, it provides a rich field for analysis and discussion.

Rhetorical Perspective on Communication Ethics and Popular Culture

The rhetorical perspective shared by contributors to this volume is grounded in the assumption that humans construct meaning in and through symbol systems and that these constructions are imbued with ethical implications and rhetorical potential. Brummett (2003) sums up the perspective with the term *constructedness*:

> Perceptions are constructed rather than natural or necessary ... [which] means that human neurological, physical, social, psychological or cultural mechanisms have intervened to shape an experience. No experience is natural in the sense of being "just so," or necessary or "that way" for everyone. Whatever is constructed might be constructed differently ... whoever constructs can also be influenced to construct differently. (p. 25)

Thus, the process of understanding is a rhetorical process, in that we persuade ourselves—complicit with or pushing against the persuasive energies of others—of the reality, authenticity, and acceptability (or not) of the symbolic constructions we engage.

Given this orientation, the chapters that follow focus less on the techniques of production or on the mechanics of dissemination and more on the process of consumption. Certainly the former are important aspects of mediated popular culture. However, Hermann Lubbe (1996) argues that "[t]he ethics of the use of media have become far more important than the ethics of media themselves" (p. 57). He goes on to explain, "In a context in which such motivations [public interest of media decision makers] cannot be guaranteed, the primary ethical question becomes a matter of the consumers of media making the best use they can of the ever more pervasive presence of the media in their daily lives and of the advantages and disadvantages of living in our 'media-saturated' age" (p. 57). A rhetorical perspective positions consumers as critics and moral agents rather than passive auditors of messages. Kenneth Burke, perhaps the most frequently cited theorist in the chapters that follow, envisions humans as symbolic actors, constructing meanings out of the vast socially shared repertoire of words and images within which they dwell and through which they constitute what they experience as reality. And as Burke (1984) asserts, such constructed meanings are inherently ethical, as they involve choices of how we define ourselves and our world (pp. 29–36).

Ethical Flashpoints in Mediated Popular Culture

As Lubbe notes, "the morality of media usage now belongs to the most important cultural competences on which the individual is reliant for providing practical guidance in her/his daily life" (p. 64). To competently engage mediated popular culture, consumers can learn to recognize "ethical flashpoints" in mediated texts, those moments when ethical awareness is engaged, when action moves one way or another, when we sense—however dimly—the implications that hang on that moment, when we realize there is "more to the story" than the simple problem/solution of surface scripting. For example, in *Home Improvement*, a popular ABC family sitcom of the '90s, Tim, the father, is continually faced with the choice of lying his way out of a predicament or telling the truth and facing the consequences. Often we can clearly identify those moments when he makes his choice. Seldom is there an overt discussion of the dilemma; frequently it is marked only by a fleeting facial expression as he considers and rejects truthfulness. Or we may not even have that subtle visual marker as Tim rushes headlong into evasion or outright deception. The fact that the audience knows how Tim will choose at an ethical flashpoint is part of the enjoyment of the program. Frequent viewers expect the lie, expect that Tim's deceitfulness will be discovered, that when found out he will be sorry, that he will be forgiven, and that, without question, he will repeat such behavior again and again. His character is established as morally challenged, at least as far as truthfulness is concerned. In his efforts to be "manly," Tim rejects coworker Al's ethic of concern for others and is completely puzzled by neighbor Wilson's abstract philosophical axioms. But Tim's moments of choice are ethically charged and invite reflection beyond his life as a fictional character in an ongoing narrative. Tim can repeat the same mistake over and over, and we—the uninvolved audience as well as his fictional family—can find it excusable, familiar, and even endearing. In real-life relationships, however, consistent self-serving untruthfulness doesn't come with a laugh track and isn't resolved in thirty minutes minus commercial breaks. Few marriages could survive such an assault on trust. So this fiction invites us to reflect upon real relational life, to consider how we make ethical choices of truth or deception, and how those choices might affect our own relationships.

Overview of the Chapters

The essays that follow engage a variety of ethical flashpoints in mediated popular culture, moments that reveal choices of secrecy or openness, inclusion or exclusion, manipulation or cooperation, courage or cowardice, attributions of good or evil, marginalizing or empowerment of others. Exploring a variety of media—newspapers, television, film, the Internet, music, and fan fiction—the authors raise issues of integrity, truthfulness, care, civility, identity, and community as these are enacted in mediated popular information and entertainment. The following two chapters provide a theoretical and methodological orientation, Jeffery L. Bineham's to the ethics of doing popular culture criticism and Phyllis M. Japp's to the process of engaging the ethics of representation. Taken together, these two chapters raise issues and questions that resonate throughout this book.

The rest of the chapters are arranged thematically rather than according to media genres, although several could easily fit into more than one category. Two chapters deal with the ethics of mediated information. Mark Meister addresses the ethical (or unethical) relationship between humans and environment as exemplified in automobile advertising. Bineham considers the framing of transgression in popular sports reporting and the implications of alternate frames for the fate of the transgressor. Three chapters explore ethics of character development in mediated entertainment. Paula S. Tompkins finds alternate constructions of integrity in two popular television series, *Star Trek: The Next Generation* and *Star Trek: Voyager*. Jon A. Hess and Joy Piazza also consider issues of integrity, in this case political integrity, as exemplified in the popular film *The Contender*. Jennifer McGee looks at ethical implications of reformulating characters' sexual orientations in fan fiction circulated on the Internet, especially that generated by the *Lord of the Rings* trilogy.

The ethics of mediated identity construction is explored in two very different contexts: Dan T. Molden considers the concept of "getting real" and what that characteristic means in the construction of mediated personas, with special reference to the rap musician Eminem. Scott Titsworth and Jeffery St. John consider the construction of identity in representations of the Vietnam War, comparing visits to the real and the virtual Memorial Wall. Finally, three chapters consider ethics of personal relationships in popular entertainment. Diana L. Rehling addresses the issue of deception among friends in the popular sitcom *Friends*. Greg Carlson analyzes ethics of familial relationships in three Wes Anderson films. Debra K. Japp turns to afternoon talk shows to evaluate the ethics of advice giving by the hosts of two extremely popular shows, *Dr. Phil* and *Judge Judy*.

We sincerely hope that these chapters are not read as answers to the very complex questions surrounding communication ethics and popular culture. Rather, we envision this book as a springboard to discussion and disagreement about what it means to be an ethical communicator and how consumers can engage popular culture with that lens in place. A careful reader will note differences among the authors about ethical issues such as integrity, civility, dialogue, and other important concepts. We prize our differences as well as our agreements; differences have proven to be the basis of many provocative discussions as we compiled this volume. So this book is both an invitation for readers to engage each other in ongoing conversations about important ethical issues and an assignment (we are teachers, after all!) for readers to locate additional examples from a variety of venues of popular culture that support or call into question our interpretations as they generate their own.

References

Brummett, B. (1994). *Rhetoric in popular culture.* New York: St. Martin's Press.

———. (2003). *The world and how we describe it: Rhetorics of reality, representation, simulation.* New York: Praeger.

Burke, K. (1984). *Permanence and change,* 3rd ed. Berkeley: University of California Press.

Johannesen, R. (2001). Communication ethics: Centrality, trends, and controversies. In W. Gudykunst (ed.), *Communication Yearbook 25* (pp. 201–35). New York: Lawrence Earlbaum.

Lubbe, H. (1996). The ethics of media use: Media consumption as a moral challenge. In K. Dyson and W. Homolka (eds.), *Culture first: Promoting standards in the new media age* (pp. 57–65). London: Cassall.

Meister, M., and P. Japp (eds.). (2002). *Enviropop: Studies in environmental rhetoric and popular culture.* New York: Praeger.

CHAPTER TWO

The Construction of Ethical Codes in the Discourse and Criticism of Popular Culture

Jeffery L. Bineham

One irony of popular culture is that while we are surrounded by its numerous artifacts (advertisements, television shows, movies, music videos, and so on), most of us believe that we are uninfluenced by these artifacts. "TV commercials use all kinds of gimmicks," we say, "but I'm aware of them. They don't persuade me." "*The Lion King* is just a cartoon; it's for fun. Don't read so much into it." Or: "Cut Barbie some slack. Playing with dolls never distorted my self-image."

But the discourse of popular culture is all around us all of the time. And it has been since birth. Wayne Booth (1988a) writes that "all of us are naturally tempted, of course, to think that ... by the time we reach maturity, *we* have learned to be 'critical' and are thus somehow immune to the effects others may suffer" (p. 41). But are we immune? And what effects might we suffer upon consumption of the toys, clothes, and mass-mediated messages of our culture?

Children do not walk out of *The Lion King* as newly enthused patriarchs, nor does playing with Barbie lead them directly to a desire for the unattainable body. But these products do wield influence. Here's how: People always make their worlds meaningful. None of our experiences comes to us in some pristine state complete with an obvious meaning about which everyone agrees. Instead we often struggle (both internally and with others) over the meaning of daily occurrences. Do those Express jeans signify comfort, a good fashion sense, or an air of superiority? Is *Seinfeld* simple comedy, distasteful, or social commentary? (Should I laugh at Kramer whooping it up with his cigar store Indian?) Are Bush's actions toward Iraq intelligent foreign policy, intrusive militarism, or political profiteering? We always make these experiences meaningful in one way or another.

Most often we get the meanings for these experiences from the discourses of popular culture. We see television commercials for Express jeans; we watch *Seinfeld* and read articles about it in the newspaper or in *TV Guide*; we are bombarded by commentaries about Bush's policies on the CBS news, Rush Limbaugh's radio show, and in editorials. From these and numerous other sources we learn the range of possible meanings by which we make sense of our daily experiences. This is not to say that we read the texts of popular culture uncritically, for we can and do argue with the meanings suggested to us. But if we reject one set of meanings, we do so in favor of another set of meanings that comes from other popular texts and artifacts.

The various texts and artifacts of popular culture, then, are constantly telling us how to think, how to dress, how to talk, what vocations are significant, and what we should do politically and economically; in sum, they tell us who to be. Some texts do this overtly, like speeches or debates we see on C-Span. Other texts advocate meanings more subtly, and artifacts like *The Lion King* and Barbie are in this category. They operate subtly because we tend to not even think of them as texts, and we are thus likely to assume that they do not influence us.

One particularly striking example illustrates the degree to which these subtle texts have power to establish meanings. Several years ago Anna Quindlen argued in her column that Barbie creates an ideal body image for girls that is distorted and damaging. Quindlen (1994) reported about a University of Arizona study that found that white teenage girls were overwhelmingly dissatisfied with their bodies and engaged in extensive dieting to reach their desired weights, even though most of them weighed within the normal range for girls of their age and height. The researchers' conclusion: "the ideal girl was a living manifestation of the Barbie doll." Quindlen traces Barbie's influence ("the most popular toy ever created") and states that the doll's "preposterous physique" (40-18-32 if life sized, with too little body fat to sustain menstruation) has established some dangerous meanings about desirable female body shapes.

But Quindlen's column was not the striking example. The striking example was a letter in response that questioned Barbie's influence. Barbie is "just pretend," the writer asserted, so don't take her so seriously; she "hasn't distorted my body image one bit." But the writer then recounts with pleasure her girlhood memories of Barbie playtime: when she dressed Barbie and Ken for a night on the town, she writes, "I was transplanted to a swell party in Palm Springs"; when Barbie wore her stewardess outfit, "it was I who was serving coffee on a 727"; and when Barbie sunned by the pool, "I was a teenager getting a tan" (Koch 1994). Could we have clearer testimony to Barbie's influence? Here Barbie helps define standards for fashion, entertainment, job possibilities for women, and beauty. And if Barbie is influential in these areas for the letter writer, why not assume that for others she is influential with respect to body image? Especially when Quindlen provides such compelling evidence for that influence. In each of these cases, Barbie functions as a text that offers meanings by which people organize and interpret past experiences, present events, and future possibilities.

Surely Barbie is not solely responsible for setting such meanings, nor does *The Lion King* alone sustain a system of patriarchy, nor does any one message convince us all to think a certain way about Iraq. But when these items enter into an environment of texts and cultural artifacts that encourage particular ways of thinking and acting, the cumulative influence is difficult to dismiss. The message of Barbie is reproduced continually in movies, television programs, advertisements, and fashion shows, so even if we resist it in one incarnation we are likely to absorb it in a multitude of other incarnations. Its ubiquity makes it influential. We need not claim that every toy, movie, and television show is evil; but we would do well to recognize the possible influences of these things, rather than to assume we are immune to the messages we consume on a daily basis.

This book explores how we might assess these possible influences, with a special focus on how the discourses of popular culture construct ethical codes. My effort in this chapter is to underscore both how the discourses of popular culture construct such codes and how the critical assessment of popular culture is itself an ethical act. Two assumptions underlie this effort.

The first is that rhetoric's primary effect is to create people's identities. Booth (1988b) calls this rhetoric's "epideictic center": "when words make your past, present, and future, what they really make is *you*" (p. 36); and he relates this effect to students and, by implication, to other publics and audiences: "The reality that is most decisively made, in every kind of rhetoric our students meet, is people, the very *shapes of their minds and souls*" (p. 41, emphasis added). This is the critical point in the Barbie example above. Popular culture's texts and artifacts tell us who to be. Such an effect differs from the mechanistically causal effects we often associate with neo-Aristotelian criticism or with some types of mass communication research. Much of the discourse of popular culture encourages us to remain the same rather than to change in any measurable way, so while its influence is profound, its effects are difficult to discern. They are important, nonetheless, because they are ethical effects. Edwin Black's classic essay "The Second Persona" (1970) demonstrates that apart from any "actual auditors" one might identify, every discourse *implies* an auditor, or a persona, and "the critic can see in the auditor implied by a discourse a model of what the rhetor would have his real auditor become" (p. 113). The discourses of popular culture advocate second personas, and in so doing they help to shape people's identities by modeling a collage of convictions and viewpoints for their implied ideal auditors. That collage constitutes a sense of character, it identifies the moral qualities and habits that we associate with a virtuous demeanor, and it thus advocates an ethic by which to evaluate individual and community actions.

The second assumption is also embedded in Booth's idea of the epideictic center. To emphasize a different clause in the quotation cited above, "The reality that is most decisively made, *in every kind of rhetoric our students meet*, is people, the very shapes of their minds and souls" (1988b, p. 41, emphasis added). It is nothing new to note that rhetorical criticism is itself rhetoric (e.g., Brockriede 1974). But as we engage in the rhetorical criticism of popular culture, we should recognize that just as the discourse we examine implies an ideal character and thus endorses particular ethical qualities, so does the discourse we produce imply an ideal character and thus endorse particular ethical qualities. Assessments of critical invention have clarified the ways in which critics work from political perspectives and in support of professional interests (e.g., Nothstine, Blair, & Copeland 1994; Blair, Brown, & Baxter 1994). Like the discourse of popular culture, the discourse of criticism speaks to issues of power. When we present criticism, whether in the popular press, in academic publications, in the classroom, or in conversations with our friends, we encourage our audiences to be a certain kind of people, to understand the world in particular ways, and to assume a particular set of convictions about how communication works in that world. Like all discourse, any critical act constructs a second persona that models the ideal character the critic would like his or her auditors to become.

Naomi Rockler's excellent critique of *Beverly Hills, 90210* illustrates the two assumptions I have outlined above, and emphasizes the importance of critical skills even (and perhaps especially) for those who are not professional or academic critics. Rockler (1999) first provides an ideological analysis of the television show that demonstrates how it has constructed both "an ideology of traditional, idealized femininity" and an "ideology of consumption" (p. 77) that instruct us how to think about beauty, sexuality, romance, our status as consumers, and specific products. The implied auditor of the show embraces particular values: heterosexuality is normal, the display of sexuality is good, and the acquisition of material goods is unquestioned. While various storylines temporarily emphasize alternative values—like women should be intelligent and strong, for example—the show's pervasive themes consistently create a second persona in line with traditional patriarchal and capitalist values.

Rockler next reports her analysis of viewers' responses to *Beverly Hills, 90210*. She conducts focus group interviews with female college students and discovers that most are unable to generate any critical responses beyond the observation that the show is "just entertainment" and therefore—they assume—not worthy of evaluative critique. These friendly critiques of the program also suggest a persona for the focus group participants. They should watch the show for its entertainment value, recognize that it is unrealistic, and not concern themselves with any potential ideological or ethical effects. Rockler's assessment is that these viewers are constrained from more meaningful evaluation of the show by their lack of a critical vocabulary (pp. 90–91). Her ideal auditor is a more sophisticated critic who recognizes the ideological dimensions of the communication he or she encounters in daily experiences.

The remainder of this chapter is divided into two sections. The first section suggests that the most significant influence rendered by the discourse of popular culture is its influence on the strategies of interpretation that people use to construct their experiences and their identities. The second section argues that this influence is an ethical effect and that the rhetorical criticism of popular culture can render a similar ethical effect because it, too, can influence those strategies of interpretation.

Communication as a Medium of Experience

In earlier work I developed the idea that communication comprises a medium within which all of human experience comes to exist (Bineham 1995). I want to revisit that idea here and to recast it so that it accounts clearly for how the discourse of popular culture creates identities for people.

James Carey (1989) notes that in western culture and research the most common view of communication is the transmission view. Communication in this view is a medium by which to transport messages from one place or person to another place or person, and an examination of the models of communication in almost any textbook reveals the dominance of this view. The medium is the delivery system, the intermediate channel that stands between source and receiver. But Carey also notes the existence of a less common view of communication, which he calls the ritual view. In this perspective the function of communication is not simply to transmit messages; communication creates and sustains a "meaningful cultural world" that serves as a "container for human action" (p. 19), and is thus a "symbolic process whereby reality is produced, maintained, repaired and transformed" (p. 23). Just as water comprises the "medium that forms [the] ambience and supports [the] existence" of a fish, so does communication comprise the ambience of existence for humans (p. 24).

The term *medium* here does not refer to a delivery system but to the symbolic substance within which humans live; it is the culture of meanings from which people create their personalities, their experiences, their convictions, and their worlds. This symbolic medium is comprised of language in its various manifestations: words, titles, meanings, definitions, reasons, arguments, structures of rationality, narratives, characterizations, symbolic forms, visual images, and the like. We are quite literally born into this ongoing medium, and as we develop within it we acquire the sentiments that it features. The medium contains the categories of thought that enable us to understand what it means to be male or female. The medium contains the narratives of self-defense, the noble rescue, and the heroic quest that help us to make sense of U.S. foreign policy. And the medium contains visual images that help frame our conceptions of the Middle East, Africa, South Los Angeles, and other places with which most of us have little or no direct contact. The medium always predates the individuals who inhabit it, so those individuals enter a world that is already structured and interpreted, and they inherit the dominant storylines of the culture. Throughout this chapter, the phrase *the medium* will denote this encompassing and pervasive amalgam of language that makes experience possible.

Popular culture supplies most of the meanings that make up the medium. As I have already suggested, and as numerous scholars have established, the discourses of popular culture are not neutral. The medium, consequently, is more than a simple structure that has developed by chance and now happens to prefer some meanings over others. The medium is ideological.

Stuart Hall provides a description of ideology that pertains to this conception of the medium. Ideology, he says, is "the web of meanings and discourses, the strings of connotation and their means of representation, within which social practices, consciousnesses, identities, and subjectivities are placed" (Grossberg & Slack 1985, p. 89). To say that the medium is ideological means that it consists of *particular* webs of meanings and discourses with *particular* strings of connotation and *particular* means of representation. When the texts and artifacts of popular culture influence the medium—when Barbie or the evening news do their work—they help to establish a particular range of languages, concepts, categories, and images that people use both "to make sense of, define, figure out and render intelligible the way society works" and to construct their own and others' identities and subjectivities (Hall 1983, p. 59). Because all experience occurs within the medium, all experience is ideological. Indeed, the medium *is* the webs of meanings and discourses, the strings of connotation, the concepts, categories, and images that Hall describes as the components of an ideological system.

The medium, then, provides possibilities for experience and interpretation that are congruent with its ideological structure. But when the medium creates one configuration of realities, it displaces other possible configurations by rendering them unreasonable and locating them outside the horizon of probable interpretations. At any given point in time the medium limits the range of socially constructed scenarios that we might accord the status of reality. And as the term *ideology* suggests, the medium's configurations and tendencies serve particular interests and often come to "dominate the social thinking of a historical bloc" (Hall 1983, p. 59).

An empowered social group can construct texts and artifacts that advocate conceptions of "family life, civil society, gender and economic relations" that become entrenched as part of the medium's ideological structure (Hall 1985, p. 93). At each of these contested sites the medium makes possible a range of interpretations that comply, to different extents, with dominant interests. So the medium tends to reify a particular range of perceptions and to limit the possibilities for new, perhaps radical, perceptions and interpretations.

One example that illustrates how the rhetoric of popular culture helps to create the medium's ideological structure is the treatment of crime and criminals in popular television news magazine programs. Maria E. Grabe (1999) assesses tabloid programs like *Inside Edition* and *Hard Copy*, and more traditional programs like *48 Hours* and *60 Minutes*, and finds that in their coverage of crime these programs construct a morality based upon clear distinctions between good and evil, and the marginalization of African Americans as criminals and women as helpless victims. Grabe links these assessments to Carey's ritual view of communication and demonstrates that these programs help to construct our "net" (or medium) of social relations because they create a moral order that imposes control and reaffirms power relations.

J. M. Fishman (1999) examines two television crime programs, *America's Most Wanted* and *Cops*, and finds that while they feature different narrative forms, they serve to reproduce the dominant philosophy of criminal justice. *America's Most Wanted* accentuates ordinary citizens as the heroes who solve crimes, often despite the legal system, while *Cops* accentuates the heroic actions of police officers. Though the programs advance different narrative forms and thus provide the symbolic resources for different interpretations, they still replicate the "central notions constituting the dominant hegemonic order": the notions of a punitive legal system (p. 283). Both Grabe and Fishman illustrate how popular texts create the medium's symbolic forms. The texts they examine produce narratives, characterizations, and visuals that then become strategies for future interpretations of events and issues.

The medium's tendency, then, is to direct those who live within it toward interpretations that serve dominant sets of ideas, interests, and values. The medium presents these dominant ideas, interests, and values as inevitable, and thus reduces the possibilities that other ideas and interests might guide experience. Its ideological character generally remains unexamined, even unnoticed, so that the realities endorsed by the medium seem natural and objective, a matter of common sense. The medium thus exerts powerful pressures and constraints on human interpretation and action, and the discourses of popular culture are forces that both shape and express the medium's structures.

Because the medium limits interpretive possibilities, it provides a sense of permanence to the world. It exerts "certain real pressures and limits—genuine determinations—within which the scope and commitment of individual action and gesture must be defined" (Williams 1977, p. 99). These determinations, however, do not guarantee one specific outcome. Instead they set boundaries within which a range of outcomes is possible. That is because the medium always contains perspectives and interpretations that diverge from the established range of alternatives, even if they are not customarily featured.

And while the medium's structures might seem to be objective conditions of existence, they actually are the result of previous discourses, interpretations, and arguments. Determinations, in this sense, are social constructions that exist in the ongoing medium of communication. Because the structures of permanence are created and sustained in communication, they can be changed through communication as well. Thus, the texts and artifacts of popular culture are sites of contest where different social groups work to advocate or to resist dominant meanings (see Storey 1993, p. 13). Their influence is a function of the access they have to the means of communication and the extent to which they offer convincing interpretations that become part of the medium's structure.

Williams (1977) notes that no structures of meaning exist passively. They have "continually to be renewed, recreated, defended, and modified" (p. 112). Because those structures are never totally exclusive, they cannot guarantee the elimination of interpretations and arguments that challenge dominant interests and values. People are not only born into and shaped by their social medium, they also contribute actively to it and can transform it via specific acts of communication. The medium, in William's words, is "continually resisted, limited, altered, [and] challenged" (1977, p. 112). While the medium possesses a definite continuity, there is also some indeterminacy about the various directions in which it might continue, and that indeterminacy makes it possible for critics of the dominant structure to reform the medium so that alternative realities that oppose established interests become more probable.

All of this is to say that the medium bequeaths to us our common sense. Certain meanings and definitions occur to us more easily (we are quick to think of Saddam Hussein as an evil tyrant), some kinds of arguments are more commonly available (it's easier to construct a case for self-defense than for pacifism), and certain symbolic forms present themselves more vividly (the quest story reproduces our desire to settle uncharted domains and thus justifies various explorations). While the dominant conceptions are most readily deemed reasonable, the empowered structure's domination is never total because the medium never completely excludes alternative concepts and interpretations.

These manifestations of language—the meanings, definitions, arguments, and symbolic forms that make our common sense—exist in material form in the sinews of the medium. They are concrete instances of communication that reinforce the medium's prevalent interpretations, or that call to attention less prevalent minority interpretations that the medium does not feature, but that it contains nonetheless. So presidential speeches and Fox news accounts contribute to the medium a range of interpretations about the nature of unrest in the Middle East and the United States' responsibility to intervene in that part of the world. The Guerilla News Network and the Friends Committee on National Legislation contribute their interpretations, too, but given the established structure of the medium and the relative lack of influence these organizations enjoy, those minority interpretations don't find the same audience that mainstream ideas do. The medium, nonetheless, is a site of contest. And into that contest enter the variety of texts and artifacts that make up popular culture. Barbie reinforces one set of values and Anna Quindlen reinforces another. *The Lion King* proffers one symbolic form and *Thelma and Louise* proffers another. *Friends* suggests one perspective on relationships, *Star Trek* suggests another, and Dr. Phil and Judge Judy advocate a third.

The conception of the medium I have outlined here accounts both for permanence and change within a given social structure. Determinations are a part of the medium's structure that establishes a sense of permanence, and constrains thought and action. But those determinations are themselves social constructions present in the ongoing medium of communication. Because the medium is a product of rhetorical discourse, it is malleable; it is created, shaped, and can be altered through interpretations and communicative practices that extend the medium's current horizons or reshape its internal dynamic. The medium sets conditions that are not of one's own making, but within which one must act either to reaffirm those conditions or to call them into question.

Kenneth Burke's well-known account of the unending conversation provides a clear summation of how people are born into a social medium of communication that establishes limits and pressures on human action, and yet can be altered through rhetorical intervention. I cite the passage here in full so we can see how it illustrates the idea of the medium that I have developed in this section.

> Imagine that you enter a parlor. You come late. When you arrive, others have long preceded you, and they are engaged in a heated discussion, a discussion too heated for them to pause and tell you exactly what it is about. In fact, the discussion had already begun long before any of them got there, so that no one present is qualified to retrace for you all the steps that had gone before. You listen for a while, until you decide that you have caught the tenor of the argument; then you put in your oar. Someone answers; you answer him; another comes to your defense; another aligns himself against you, to either the embarrassment or gratification of your opponent, depending upon the quality of your ally's assistance. However, the discussion is interminable. The hour grows late, you must depart. And you do depart, with the discussion still vigorously in progress. (1973, pp. 110–11)

We enter a parlor, and we must. No choice exists but to find ourselves in the context of language and tradition and power that is the medium of existence. And we enter late. Again we must. Entrance is into an ongoing flow of communication, a world of texts and artifacts and interpretive strategies, and no one is present who was not late. No one currently present, as Frank Lentricchia (1983) states, "was there at the beginning, when the conversation started" (p. 161). The origins of this medium, the initial premises of this pervasive and enveloping "conversation," are forever inaccessible; no one knows more than what has been gleaned from the discussion, a discussion comprised of various texts—the interpersonal, academic, scientific, religious, and of course popular texts we encounter throughout our lives.

Our entrance into the parlor does not guarantee equal access to the conversation, but once we have "caught the tenor of the argument," we begin to participate. How we participate is constrained by the conversation's structures and determinations—its limits and pressures—so that we cannot do or say or believe simply anything. The history and current status of the medium render legitimate a particular range of topics and particular groups of contributors; if you don't speak the idiom, your access to the conversation is limited. And to learn the idiom is to commit to an acceptable way of talking about the legitimated topics. But our participation, nonetheless, is influential. We influence those actively engaged in the conversation and, perhaps more important, we influence the medium of the conversation itself. Our interjections shape the medium so that new narratives and characterizations are possible, and so that new interpretations and actions gain entrance into the discussion. So while we help to shape our own experiences, we also propel the medium forward; we help to sustain and to alter its existence, and in so doing to establish the conditions into which others will enter. Through the discourses of popular culture that we create and interpret, we participate in the continual creation and re-creation of the medium within which reality is shaped. And when we depart, we leave behind an ongoing medium into which other interlocutors will come, always late, always shaped by conditions for which they are not responsible, and always engaged in the conversation which continues to shape the medium.

Ethical Dimensions of Popular Culture
and Popular Culture Criticism

Although I have referred to different kinds of texts in my discussion of the medium, I have made no effort to distinguish between texts that are a part of popular culture and those that are not. This is because I believe that any text can become a text of popular culture. I find most useful the fairly simple definition offered by Barry Brummett (1991): a popular culture is comprised of the texts and artifacts to which most people in a given social group have easy access (p. xx). We can easily identify some texts as texts of popular culture—television shows and newspapers, for example. But while we typically do not give the label "popular culture" to a long address by the U.S. Secretary of State to the United Nations, that address can become a text of popular culture as it is reproduced in segments by the news media, or extolled by some commentators and lampooned by others. Thomas Rostek (1999) notes that critics need make no distinctions between politics and popular culture or between artifacts of high culture and low culture (p. 237). Elizabeth W. Mechling and Jay Mechling's (1991) analysis of civil defense campaigns in the 1950s and 1960s illustrates how a myriad of texts entered the domain of popular culture and propounded themes and metaphors that influenced American thinking. They analyzed newspaper and magazine articles, government and social movement pamphlets, speeches, television shows, movies, editorials, survey results, architecture, novels, and scholarly articles by historians, sociologists, and scientists; all of these became texts of popular culture.

Popular culture is comprised of the texts and artifacts that work most actively to win public favor and shape public sentiment (Brummett 1991, p. xxi). Any text's most significant public influence is its influence as a text of popular culture. That influence is not restricted to whatever immediate results might follow from the text, but is most pronounced in the maintenance or alteration of the medium. This is because the medium provides the resources by which people make sense out of their experiences and bring order to their worlds, and that influence stretches far beyond any immediate decision to support a policy, buy a product, or adopt any other mind-set or engage in any other action. The discourse of popular culture constructs ethical codes as it advocates particular forms and strategies of interpretation. Its ethical effects lie in the symbolic worlds and identities that it creates.

Brummett (1991) argues that when people learn how to interpret their experiences and their worlds, they also learn to be a particular type of person. They construct an identity out of the same symbolic resources they use to construct the world. He states: "The process of socializing people, begun in childhood and continued throughout life, is the process of showing people how to order the world and simultaneously to construct themselves within those orders. When we know how to make sense of the world we also, then, know who to be in that world" (p. 82). Every discourse, as it enters the domain of popular culture and shapes the medium, advocates that its audiences assume a particular character and adopt particular ethical qualities. And in its endorsement of whatever virtues it features, the discourse is itself an ethical act and thus subject to ethical judgment, for it works to shape the minds and souls of those who consume it.

The medium functions in two basic ways. It provides the resources by which each person constructs a self, and it provides the resources by which each person constructs a world. The rhetorical critic's primary ethical responsibility is thus to disclose the ways in which the texts and artifacts of popular culture might influence the configurations of the medium.

The rhetorical criticism of popular culture can help to avert the possibility that some specific vocabulary, some one mode of explanation and thought, might become reified in the structures of the medium and thus secure the permanent establishment of a particular social structure. Richard Rorty (1979) identifies this possibility of reification as "the dehumanization of human beings" (p. 377): when a single view of any dimension of human reality becomes entrenched as *the* view, humans do not recognize their ability and attendant responsibility to participate in the production of their worlds. If a limited range of views dominates completely, it "provides a defense behind which social prejudices and interests lie hidden and thus protected" (Gadamer 1976, p. 93). The concept of the medium provides the framework for a critical perspective that will strive to make evident the prejudices and interests that undergird popular vocabularies and theories, and thus to establish the possibility for alternative interpretations.

We can ground this critical perspective in the postulate that the medium's established structures are never totally dominant. While they do guide most interpretation and experience, the prospect remains for interpretations that question and perhaps change the established medium. Alternative meanings are always available. The

medium does provide the resources from which a dominant structure is composed, but it also provides the resources from which
people can construct alternative configurations.

Raymond Williams's (1977, p. 116) cogent argument for the
availability of alternatives in history helps to explain a critical perspective that is informed by the concept of the medium. Williams
writes, "It is at the vital points of *connection*, where a version of the
past is used to ratify the present and to indicate directions for the
future, that a selective tradition is at once powerful and vulnerable." A tradition is powerful because it is adept at "making active selective connections." Because the tradition is established, its
links to the present and future seem obvious and appear as common sense. A tradition is vulnerable, however, because alternative
records remain "effectively recoverable" and render accessible "opposing practical continuities." While these opposing continuities
are accessible, they do not present themselves as readily apparent;
they do not stand within the medium's established forms because
the discourses of popular culture do not reinforce them as obvious
interpretations and meanings. They are marginal, not central, to the
popular medium.

One task of the rhetorical critic is thus to "re-read culture so as
to amplify and strategically position the marginalized voices of the
ruled, exploited, oppressed, and excluded" (Lentricchia 1983, p. 15).
A critic can demonstrate how accepted interpretations are just that:
interpretations. And the critic can then point to alternative interpretations that typically are marginalized but that can help to explain
in nontraditional ways the discourse or event in question. This
critical activity can divulge how the texts and artifacts of popular
culture help create the medium by sanctioning conventional or un-
conventional symbolic forms and strategies of interpretation. These
forms and strategies influence the medium's composition and endorse a particular range of experiences and understandings. How
a particular message or set of messages confirms or challenges the
medium's dominant structure is not necessarily obvious. The critic
can illumine that which is not obvious and reveal how discourses
influence, and are influenced by, the medium within which they
are articulated. Rhetorical criticism, in this view, elucidates how

humans have made and continue to make their medium or world of experience. It elucidates, also, how they can develop alternative meanings and thereby remake that medium.

The case of Christian feminist discourse illustrates how a particular tradition can be both powerful and vulnerable, and how critical intervention can reshape the medium through the creation of alternative meanings (Bineham 1993). A dominant tradition in orthodox Christianity describes God as exclusively masculine and thus legitimates the domination of men over women. Church leaders from Jerome in the fourth century to Thomas Aquinas in the thirteenth century to John Calvin and Martin Luther in the sixteenth century produced numerous documents that restated a specific message: males were superior because they possessed God's image to a greater degree than did women and because the female body was a source of debasement and inferiority. Numerous popular speakers and writers reproduce these characterizations in the medium of twentieth-century evangelical Christianity. People like James Dobson, head of Focus on the Family, use their writings and radio and television shows to articulate interpretive codes that render key scriptural passages to say that women should be submissive to men and rely upon them for protection, teaching, and authority. This dominant tradition is powerful because it contains the prominent symbolic codes that many Christians use to construct their views of women.

But this tradition is also vulnerable, for it contains alternative codes and texts that interested parties can recover and use to create oppositional interpretive possibilities. Many Christian feminists, for example, see the Bible as the basis for their tradition, and call attention to egalitarian texts that have been submerged within the dominant tradition but that provide a biblical basis for nonpatriarchal structures in the church and in society. They affirm the Bible as a central text but posit interpretive codes that yield feminist readings of those texts. One example of such a code is the location of authority in female experience or in the intersection between female experience and scriptural texts. This code counters the dominant code, which locates authority solely in specific scriptural texts, and it has specific implications for biblical interpretation, as it leads to an emphasis on female role models and images within Scripture. To cite such role models and images affirms women's experiences and illustrates how the dominant interpretive tradition has ignored portions of the scriptural text. Christian feminist texts thus provide a critical intervention that reveals how humans have constructed their medium of experience and suggests ways to remake that medium. And significantly, the critique of orthodox and feminist texts serves a similar function.

This kind of critical activity is an ideological enterprise because it engages the critic in the struggle either to maintain the medium's established structures and meanings, or to disrupt and displace those established structures and meanings in order to make possible alternative experiences and interpretations. The critical activity I advocate here does not merely explain *how* the medium is constituted through discourse. Criticism, instead, is an *active force* in the processes of constitution; it helps generate the histories and vocabularies, the theories, concepts, and interpretations, and the narrative and symbolic forms that comprise the medium's structures. Criticism becomes every bit as political as the texts, artifacts, and events that it examines. We can thus conceive of rhetorical criticism as a form of social, cultural, intellectual, and political intervention into the medium's structure. It is a way to participate in the ongoing construction of the medium in which people live.

We can see in this perspective one clear way in which the analysis of popular culture advocates ethical codes. When we construct the kinds of analyses I describe above, we advocate a second persona. We say to our audiences that they should become aware of and challenge the dominant meanings to which they are most accustomed. Even if, given the choice, they choose to reject subordinate meanings in favor of dominant meanings, we still have suggested that they should have a choice, that they should see the world as a puzzle of symbolic forms and competing interests rather than as a master narrative or a set of established truths given by God or by nature. To advocate that view is, at the least, to advocate a relativist rather than an absolutist ethic. But while the suggestion of a worldview is one way in which criticism posits an ethic, it is not the only way, nor perhaps is it the most significant.

Brummett (1991) emphasizes another way in which the type of criticism I describe here serves to construct ethical codes. He notes that the primary goals of criticism should be to raise people's consciousness about how the dominant medium limits their interpretive possibilities and to expand the range of symbolic forms by which people create their realities. When a critic teaches people how they are encouraged to structure their worlds now and how they might structure them in the future, that critic produces discourse that is as much involved in the creation of identities as the texts and artifacts of popular culture that the critic examines. "To the extent that experience is reality," Brummett writes, "and experience is created through symbolic ordering, then teaching people how to order is the process of teaching people *who to be* and how to make the world" (p. 102, emphasis added). To suggest interpretations, in other words, is to suggest identities.

When we ask people to recognize the possibility of multiple ways of ordering the world, we ask them to embrace an ethical and political code that calls them to challenge established ways of ordering that world. Criticism, whether in academic journals, newspaper columns, or classroom or coffeehouse conversations, becomes a form of political action. And when we recognize it as political action, we see clearly that it advocates an ethic, a course of action of one kind or another and a way of being of one kind or another. It is a statement about how people should live. "When people learn that a particular way of making sense of a rhetorical transaction is one option for experiencing rather than *the* option, then the partiality and limited nature of that logic makes hegemony partial and limited, too; and nothing could be more oppositional" (p. 104). So the rhetorical criticism of popular culture advocates ethical codes because it encourages people to decode texts and artifacts oppositionally, or at least to recognize the possibility of such oppositional readings.

The Epideictic Center in Popular Culture and Rhetorical Criticism

I can summarize my argument about the relationships among the medium, popular culture, and criticism in several basic points. The

texts and artifacts of popular culture exist in a reciprocal relationship with the medium of experience into which all people are born.
Those texts and artifacts help to construct the medium because to
greater or lesser extents they reproduce or challenge the traditional
and dominant structures of meaning that comprise the medium.
But those texts and artifacts are themselves produced within the
medium and according to its logics and symbolic forms. Any medium makes some meanings and interpretations reasonable and
others unreasonable. It thus endorses a particular manner of understanding; it makes a limited range of experiences probable for
those who live within it. A particular text or artifact may not have,
in and of itself, a clearly evident persuasive goal or result. But any
discourse will influence the medium. It may reinforce those meanings and structures already dominant and thus help sustain the
medium, or it may alter those structures in some significant or insignificant way.

Criticism is one form of discourse that helps to shape the medium. While one important source of such discourse is the professional critic, I have also intimated in this chapter that all people are
critics and that criticism can appear just as surely over a beer as in
an academic journal. Whether we realize it or not, whenever we
engage the texts and artifacts of popular culture, we engage in critical activity because we make choices about what to accept, what to
question, and how hard to work at the processes of interpretation.
If we raise this everyday critical activity to a place of conscious attention, so that we retrain our critical capacities and refresh our
repertoires of interpretive possibilities, we prepare ourselves to
discover more fully the ethical dimensions of popular culture, of
the critical process itself, and of the medium that both shapes and
is shaped by popular and critical discourses.

Two examples related to the war in Iraq can help to illustrate
the principles of the medium and the importance of critique. Both
examples demonstrate the influence of symbolic forms in the framework of the medium: the first example features metaphor and the
second features narrative.

Metaphor in the Medium

Since the beginning of the first Gulf War in 1991, Americans' hatred for Saddam Hussein has been palpable. President Bush has called for his execution. Colin Powell pronounced in his February 2003 speech to the United Nations that Saddam's "inhumanity knows no limits." And in Minnesota, where I live, one citizen remarked after Hussein's capture, "I hope he ends up being dragged through the streets of the United States" (Sternberg, Olson, & Meryhew 2003). These comments are representative of most Americans' general sentiments toward Saddam Hussein.

But the United States has not always harbored such ill will toward Saddam, and numerous leaders with worse records don't incite our wrath like he does. Since 1990 we have consumed a steady diet of messages telling us that he is an evil tyrant whom we should fear and hate. The characterizations of Saddam directly after his capture are consistent with that theme, and they fuel and justify that hatred.

One characterization tells us that Saddam is an object of disgust. He is "bewildered" and "bedraggled," a "rat," a "caveman," a "vagrant," and a "hobo" (Schechner 2003). After his capture a video clip entered the domain of popular culture; we saw over and over again via cable and network outlets and via the Internet the video of a doctor checking Saddam's hair for lice and probing inside his mouth with a tongue depressor. This characterization is no accident. The checkup video was part of a White House public relations plan designed in case of a capture. A director of strategic communications gushed that Saddam helped "in ways we never dreamed possible—he allowed himself to get into such a disheveled state and to look so haggard" (Schechner 2003). In essence, he played directly into the predetermined characterization.

A second characterization suggests that this capture is a watershed event. President Bush asserted that Saddam's apprehension marks the end of "a dark and painful era" and signals that "all Iraqis can now come together and reject violence and build a new Iraq" (Bush's comments 2003, p. A8). House majority leader Tom DeLay

pronounced that "today our nation and our world are safer," as if
U.S. citizens and military personnel were in more danger the day
before Saddam's capture than they were the day after (Milbank
2003, p. A1). One Minnesotan predicted that "our troops can be sent
back home," and Minnesota state representative Peter Adolphson
remarked that Saddam's capture "will discourage further terrorist
attacks on our troops" (Sternberg, Olson, & Meryhew 2003). Each of
these comments presumes that his capture marks a significant turn
in the war in Iraq and in the war against terrorism.

These characterizations are significant because they sustain the
metaphor that justifies most U.S. foreign policy: the "nation-as-person" metaphor (see Lakoff & Johnson 1999, pp. 533–36). The numerous justifications for this war—the search for weapons, the need to
stop terrorists, the desire to free the Iraqi people—are grounded in
this metaphor. We had to stop Saddam either to defend ourselves or
to rescue others. These self-defense and rescue scenarios are powerful justifications because they resonate with our national psyche;
they are consistent with our self-image and our core values.

But this metaphor has its downsides, too. Since it encourages
us to see a nation as a person, it implies not only how we should
think about Saddam, but also how we should think about Iraq and
the Iraqi people. Any metaphor features some concerns and hides
others, and this one is no different.

First, the metaphor focuses on an individual and hides systemic
issues. This fits nicely into the narratives of rescue and defense:
Saddam Hussein is the villain, the Iraqi people and the world community are the victims, and the United States is the hero. But it diverts attention from other factors that contribute to the situation in
Iraq: economic difficulties, ethnic rivalries, religious conflicts, and
political factions. When we see the state as a person, we simplify
these complexities out of existence.

Second, because the metaphor features the United States as
hero, it diverts attention from our complicity in the creation and
maintenance of those complex conditions. It hides motives such as
the desire for inexpensive oil, the desire for profits by oil companies, the desire to finish the job left undone in 1990, or the desire to
shift attention from the economy. When everything is the fault of

one evil man, we are not inclined to look in the mirror.

Third, the metaphor frames how we think about Iraqi civilians. George Lakoff and Mark Johnson note that in a world of nation-persons, less industrialized countries are conceived as backward and underdeveloped children who must be disciplined into maturity (1999, p. 534). One Iraqi man told the *New York Times* that although he hated Saddam "to the core of my bones," he felt an unexpected sympathy for him. "I feel sorry for him," he stated, "to be so humiliated. It is as if he and Iraq have become the same thing" (Schechner 2003). Perhaps this metaphor explains why Americans tend to measure the war's cost in U.S. lives: we see a Saddam in every Iraqi person.

While the nation-as-person metaphor influences how we think about Iraq and Saddam Hussein, we can imagine its even more significant influence when we recognize that the metaphor is part of the medium; as we employ it in discourse and in interpretation, we imbed the metaphor more deeply into the structures of the medium. Its repetition in this historical context makes more likely its use in future contexts. The metaphor becomes a part of who we are. And of course the critique of this metaphor calls this process to consciousness and enables us to live more thoughtfully in the world of popular culture. But as the next example shows, metaphor is but one of the symbolic forms that comprise the medium.

Narrative in the Medium

Humans are storytellers. We make decisions based upon the narratives we deem most believable. Some stories become dominant. Their plot and moral assume a featured place in the medium. Officials repeat them in various contexts and cite them to support policies and actions. The more this repetition occurs, the more likely we are to accept those stories uncritically.

The tale of General Hussein Kamel illustrates this phenomenon well (see Ackerman 2004). Kamel was Saddam Hussein's son-in-law and supervised Iraq's weapons production until he defected in August 1995. He provided to the United Nations materials that contained evidence about past weapons programs. This prompted

Iraq's government to release documents that indicated they had lied about their efforts to develop weapons of mass destruction. Kamel returned to Iraq in 1996 and was promptly assassinated. Kamel's story became international news and provided justification for U.S. policies during both the Clinton and Bush administrations. Officials referenced the story repeatedly to justify efforts toward regime change.

In February 1998, for example, President Clinton stated that "Iraq still has stockpiles of chemical and biological munitions," and cited as evidence Kamel's revelations to the United Nations. National Security Advisor Sandy Berger said that Kamel's defection led Iraq "to reveal additional weapons stockpiles and production capacity it had insisted it did not have." Secretary of State Madeleine Albright pronounced Kamel's defection "a turning point" in Iraq's efforts at deception. And Defense Secretary William Cohen said that because of Kamel's defection, "Iraq confessed to having materials and munitions it had lied about for years" (Ackerman 2004).

The Bush administration also uses the Kamel story to justify foreign policy. Secretary of Defense Donald Rumsfeld stated to Congress that Kamel provided important information unavailable to weapons inspectors, a claim repeated by Vice President Cheney in August 2002. Secretary of State Colin Powell stated to the United Nations in February 2003 that Iraq's admission that it produced nerve agents came only "as a result of the defection of Hussein Kamel." President Bush asserted in October 2002 that Iraq "was forced to admit that it had produced more than 30,000 liters of anthrax and other deadly biological agents" only after "the head of Iraq's military industries defected." Kamel's defection, Bush concluded, revealed "a massive stockpile of biological weapons that has never been accounted for" (Rangwala 2004).

The point of the story is clear: Iraq had weapons of mass destruction; its leaders lied about their existence; Kamel revealed the truth about Iraqi weapons programs. Despite the numerous references to this story, several important statements received no public attention until February 2003, when United Nations authorities released a transcript of Kamel's interview. They have received only scant attention since then.

Kamel stated, for example, "I ordered destruction of all chemical weapons. All weapons—biological, chemical, missile, nuclear were destroyed." When asked about anthrax, he stated that "nothing remained." When asked about the nerve agent VX, he asserted that "the program was terminated" and "we changed the factory into pesticide production." And when queried about prohibited missiles, he said that while "they had blueprints and molds for production, all missiles were destroyed" (Rangwala 2004). All of this occurred in 1991. Kamel revealed the information to the United Nations in August 1995, and that same month it appeared in a CIA intelligence report. So while the Clinton and Bush administrations used the Kamel story as evidence for the existence of weapons and as justification for military strikes against Iraq, Kamel actually attested to the past existence of such weapons and stated unequivocally that all of the weapons had been destroyed before Clinton took office.

We could offer many explanations for this. We could say that Clinton and Bush lied about the existence of weapons. We could point to a conspiracy to mislead the American people. We could presume that imperialist ambitions or a desire for personal revenge led our leaders to engage in a campaign of misinformation. Critics of both administrations have offered all of these explanations. But we need not surmise evil intentions to explain this phenomenon. A simple communication principle will suffice: stories take on lives of their own. They embed themselves in the structures of the medium and ensure that we see what we are prepared to see. We believe evidence that supports the narratives that frame our perceptions, and we ignore evidence that contradicts those narratives. Perhaps we will be better prepared to confront our problems and each other if we recognize that even those with whom we most vehemently disagree do not necessarily operate from surreptitious and evil motives. They may simply be doing what we all do as human beings who share a unique characteristic: we tell and consume stories.

These examples of metaphor and narrative illustrate two specific cases in which both the discourse and criticism of popular culture shape the medium. Whatever the object of study, the critic's primary task is to explicate how the medium influences the ways in which people understand, interpret, and experience their worlds.

The critic's work should make evident how popular forms and structures are part of a symbolic medium, and it should make possible alternative interpretations by calling attention to marginalized forms and structures. Embedded in this critical activity are several assumptions. One is that the discourse of popular culture has ethical effects; all of the texts and artifacts of popular culture encourage us to be particular kinds of people, and our experiences with those texts and artifacts are sometimes beneficial and sometimes harmful. A second is that the medium makes available to people a variety of interpretive strategies; we can construct our selves and our worlds in different ways. And a third is that the rhetorical criticism of popular culture is itself an ethical act; it identifies the possibilities for alternative worlds and selves, and it demonstrates the virtues of those alternative constructions. Criticism, like the texts of popular culture it examines, contributes to rhetoric's epideictic center, for the reality it most decisively makes is the very shape of our minds and souls.

References

Ackerman, S. (2004). A legacy of lies. *Mother Jones*, January/February. Available at: www.motherjones.com/news/update/2004/02/02_402.html.

Bineham, J. L. (1993). Theological hegemony and oppositional interpretive codes: The case of evangelical Christian feminism. *Western Journal of Communication* 57: 515–29.

———. (1995). The hermeneutic medium. *Philosophy and Rhetoric* 28: 1–16.

Black, E. (1970). The second persona. *Quarterly Journal of Speech* 56: 109–19.

Blair, C., J. R. Brown, & L. A. Baxter. (1994). Disciplining the feminine. *Quarterly Journal of Speech* 80: 383–409.

Booth, W. C. (1988a). *The company we keep: An ethics of fiction.* Berkeley: University of California Press.

———. (1988b). *The vocation of a teacher.* Chicago: University of Chicago Press.

Brockriede, W. (1974). Rhetorical criticism as argument. *Quarterly Journal of Speech* 60: 165–74.

Brummett, B. (1991). *Rhetorical dimensions of popular culture.* Tuscaloosa: University of Alabama Press.

Burke, K. (1973). *The philosophy of literary form.* Berkeley: University of California Press. (Original work published 1941.)

Bush's comments on Hussein capture. (2003). *Washington Post*, December 15, p. A8.

Carey, J. (1989). *Communication as culture.* Boston: Unwin Hyman.

Fishman, J. M. (1999). The populace and the police: Models of social control in reality-based crime television. *Critical Studies in Mass Communication* 16: 268–88.

Gadamer, H. G. (1976). *Philosophical hermeneutics.* Berkeley: University of California Press.

Grabe, M. E. (1999). Television news magazine crime stories: A functionalist perspective. *Critical Studies in Mass Communication* 16: 155–71.

Grossberg, L., & J. D. Slack. (1985). An introduction to Stuart Hall's essay. *Critical Studies in Mass Communication* 2: 87–90.

Hall, S. (1983). The problem of ideology: Marxism without guarantees. In B. Matthews (ed.), *Marx 100 Years On* (pp. 57–85). London: Lawence and Wishart.

———. (1985). Signification, representation, ideology: Althusser and the post-structuralist debates. *Critical Studies in Mass Communication* 2: 91–114.

Koch, T. (1994). *Minneapolis Star Tribune*, September 18, p. 24A.

Lakoff, G., & M. Johnson. (1999). *Philosophy in the flesh: The embodied mind and its challenge to western thought.* New York: Basic Books.

Lentricchia, F. (1983). *Criticism and social change.* Chicago: University of Chicago Press.

Mechling, E. W., & J. Mechling. (1991). The campaign for civil defense and the struggle to naturalize the bomb. *Western Journal of Communication* 55: 105–33.

Milbank, D. (2003). No gloating as Bush lauds "hopeful day." *Washington Post,* December 15, p. A1.

Nothstine, W. L., C. Blair, & G. A. Copeland. (1994). Professionalism and the eclipse of critical invention. In W. L. Nothstine, C. Blair, & G. A. Copeland (eds.), *Critical questions: Invention, creativity, and the criticism of discourse and media* (pp. 15–70). New York: St. Martin's Press.

Quindlen, A. (1994). Impossibly curvy shadow of Barbie at 35. *Minneapolis Star Tribune,* September 13, p. 11A.

Rangwala, G. (2004). The interview with Hussein Kamel. *Traprock peace center.* Retrieved April 4, 2004, from http://traprockpeace.org/kamel.html.

Rockler, N. R. (1999). From magic bullets to shooting blanks: Reality, criticism, and *Beverly Hills, 90210. Western Journal of Communication* 63: 72–94.

Rorty, R. (1979). *Philosophy and the mirror of nature.* Princeton, NJ: Princeton University Press.

Rostek, T. (1999). A cultural tradition in rhetorical studies. In T. Rostek (ed.), *At the intersection: Cultural studies and rhetorical studies* (pp. 226–47). New York: Guilford Press.

Schechner, S. (2003). Widely read dawn. *Slate,* December 15. Microsoft Corporation. Available at: http://slate.msn.com/id/2092525.

Sternberg, B. V., R. Olson, & D. Meryhew. (2003). Stunned—but not speechless. *Minneapolis Star Tribune,* December 15, p. A9.

Storey, J. (1993). *An introductory guide to cultural theory and popular culture.* Athens: University of Georgia Press.

Williams, R. (1977). *Marxism and literature.* New York: Oxford University Press.

CHAPTER THREE

Representation as Ethical Discourse: Communicating with and about Mediated Popular Culture

Phyllis M. Japp

A 1970s television game show, *To Tell the Truth*, presented three contestants, one "real" person and two imposters who pretended to be the real person. After a brief narrative biography, each of the three contestants was queried about details of the real person's life. At the end of the questioning, the studio audience voted to select the real person, at which point the host requested, "Will the real Mr. X please stand up?" The audience, most having no knowledge other than that presented by the contestants, chose as real the person who told the most believable story. The format made for an interesting game show, for those of us old enough to remember it. But in recent months I and undoubtedly many others have felt much the same toward current events. For example, as I watched the saga of Jessica Lynch, the POW recovered from an Iraqi hospital, unfold, I wanted to plead, "Will the real Jessica please stand up?"[1] In the media event, spread across a variety of genres—news reports, talk shows, and docudrama—fact and fiction were so intertwined that there appeared little difference between a network news spot, a *Primetime* interview, and a made-for-TV movie. And whose "facts" were truth—the Pentagon reports, the accounts of other soldiers, the fragmented memory of Lynch, explanations of Iraqi medical personnel, or the news reports and images that described her capture and recovery? Was she "rescued" by U.S. forces at great risk, or was she simply "retrieved" from those who were caring for her?

For most viewers, truth came down to what they believed to be the most compelling story filtered through their own values and biases. Was she a hero, a damsel in distress, or a pawn manipulated by the military and the press? Or all or none of the above? Various representations were accepted as "fact," in large part because they fulfilled what people wanted to believe.

As the Lynch event reminds us, we are so often in the same situation as the *To Tell the Truth* studio audience. Kenneth Burke (1966) graphically presents our dilemma:

> Take away our books, and what little do we know about history, biography, even something so "'down to earth" as the relative position of seas and continents? What is our "reality" for today (beyond the paper-thin line of our own particular lives) but all this clutter of symbols about the past combined with whatever things we know mainly through maps, magazines, newspapers, and the like about the present.... And however important to us is the tiny sliver of reality each of us has experienced firsthand, the whole overall "picture" is but a construct of our symbol systems. (p. 5)

As Burke notes, most of our "realities" are representations, stories told to us rather than events experienced firsthand by us.

Thus, we live in a world composed mostly of representations. Burke further warns us that there are no innocent or unbiased representations: "Even if any given terminology is a *reflection* of reality, by its very nature as a terminology it must be a *selection* of reality; and to this extent it must function also as a *deflection* of reality" (1966, p. 45). What we assume are accurate reflections, even if attempting to be faithful to some original event or idea, are of necessity selections of some elements of that original and thereby wittingly or unwittingly are deflections; that is, they construct a trajectory that excludes or deemphasizes some aspects of that original. And because "any nomenclature necessarily directs the attention into some channels rather than others," we cannot avoid bias; it is encoded into our selections of words and images (p. 45). Michael J. Shapiro (1988) concurs: "To the extent that a given image accords with the familiar and already known, it is naturalized and read as an unproblematic representation.... Indeed, an image is taken as 'real' to the extent that the interpretive codes with which it is received function unnoticed" (p. 150).

Indisputably, much of what we understand about the world comes to us already selected and shaped, as stories we assess for their veracity, credibility, and coherence (Fisher 1987). But we are not only consumers of representations, we are co-constructors as well. As we process representations, we make our own selections, choosing elements of what we see and hear that are important to our understanding, thereby deflecting some aspects of the whole. Thus, our own interpretations and elaborations are layered onto and embedded within our understanding of any representation we access. For example, in a conversation I overheard about Jessica Lynch, her story was cited by one discussant as evidence that women belonged in combat and by another as evidence that they did not, each person having selected from the Lynch story those details that supported his or her opposing point of view.

Ethics and Mediated Popular Culture

What, then, does a consumer do with the hundreds (if not thousands) of popular culture representations she processes daily, from the anecdote told by a colleague to the news story on the front page, from the ad on a billboard to the evening's entertainment at the theater or on television? And how is this activity related to communication ethics? I argue in this chapter that, consciously or unconsciously, consumers of mediated representations are value seekers. We search for the meaning, the worth, the authenticity, the purpose, and the usefulness of a representation for our lives. Some representations we deflect as irrelevant; some we make selections from—that is, we extract those elements we find interesting or relevant; some we accept uncritically. In all these instances we are necessarily engaging in a dialogue about meaning, importance, and value.

Dialogue, explained more fully below as an ethical construct, here refers to the co-construction of meaning, an acknowledgment that meanings are not formulated in isolation but in interactions with others, in the commonly shared symbols, forms, and formulas we must use to understand and communicate with others. Thus, to engage a representation is to be in conversation with that representation, whether in affirmation, contestation, or repudiation.

Moreover, we not only engage in dialogue *with* representations, we engage in dialogue *about* them, using selected elements to formulate arguments, make connections, or locate supporting evidence as we explain and justify our daily decisions in our dialogues with others.

As value seekers, whenever we enter into conversation with and about mediated representations, we are of necessity engaging in communication ethics, as we ponder stories of human behavior, their outcomes and implications. Christina Slade (2003) argues that there is "philosophical depth and complexity" in the mediated world, but that it is the responsibility of "the viewers and consumers of the media to explore this complexity in a rigorous and philosophically sensitive way" (xi). Certainly much has been written about the ethics of those who construct mediated representations. The ethics of journalistic practice—that is, the choices made in how a news story is framed and visualized—is the subject of several decades of scholarship. An equally large body of work addresses the ethics of representations in entertainment—for example, racial and gender stereotypes, unnecessary violence and sexuality, and other ethically suspect forms of characterization and action. A new genre of entertainment—reality television—confounds the usual information/entertainment, fact/fiction dichotomies as real people in supposedly real situations are fictionalized to produce the desired dramas that hold audiences' attention. The ethical dimensions of these practices beg scholarly reflection, which certainly is in progress. But important as it is to reflect on the ethics of producing mediated representations, we need equal consideration of the ethics of consumption; that is, how audiences of popular media read ethical issues into and out of such representations as they are also simultaneously constructing their own second-order representations from the mediated representations they access.

I could quickly become mired in complex debates about the nature of representation and its relationship to truth, of the power of media, of the features of mediated forms, genres, and formulas. Instead, I draw a few concepts from selections of that literature to articulate a critical process for engaging in dialogue with and about representations. First, I consider the ethical terrain of mediated representations, then how consumers of representations can pose ethical questions to those representations, and finally, how consumers can ethically communicate about the representations in popular culture.

The Ethical Terrain of Mediated Representations

Mediated representations encompass a vast field of forms and genres: popular literature and print media, self-help books, newspapers and magazines, film, television, ritual behaviors and practices, music, and the Internet. I concentrate primarily on television, film, and popular news, since most of the chapters to follow engage those media. However, the issues and processes outlined below are equally applicable to other genres of popular culture.

Varieties of "The Real"

If the simple oppositions of fact or fiction can ever be applied to the evaluation of representations, those distinctions are inevitably blurred in mediated domains. Supposing a continuum with fact/actuality at one end and fiction/imagination at the other, mediated representations fall at all points. Beginning with the supposedly factual end of the continuum, television news draws from the flow of daily events, makes its selections, reductions, interpretations, and elaborations and works these into a predetermined template—for example, a sixty-second feature, a two-minute "in-depth" report, or a longer segment on a program like *60 Minutes*. Yet mingled with whatever facts are verifiable we find summarizing, elaborating, abstracting, imaging, and editorializing, if not re-creations. While some aspects of the chosen event are not selected and thus go unreported, other important events of the day are entirely unnoticed, deflected from our attention. News, as Anne Norton (1993) notes, "gives currency to events. The selection of a set of circumstances, actions, conditions, and actors, the association of these, their transformation into literary form, their publication and dissemination invest certain acts, actors, places, and events with value and diminishes the value of others" (p. 34). As news stories are constructed with beginnings and endings, settings, characters, and plots, they come to represent, as Burke noted above, the "reality" of events for those not physically present and even for many who are. However accurate or inaccurate their rendition of actual events, such representations construct an implicit or explicit moral argument about the world of people and situations they claim to represent.

At the other end of the continuum, those representations overtly coded as fictions are free from the obligation to represent actual events, yet nonetheless are moral arguments about what could, might, should, or should not be so in the worlds they construct for our entertainment. These also are stories, constructed according to formulaic conventions, with selections of plot, characters, and settings. Films and television programming, like literary fiction, embody attitudes and values that are often—and often intended—to carry over into what we label the "real" world of thought and action. *ER*, *Law & Order*, and *The West Wing* depict the moral universes of our institutions of medicine, justice, and politics, respectively. *Friends* and *Seinfeld* give us visions of the ethics of friendship. Family sitcoms, from *Happy Days* to *Rosanne* to *The Simpsons*, provide images of family relationships and values. These texts, like those of great literature, engage the consumer in moral reflection about how life is to be lived, what relationships ought to be, and what integrity means in various situations.

In between these ends of the continuum lie a variety of mixtures of supposed fact and fiction. Docudramas dramatically configure the experiences of actual people into scripts that are a blend of fact and imagination. Television dramas advertise their plots as "ripped from the headlines." Reality television substitutes ordinary people for professional actors and supposedly spontaneous behavior and dialogue for prewritten scripts. Feature films re-create historical events, such as wars, murders, trials, assassinations, and assignations, blending and blurring fact and fantasy in a suitably dramatic script.

For example, while I was writing this essay, the docudramas of Elizabeth Smart and Jessica Lynch played on prime-time television while the Ronald Reagan television miniseries was *not* shown on CBS due to protests about its accuracy. Each was an imaginative reconstruction of actual people and events.[2] In the case of the Reagan programming, Reagan the historical figure, Reagan the myth, and Reagan the character in the television narrative were decidedly different, thus inciting a dispute over what was fact, what was fiction, and what collective political memory declared to be true or false. The accuracy of the docudrama and thus its moral value was read through the conflicting memories and ideologies of liberal and conservative politics.

So if we acknowledge that all representations are constructions and not reflections, how can we—or need we—make distinctions between fact and fiction? Norton (1993) suggests that engagement with media is "for most of us most of the time, an act of faith" (p. 36). And as John Fiske (1994) warns:

> In a postmodern world we can no longer rely on a stable relationship or clear distinction between a "real" event and its mediated representation. Consequently, we can no longer work with the idea that the "real" is more important, significant, or even "true" than the representation. A media event, then, is not a mere representation of what happened but it has its own reality, which gathers up into itself the reality of the event that may or may not have preceded it. (p. 2)

Yet for practical action in the world, we consider "did happen" and "could happen" as vitally different assertions that require different attitudes and actions. As Bernadette Casey and colleagues (2002) reflect, "by our everyday use of the term 'realistic' we try to judge how far a media representation is like some reality that we understand or have experienced." Since our knowledge is partial, our decision "relies on the quality of the text" to guide us in our judgment (p. 194).

In mediated representations, then, what is presented as "real" is coded via a set of conventions to create an argument of authenticity, urging consumers to accept it as such. R. V. Ericson (1998) asserts that "fact—defined simply as that which is accepted as reality—is an artifact of communication processes" (n.p.). Norton (1993) concurs: "One's own reliance on convention for judgments of truth and falsity, reveals the cultural significance of convention in the construction of truth" (p. 37). This does not, of course, mean that facts do not exist, only that we define and access those facts through a communication strategy that essentially says to us, "Take notice, this is a fact." Of course, that coded as fact may not be so; the "real" Mr. X on *To Tell the Truth* could be an imposter and who would know, since he was coded as authentic on the program when he stood in response to the request. Without doubt, Jessica Lynch is a living person who enlisted, went to Iraq, was injured, and returned. These facts can be verified in birth and Army records. But Jessica's mediated persona, coded to be authentic, is a creation of her representations. So our dilemma remains, what should we take as real, or actual, and what not? How do we define ourselves, others, and our world depending upon whether we categorize a given representation as fact or as fiction? If we cannot establish factuality, what ethical criteria *can* we bring to our assessments?

Norton (1993) suggests that the realization that we cannot know the "reality" behind representations can engender skepticism if not paranoia in audiences (pp. 36–37). Although the need for accuracy and authenticity can never, in my opinion, be considered irrelevant, neither can it ever be satisfied beyond doubt. We all in this volume believe that between passive, uncritical acceptance of representations as true and utter skepticism about any possibility of truth lie midpoints where consumers, as Fiske advises, can understand a representation as its own reality, and evaluate it accordingly.

Consumers clearly understand the "reality" of media texts to mean different things, factuality being only one. Alice Hall (2003) found that audiences use six criteria to determine the "reality" of mediated representations. In order of importance, these are plausibility, the belief that the events depicted "have the potential to occur in the real world" (p. 629); typicality, the conviction that the text is a "representation of events or characteristics that are common among a particular population" (p. 632); factuality, not only the belief that the text reflects actual events but the sense that it appears to "agree with representations in previously encountered texts" (p. 634); involvement, the sense of identification with characters and situations, when they "could either feel the characters' emotions or have an affective response to the characters the way they would to a real person" (p. 635); narrative consistency, the sense of an internally coherent logic in the story, whether news, fiction, or fantasy (pp. 636–37); and perceptional persuasiveness, the presence or absence of a "compelling visual illusion" that is believable (p. 637).

As Hall's research demonstrates, the fact/fiction dichotomy appears far too simplistic to describe the complex issues involved as consumers evaluate representations and search for their relationship to life. Slade (2003) points to the "paradox" of reality television in particular but of all mediated representations in general as simultaneously real and unreal (p. 208). Reflections are unreal, or in essence untrue, in the sense that whatever they claim to reflect they are both less and more than the original. Yet in another sense they are real and thus true, constituting an empirical phenomenon in their own right, an authentic product of culture and communication. And as Barry Brummett (2003) notes, all representations are inescapably moral in nature; "because representations are epistemic, the judgment of their epistemic efficacy is often moral" (p. 6). Thus, ethical analysis is appropriate for any representation, those argued as fact, fiction, or in-between, employing criteria such as honesty, integrity, fairness, care, and other values embodied and exemplified in the worlds they construct for our contemplation.

Communicating with Mediated Representations

As noted, the common form across all genres of mediated representations is the narrative structure. Shapiro (1988) insists that "a recognition that the real, or the what of our knowing, is inseparable from how it resides in our modes of representation must lead us to questions of style" (p. 8). And in popular culture, as with life in general, narrative is that style. According to Wayne Booth (1988), a narrative is any "presentation of a time-ordered or time-related experience that in any way supplements, re-orders, enhances, or interprets unnarrated life" (p. 14). Essentially every aspect of life as we know it, from birth to death, is constituted and experienced via narratives that define, explain, justify, and give meaning to what is happening. Narrative structuring of experience is virtually universal, since "no human being, literate or not, escapes the effects of stories," the "daily and hourly impact of stories that human beings have told to one another and to their own private selves awake and sleeping" (pp. 38–39).

Every narrative, Booth (1988) asserts, is didactic—that is, morally instructive (p. 144). All stories imply norms, reveal what is taken for granted in a culture as well as what is contested. The very fact that something is told, repeated, and dramatized infers that it is acceptable to do so. The "what, when, where, who, why, and how" of a narrative of necessity draws upon the common assumptions and expectations of the culture in which it is constructed and circulated. Narrative strategies such as "of course," "it goes without saying," or "once upon a time," are inherently evaluative; they encourage acceptance and investment in the story being told and discourage reflection or challenge outside the parameters of the story. The characters, real or fictional, embody qualities recognizable to readers/listeners as the vices and virtues prevalent in that culture as they act with integrity, honesty, respect, or lack of these qualities. The conflicts and relationships of the narrative, the ethical dilemmas, the opportunities to act or fail to act, resonate as understandable in that culture. Thus, embedded in any narrative are multitudes of moments or ethical flashpoints that invite reflection on what is happening in the story, on how that story connects to other stories, and on the relationship of the story to life in that culture. Below I draw from several theoretical approaches to narrative analysis to construct suggestions for engaging the ethical issues in mediated representations.

Dialogism as Ethical Inquiry

All narratives invite dialogue with their implicit or explicit moral arguments. As Brian Edmiston (2000) explains, dialogue is more than simply talk, it is the juxtaposition of orientations such that each is "seen through" the other. When two discourses or narratives are placed in dialogue, each engages the other, attempts to see the world as articulated by the other, and as a result is able to view its own world a bit differently. "Dialogising discourses produces the kind of 'both/and' thinking needed to create more complex understandings. When discourses are not being dialogised then people can easily drift into the kind of 'either/or' thinking that can result in an experience of a dichotomous binary" (p. 73). And, Edmiston continues, the process of ethical reflection is always dialogic:

> Being and becoming ethical is a social project, not an individual journey.
> Values are not acquired from outside us, but rather, are forged in dia-

logue among people and texts.… Thus encounters with stories or people, in everyday life and in the imagination of drama, are sites for dialogue through which we can become clearer about the ethical views we or others already hold and through which our ethical positions can change … ethical views are a facet of all the language and thought we use and encounter daily." (p. 64)

As a story states its case and lays out its view of the world, consumers enter into a dialogue in order to understand, question, comment, critique, and tease out its implications. While some arguments are overt and others more subtle, all are constructed from the ideas and experiences circulating in a culture that provide the basis for dramatic conjecturing about what our world is or might be. In all, such representations implicitly instruct the consumer to occupy a position or stance toward the story, one that suggests that he or she accept, believe, challenge, speculate, approve, or disapprove the characters and action therein and their implications beyond the narrative. If the objective "truth" of a narrative is not decidable, narratives nonetheless position readers to consider the world created therein for their truth-value. Even fantasy creates a world that one is invited to assess for its relationship to the actual world one inhabits.

Ethicizing Connections

Narratives, as noted above, connect elements and ideas. Donald Polkinghorne (1988) asserts that meaning and cognition are relational: "the question 'what does that mean?' asks how something is related or connected to something else" (p. 6). He posits several types of connection, three of which seem especially relevant to mediated representations. These connections depend upon what Burke (1969b) calls identifications and divisions—that is, determinations of what goes with what and correspondingly what does not go with what (pp. 19–29). As a narrative constructs identifications or connections between selected components, it simultaneously constructs divisions or disconnections between other components of the representation, or those components not selected for inclusion.

Polkinghorne's strongest identification is *sameness*, in which the elements being connected are presented as virtually identical

(1988, p. 4). When two elements are grasped together as one, what is true of one is automatically assumed to be true of the other. Thus, the emotions invoked by one—for example, affection, suspicion, or horror—are assumed to be felt for the other. The sameness argument is a profoundly moral declaration. Yet it is only when such a connection feels strange or objectionable that we become aware of its moral implications. When it fits our personal and cultural preconceptions, we tend to accept it uncritically.

Consider, for example, the controversy surrounding a recent PETA (People for the Ethical Treatment of Animals) campaign. When PETA chose images of Nazi concentration camp inmates to represent the plight of animals waiting for slaughter, there was moral outrage from many quarters. The connection, obviously selected for its shock value and ability to solicit media attention, was not an ethical one in most consumers' minds.[3] Consumers found the differences between the two realms of experience—human versus animal life—so great that they overwhelmed the proposed sameness identification, the fact that both humans and chickens were imprisoned and headed for death. If chickens and concentration camp prisoners were to be accepted as equal, the fate of one should evoke the same horror as the fate of the other. But in this instance, the comparison was repugnant to many, who refused the moral imperative of the sameness connection.

A strong but less essentialist connection is *similarity/dissimilarity*, the assertion that elements under consideration are like or unlike enough to justify the identification or division (Polkinghorne 1988, p. 4). An analogy, for example, claims that X is like Y to the extent that we should understand them as alike for a given purpose. If chickens and holocaust victims are similar primarily in their eventual fate, both being murdered for the gain of powerful others, we are invited to feel similar outrage over their deaths without feeling obligated to view them as alike in other respects. Again, many analogic connections are accepted uncritically, unless they happen to challenge a consumer's beliefs or values. In the PETA representation, the similarity connection was also rejected by many observers, the differences between the death of chickens at human hands and the death of humans by other humans not accepted as similar in intent or in repercussions for present and future action.

A third type of identification, collapsing several of Polking-horne's concepts (1988, p. 4), can be called *commonality*. Here the elements being connected are both members of a larger category, and thus can be used to "stand for" each other. Differences are acknowledged, but attention is focused on qualities that justify commonality. For example, one could legitimately place holocaust victims and chickens in a larger category of victims of human cru-elty or one of victims of mass execution. Such categories are usually broad enough to encompass a wide variety of historical instances across time and space—instances that might differ in many other particulars. Based on one selected particular, however, they are characterized as belonging to the same group. Commonality usual-ly requires justification, support for the assertion that shared char-acteristics justify placement together. Yet commonality also implies that members in the category deserve similar treatment by virtue of their membership. In the PETA case, the inclusion of both humans and animals as victims of inhumane treatment did not deny differ-ences between the species. Yet many could still not accept the argu-ment that these two experiences belonged together and certainly objected to the appeal for similar emotional responses to their fate.

Representative Anecdote as Moral Exemplar

The above discussion leads us back to Burke, for as he explains, often one member of a category becomes a paradigm narrative or image that over time comes to represent the entire category. Burke's (1969a) "representative anecdote" is an inquiry into the ethical is-sues involved when a part, or one of a group, is selected to "stand for" the whole. In simplest terms, a representative anecdote is a sto-ry that argues its adequacy to represent an idea, experience, event, or category with at least some of the necessary breadth (complexity and inclusiveness) and in some of the necessary depth (specificity and particularity) that allow it to be accepted as representative of all in the category. The representative anecdote can become, over time, the way we think and talk about the entire category; ultimately it may serve as our criteria for inclusion and exclusion from that cat-egory. And as Burke explains, a representative anecdote encapsu-lates the "moral of the story," identifies who or what is responsible;

who is to be praised, blamed, or scapegoated; with whom we are identified; from whom we are divided. If, for example, the holocaust were to become a representative anecdote for animal rights, as PETA proposes, it would be a profoundly moral indictment of current dietary practices and the industries and governments that support those practices.

However, Burke (1969a) warns that if an "anecdote is not representative, a vocabulary developed in strict conformity with it will not be representative"; that is, it will privilege some positions and understandings while denying representation to other elements that ought be given voice (pp. 59–60). C. Hanson (2003) argues that Jessica Lynch's story became a representative anecdote in media coverage of the war in Iraq. As he notes, "Central casting could hardly have contrived a better symbol of wholesome small-town values and American purity" (p. 58). The *Cleveland Plain Dealer* asserted, "the face of Gulf War II will forever be the smiling young woman under the camo-colored Army cap against the background of the American Flag" (quoted in Hanson 2003, p. 58). However appealing this story became as it was spun out by various media, did it deserve to "stand for" the war? Was Lynch's experience truly representative of the hundreds of soldiers wounded or killed in combat?

In my judgment and by Burke's criteria, the Lynch story constitutes an inadequate or faulty anecdote that ought not be accepted as representative, for it deflects consideration of other equally important lives and traumas, of issues, decisions, and the implications of those decisions that ought to be voiced. And with the PETA example, we can clearly see the perils of an anecdote that equates human and animal victims. Such equations are always open to use in reverse; the equation could comprise in other hands a powerful argument that human slaughter is of no more import than killing chickens. Thus, an anecdote that originated as a statement against animal cruelty could, in alternate circumstances, be used to support human genocide.

Narrative Interconnections

Finally, one must consider not only the narrative of a given representation but also other narratives that are connected to or are referenced within that narrative. Margaret Somers (1994) posits several dimensions or levels of narrative, from individual stories of experience to the master narratives that are the grounds of cultural knowledge and identity. At the personal level, what Somers terms *ontological* narratives explain the identities of individuals, families, and groups (pp. 618–19). Connected to these stories are larger, more *public* narratives, the institutional and political stories that form the context for our personal stories and within which we understand those stories (p. 619). Finally, there are *master narratives*, the overarching mythic structures of a society that feed both the public and personal narratives and for which they serve as explanatory frameworks (pp. 619–20). The saga of Jessica Lynch, for example, is the story of an individual nested in the public narratives of foreign policy and military service, these in turn nested in master narratives of gender, race, war, politics, and U.S. cultural values, among others.

Such nestings of narratives constitute a subtle but powerful moral argument. Framing the story of an individual within an accepted myth or taken-for-granted master narrative imbues that story with the values of the frame. A story of individual action, when framed in the myth of heroism, confers heroic status. A story of individual achievement, when framed in the myth of success via hard work, confers social approval on that individual. And, of course, narrative connections work negatively as well as positively. An individual story framed in a master narrative of deviance labels the personal story, and thus the person, as socially unacceptable.

Ethical Conversations with Representations

The above concepts invite consumers to engage in moral dialogue with mediated representations. In conversation with friends, for example, we might ask (or think to ourselves): "What is it you are asking me to believe?" "How will I be obligated to think/feel/act if I accept your story?" "What did you leave out of or add to your story?" "What is the moral of your story?" Or we object: "You're using this to support your belief in X, your condemnation of Y" or "You're leaving out Z, an important consideration for this issue."

The same questions can and ought to be addressed to mediated representations.

In writing this chapter, I've used the story of Jessica Lynch, the PETA campaign, and other representations current at the time of my writing. While these may be forgotten by the time this book is in readers' hands, others will have taken their place. Each week brings new representations, some enduring, some quickly forgotten, all serving as invitations to moral dialogue. Thus, as readers of this chapter consider the following questions for dialogue with representations, they are invited to choose a current event or situation to pull through the inquiry.

Critical Questions

Questioning is a time-honored method of engaging in ethical inquiry and one congruent with dialogic meaning construction. As Charles Scott (1990) notes, the process of questioning is at the heart of the ethical, and involves

> learning how to ask questions in given settings.... Learning to name things anew, to become alert to exclusions and to forgotten aspects ... to overhear what is usually drowned out by the predominant values, to rethink what is ordinarily taken for granted.... Questioning, as I use the word, is not a matter of indifference and ignorance, but a way of relating to something that holds its fascination or importance while it loses a measure of its authority. (pp. 7–8)

Such questioning, illustrated in the following suggestions for dialogue, is not hostile interrogation, but rather is a respectful engagement of the representation being questioned, an acknowledgment of its importance, and a tactic intended to uncover meanings and values that may not be apparent in a surface reading.

Reflection/selection/deflection. An important, very fundamental area for questioning representations involves their status as a reflection of some external fact or truth, consideration of how we are being asked to place the story. Does it claim to reflect or mirror real events? Is it overtly or implicitly coded as fact or truth? Whose reality is this, and why is it presented to me in this way? Concurrently, we must inquire about the processes of selection and deflection.

What has this representation selected to emphasize, feature, elaborate upon? Why those selections? Conversely, what has it deflected, chosen to conceal or deemphasize? Whose stories or points of view remain untold? How might the representation be different if these were included? What are the ethical implications of the silences or absences?

Identifications and divisions: Connections and disconnections. As the representation attempts to engage our emotions and solicit our approval or disapproval, we must also question what it implicitly asks us to accept or reject. To whom or to what will acceptance of this representation connect me? From what or whom will it divide me? Are elements in the story presented as the same, as similar, as having major characteristics of commonality? What are the ethical implications of accepting these connections or disconnections?

Representative anecdote. Another important area for questioning addresses the role of this representation vis-à-vis others. Is this representation arguing its value as representative of a category? Can it, should it, stand for others in a category? What else is included in that category? If the story is not representative, how is it inadequate or misleading? What is the moral position the story implicitly asks me to assume vis-à-vis the world and characters it constructs?

Narrative interconnections. Finally, we need to question the narrative interconnections within and surrounding this representation. To what personal, public, and master narratives is this representation connected? What cultural myths and beliefs does it reinforce or challenge, and how do these narrative connections support visions of good and evil, right and wrong, acceptable or unacceptable practices in this culture?

Ethical Conversations about Mediated Representations

Not only are we in a dialogue with mediated representations, but they also become part of our dialogue with self and others. Interpersonally, whether expressing concern about a news report, sharing laughter over a Letterman joke, arguing differences of opinion about the ending of a film, or reflecting on the latest ads, we represent representations in a variety of situations and contexts. Just as producers of media representations make selections in order to emphasize some issues rather than others, so consumers pick and choose among possibilities, gravitating toward those representations and the elements within them that reinforce their beliefs and values. Thus, a representation continues to mutate and accrue meanings as we place it in the context of other representations, past and present.

Here as well, every dialogue is a moral dialogue, every choice a moral choice. Moreover, we can and ought to pose the same questions to our own and others' use of representations as they ripple and spread out beyond the original boundaries constructed by the original. Thus, representations, the seemingly static entities we all access and construct, are the "raw material" of our ongoing communication. As narrative connects to narrative, as personal and public, moral and ideological elements are intertwined, each representation continues to live on as various interpretations, interests, and uses layer onto it and comprise the larger environment in which the original representation is embedded.

I end with two examples of ongoing engagement with representations, one historical, global, and political in its implications; the other current, local, and unimportant except to the community involved.[4] Both illustrate the vitality and interconnectedness of representations and the necessity for ethical reflection.

Is Iraq "Another Vietnam"?

In 2003, as the reasons for and against the invasion of Iraq were debated, the similarity of the situation to the Vietnam War was repeatedly suggested, supported by some and rejected by others. Except for those who actually lived the Vietnam experience, we understand that war via representations, images in newscasts, retrospective documentaries, films, memorials, and Internet sites such as those described by Scott Titsworth and Jeffery St. John in chapter 10 of this book. Personal, public, and master narratives are woven together in the collective memory and psyche of our citizens. This Vietnam of our collective memories is often invoked as an explanatory framework for more recent conflicts, as with the commonly expressed concern that Iraq might be "another Vietnam."

As the war appeared to be going well—or as well as could be expected—the Vietnam comparison was seldom heard. However, in April 2004, as Iraqi resistance to the occupation intensified and the death count of both U.S. forces and Iraqi citizens mounted, the Vietnam connection surfaced with renewed intensity. "Surely I am not the only one who hears echoes of Vietnam," declared Senator Robert Byrd, to be countered by Senator John McCain's assertion that it was "a totally false comparison" (Page, n.p.). The comparison seemed to grow more valid for many as they saw "mounting casualties, growing guerilla resistance. Skepticism about the justification for going to war in the first place. No clear strategy for finishing the job and coming home" (quoted in Page 2004, n.p.). If the Vietnam war was a mistake, a costly and immoral foreign policy blunder, then a sameness or similarity comparison charges that this one is as well. Those who reject the sameness comparison argue that differences outweigh any similarities. Certainly, for many, Vietnam has become the representative anecdote for a costly and unpopular war; as Evan Thomas (2004) writes, "To most Americans, Vietnam is the recurring nightmare" (p. 30).

Whatever the historical facts of Vietnam, that war in public memory will always be both more than and less than those facts, and will be consistently reworked in the light of contemporary issues, needs, politics, and purposes. Should we or should we not have engaged in that war, in this war? What does that event tell us about those that follow? What moral lessons should have been learned from that experience? The dialogue will continue as this current war takes its place alongside Vietnam and previous wars in history books and public memory and serves as a narrative frame for defining future conflicts.

"What? He Fired the Coach?"

And now to the local and mundane: perhaps only in Nebraska, that Midwestern state where not much happens on a given day, could the firing of a football coach push a war, a global disaster, and even Christmas shopping projections from the headlines. Upon completion of the last conference game in November 2003, University of Nebraska athletic director Steve Pederson fired Husker head coach

Frank Solich. Solich, who had a 9–3 win/loss record for the season, was the heir of legendary coach Tom Osborne, who had lob-
bied for his hire. For weeks the state was absorbed by the drama
as reflected in newspapers, television news, and editorials. Arguments and conversations debated the moral and practical implications of the action. Rumors were presented as fact; facts exposed
as rumors. Lawsuits were threatened; friendships ended; season
tickets returned; contributions to the athletic program rescinded;
judgments of God, Tom Osborne, and history invoked. Mediated
and personal dialogues centered on such moral issues as honesty,
integrity, responsibility, and openness. Coffeehouse conversations,
for a change, revolved around topics other than Nebraska weather.
Ethical concerns, although not so labeled, dominated discussions,
raising issues such as Does the end justify the means? Are long- or
short-term consequences more important? What is the role of caring and loyalty in organizational decision making? When is secrecy
justified? Is deceit ever necessary? What is the need for integrity in
individuals, organizations, and communities?

   In one especially heated conversation, I overheard the table of
morning regulars at the Mill, a local coffeehouse, debate whether
or not a winning season in 2004 would mean that the firing was
"the right thing to do." As one geezer put it, "Even if we win every game next year, it doesn't mean it was the right thing to do!"
Another disagreed: "Winning will prove he [Pederson] was right."
Another challenged, "So if we have a losing season it was wrong?"
And yet another: "It [the firing] may have been necessary, but that
doesn't mean it was right." These men, who certainly do not consider themselves moral philosophers, understood the profoundly
ethical issues at the heart of the incident. Overall, there was a sense
of ethical discomfort with the situation. A common refrain was
"We don't act that way in Nebraska," referencing what many felt to
be the moral values of the community of which they were a part.
Another comment that was received with nods of affirmation was,
"I was brought up to treat people with respect even if I have to
fire them."

   As with the public dialogue about Iraq, although of far less importance (except to a Husker football fan), the event, the represen-

tations, the connections, and comparisons made will continue to mutate and change as time passes. And we can be sure that, in Nebraska at least, the stories of the firing of the coach will be the nucleus of additional stories, explanations, justifications, praise, and censure as the decision is connected ethically and causally to the events that will succeed it. The dialogue with, and the re-presentations of, the coach's firing will continue, as future wins or losses are connected to the action of November 2003. Stay tuned!

Conclusion

Burke (1984) argues that "all living things are critics," reflecting the fact that we all, even animals, must learn to interpret what is going on around us and make distinctions or choices about what is desirable, good, and helpful and what is not (p. 5). The process of making such distinctions, at least in humans, is both a critical and an ethical process. As we choose among alternatives, from casting a vote to filling out a survey to flipping the TV remote, we are necessarily engaged in an evaluative process, are part of an ongoing conversation. There is no neutral position: to attempt to stand removed or disengaged from an issue or concern is a critical choice and thus a moral stance. Thus, it is imperative that we develop a conscious awareness of our critical choices, the grounds on which we make those choices, and the ethical implications embedded in those choices.

Thankfully, I and many of my students find this responsibility enjoyable and stimulating. Even the seemingly most mundane mediated narrative, an ad or news item or a television program, provides us with opportunities to discuss ethical values. What, we can inquire, are the values encoded into *The Apprentice*? Are they the values that we expect and desire in organizations? In sports? In politics? Why or why not? As we watch *Friends*, do we agree that it is sometimes acceptable to lie to our friends or family? In what circumstances? What if we discover they have lied to us? And what would result if we decided to emulate *Dr. Phil* when commenting on our friend's choice of yet another dysfunctional romantic partner? How do we define integrity, and what characters, from *Lord of the Rings* to the nightly news, embody that quality for us?

In these opportunities to engage a variety of mediated representations and participate in dialogue about them, we learn to articulate our own reactions, emotions, and values as well as to listen
to others who may or may not share those reactions. We become
ethical communicators by choice, not by default, using our critical awareness to consciously interpret and evaluate the mediated
popular culture in which we are immersed.

Notes

1. Lynch was the subject of many articles, news reports, and interviews, includ-
    ing an ABC *Primetime* interview with Diane Sawyer on November 11, 2003,
    and an NBC made-for-television movie, *Saving Jessica Lynch*, shown on No-
    vember 9, 2003.
2. The *Elizabeth Smart Story*, a made-for-television movie, was shown on CBS on
    November 9, 2003, opposite *Saving Jessica Lynch*. Smart is the Utah teen who
    was kidnapped and held captive for nine months. The Ronald Reagan mini-
    series, *The Reagans*, was pulled from the CBS lineup on November 4, 2003, in
    response to criticism and threatened boycotts of the network. A shorter ver-
    sion was shown on Showtime on November 30, 2003.
3. The images of PETA's "The Modern Day Holocaust" can be found on
    www.masskilling.com. The organization has included quotes from various
    individuals and organizations in a discussion about the validity of the anal-
    ogy and their defense of its use.
4. I have not referenced the multitude of sources on either the Vietnam com-
    parison or the Nebraska football situation. Both *USA Today* and *Newsweek*, as
    cited, overview the terms of the discussion about "another Vietnam." A search
    of LexisNexis will generate resources on both topics.

References

Booth, W. (1988). *The company we keep: An ethics of fiction.* Berkeley: University of
    California Press.
Brummett, B. (2003). *The world and how we describe it: Rhetorics of reality, representa-
    tion, simulation.* New York: Praeger.
Burke, K. (1966). *Language as symbolic action: Essays on life, literature, and method.*
    Berkeley: University of California Press.
———. (1969a). *A grammar of motives.* Berkeley: University of California Press.
———. (1969b). *A rhetoric of motives.* Berkeley: University of California Press.
———. (1984). *Permanence and change,* 3rd ed. Berkeley: University of California
    Press.

Casey, B., et al. (2002). *Television studies: The key concepts.* New York: Routledge.

Edmiston, B. (2000). Drama as ethical education. *Research in Drama Education* 5: 63–84.

Ericson, R. V. (1998). How journalists visualize fact. *Annals of the American Academy of Political and Social Science* (November): online edition.

Fisher, W. (1987). *Human communication as narration: Toward a philosophy of reason, value, and action.* Columbia: University of South Carolina Press.

Fiske, J. (1994). *Media matters.* Minneapolis: University of Minnesota Press.

Hall, A. (2003). Reading realism: Audiences' evaluations of the reality of media texts. *Journal of Communication:* 624–41.

Hanson, C. (2003). American idol: The press finds the war's true meaning. *Columbia Journalism Review* 42 (July/August): 58–59.

Norton, A. (1993). *Republic of Signs.* Chicago: University of Chicago Press.

Page, S. (2004). Is Iraq becoming another Vietnam? *USA Today.* Online edition, retrieved April 13 at: www.usatoday.com.

Polkinghorne, D. (1988). *Narrative knowing and the human sciences.* Albany: SUNY Press.

Scott, C. (1990). *The question of ethics: Nietzsche, Foucault, Heidegger.* Bloomington: Indiana University Press.

Shapiro, M. (1988). *The politics of representation.* Madison: University of Wisconsin Press.

Slade, C. (2003). *The real thing.* New York: Peter Lang.

Somers, M. (1994). The narrative constitution of identity: A relational and network approach. *Theory and Society* 23: 605–49.

Thomas, E. (2004). The Vietnam question. *Newsweek*, April 19, pp. 28–33.

CHAPTER FOUR

Leopold's Land Ethic: Environmental Ethics and Sustainable Advertising

Mark Meister

After Earth Day 1970, environmentalism reached its height in popularity as a social movement. Business and industry flaunted their so-called green commitments. Often called "green" advertising because of the association created between product and environmental issues, its intention was to increase product and service recognition, promote sustainability, and facilitate corporate social responsibility (Elkington, Knight, & Hailes 1991; Kinlaw 1993). As green advertising grew in popularity, it drew public criticism for not owning up to bogus environmental claims (Kilbourne et al. 1995). Federal laws were passed in the late 1980s making it illegal for industries to exaggerate their commitment to the environment.

Faced with criticism during the early 1990s by informed consumers and environmental groups (challenging the rhetoric of green advertising) and fraud investigations by the U.S. Federal Trade Commission, green advertisers began creating exceedingly implicit messages associating products with nature (Goldman & Papson 1997). Gone were the direct, often linguistic claims touting a product's environmental qualities, and in their place came less specific, visual claims using images of nature. Green advertising and marketing, predicted Dennis C. Kinlaw (1993), will, "in the future, do more than any government or environmentalist group to enlighten the public about the environment and its protection"

(p. 104). Such a claim should not be surprising given the saliency of nature imagery incorporated in contemporary advertising. Today, the association between product and nature is implicit, highly subjective, and increasingly visual. Kevin M. DeLuca and Ann T. Demo (2000) convincingly argue that nature imagery aided in shaping American environmentalism, and that these "pictures are constituting the context within which a politics takes place—they are creating a reality" (p. 242). For this reason, inquiry that investigates nature imagery in advertising is necessary because the influence of both nature and advertising in American society is profound, and because they visually create a reality (DeLuca and Demo 2000).

Yet, given the laws and regulations against explicit embellishment, we continue to witness embellished environmental themes appearing in advertisements. The embellishments today are implicitly manifested in highly stylistic and visual rhetoric ambiguously related to "sustainability" (the "balancing" of environmental concerns with those of industry and development). The "sustainable" manifestations of nature depicted in green advertising raise many ethical concerns precisely because these ads promote human lifestyles that often abuse nature. First, can the media and popular culture play a significant role in shaping public opinion to become more sustainable? Second, what type of environmentalism is prescribed in sustainable advertising? Third, what communication ethical concerns are there for how sustainable lifestyles are depicted in advertising? Environmental ethicist Max Oelschlaeger, in his book *Postmodern Environmental Ethics* (1995), refers to the "sustainability" buzzword as "primarily an apologetic for the continued wholesale exploitation of the earth and Third World peoples by multinational corporations and developed nations" (p. 7). Moreover, nature imagery in advertisements facilitates what Mark Meisner (1995) calls a resourcist or commodified reality of nature. Here nature has no intrinsic value other than what humans prescribe to it. The hybridization of nature ideology in advertising is highly visual rather than linguistic, operating as a facilitator of meaning seen rather than heard (DeLuca 1999; DeLuca & Demo 2000). In fact, the highly visual and stylistic emphasis of what Theodor Adorno and Max Horkheimer (1972) call the "culture industry" operates as a cultural mirror reflecting back both reality and fantasy (Jhally 1989).

Yet another ethical consideration involves how marketplace industries are now embodying environmental ethics. Can marketplace industries guided by profit margins actively promote environmentalism (sustainability), and if so, what type of environmental ethic (advocacy, consumerism, activism) is actually promoted? In advertising, the rhetoric of sustainability is complicated by how it portrays products in the context of idealized and desirable good life (Japp & Japp 2002). In fact, lifestyle data that are assumed to reflect market behavior are widely used by advertisers to identify and target market segments (Moore & Homer 2000). Because lifestyle measures focus on market segments only (what marketers often refer to as the measure of "affect intensity"), Basil G. Englis and Michael Solomon (1995) argue that visual representations of desirable lifestyles function as "pervasive elements of commercial and cultural signification" (p. 13). "Lifestyle" advertising is predominately visual, associating a "good life" or "quality of life" manifestation (Belk & Pollay 1985) that shapes, for example, how young people perceive alcohol consumption (Waiters, Treno, & Grube 2001) and how dieters perceive weight loss (Bishop 2001). As such, Serra Tinic (1997) contends that "advertising should be studied as a complex and contested social discourse" (p. 3) precisely because visual imagery in advertising metaphorically represents lifestyle choices through consumptive practice. Thus, contemporary advertising incorporates nature imagery and themes not in promoting the green characteristics of its products or services, but rather in displaying nature imagery and themes as they relate to a sustainable lifestyle based on consumption. Green advertising has been replaced by sustainable advertising—a shift from product and/or service to human lifestyle and consumption. Where once green advertising bolstered market share by promoting environmentalism, sustainable advertising uses nature in implicit ways: nature is not only commodified and consumed, it becomes part of a lifestyle distinct from nature.

This essay is guided by two assumptions and one definition in its inquiry about the ethics of sustainable advertising. The assumptions reflect Fredrick J. Antczak's (1991) challenge to focus on rhetorical concerns as ethical concerns. The challenge, according to Antczak, is to "articulate the moral possibilities and limits [and] to describe ... the discursive community that is constituted" in the text (p. 82). I embrace Antczak's challenge and offer Aldo Leopold's land ethic as a construct in defining the discursive community illustrated in sustainable (lifestyle) advertising.

The first assumption addresses how the ethical concerns of nature imagery in advertising often depend on the ambiguous notion of sustainability articulated by the United Nations (UN). Thus, in order to unmask, from a communication standpoint, the ethical saliency of what I call sustainable advertising, it is necessary to profile the UN discourse of sustainability. Second, can an environmental ethic perspective aid communication scholars in clarifying the tenuous claims made in advertisements steeped in sustainability? To address these questions, I rely heavily on Leopold's notion of land ethic as a critical framework in this discussion of sustainable (lifestyle) advertising. Leopold's land ethic formulates not only an ethical perspective, but also a critical one. Leopold advocates, in simple terms, moderation in resource consumption. Leopold's vision embraces ethical sustainability. Sustainable advertising involves paid-for promotions that incorporate nature imagery and themes while depicting comfortable, secure, and simple lifestyles without direct association to environmental imagery and themes. Rather, in sustainable advertising, nature imagery and themes are relegated to background status and the services and products promoted in the advertising occupy the foreground. The juxtapositioning of nature and product, nature and service, and nature and technology in sustainable advertising offers a balanced lifestyle manifestation, a vision of sustainability predicated on consumption and technology rather than stewardship for the land.

I begin by discussing Leopold's land ethic. My purpose here is not only to establish it as a credible critical lens from which to discuss sustainable advertising, but also to point out the relevance of the concept for communication ethicists. Finally, I offer an abbreviated analysis of Ford automobile sustainable advertisements incorporating Leopold's land ethic.

Leopold's (Communication) Land Ethic

Raymie E. McKerrow (1989) and other rhetorical critics interested in critical rhetoric attempt to embrace a "critique of domination" and a "critique of freedom" that seek to "unmask and demystify the discourse of power" (p. 91). The critical rhetoric inquiry provides an entry point by which to discuss the ethical considerations of sustainable advertising. Critical rhetoric focuses on the inter-relationship between communication and culture and the vital role power plays in the formulation of cultural knowledge. From the entry point of critical rhetoric, I discuss Leopold's land ethic as a construct that helps us understand communication ethics as a communication-cultural phenomenon complicated by power. This is a particularly important starting point given the role of advertising in our society, and my purpose here is to unmask the ethical tensions that surface in advertising using nature imagery.

Leopold first described the notion of land ethic in his book *A Sand County Almanac*. Since its publication in 1949, the land ethic concept has been discussed primarily by academics (for example, Attfield 1991; Bruner & Oelschlaeger 1994; Callicott 1989, 1994; Ferre & Hartel 1994; Katz 1997; McCloskey 1983; Sylvan & Bennett 1994). Because Leopold's land ethic idea has been primarily the focus of the academic community, little knowledge and understanding of it as a concept emphasizing such values as community, stewardship, and moral responsibility exists outside the academia. In short, as J. Baird Callicott (1989) states, Leopold's land ethic is "from a philosophical point of view, abbreviated, unfamiliar, and radical" (p. 76).

Leopold notes, "There is as yet no ethic dealing with man's relation to land and to the animals and plants which grow upon it.... The land-relation is still strictly economic, entailing privileges but not obligations" (1966, p. 238). Leopold resolves this gap by offering an ethic as a "mode of guidance for meeting ecological situations ... a kind of community instinct in-the-making." Leopold begins formulating his land ethic by grounding it in systems theory, noting that the "individual is a member of a community of interdependent parts" and that the land ethic "simply enlarges the boundaries of the community to include soils, waters, plants, and animals, or collectively: the land" (p. 239). Human society, Leopold argues, is founded, in part, upon mutual security and economic interdependency and preserved only by limitations on freedom of action in the struggle for existence—that is, by ethical constraints (Callicott 1989). In basic terms, Leopold's land ethic calls for what Kenneth Goodpaster (1978) calls "moral considerability" for the biotic community: "In short, a land ethic changes the role *Homo sapiens* from conqueror of the land-community to plain member and citizen of it. It implies respect for his own fellow-members, and also respect for the community as such" (Leopold 1966, p. 240). Leopold emphasizes a community theme in his notion of land ethic because it includes holistic as well as individualistic connotations. As individual members of a larger holistic community, notes R. L. Knight (1996), humans possess the moral responsibility to care for nature and "must acknowledge [their] role as … integral part[s] of an ecosystem, whose activities must be attuned to natural processes of utilization and restoration" (p. 471). In essence, our moral duty is the creation and implementation of a land ethic based on stewardship and responsibility, which specifically emphasize, according to B. Shaw (1997), three land virtues: respect (or ecological sensitivity), prudence, and practical judgment. This emphasis on ethics requires limiting how nature is traditionally used, and thus "would impose limitations on human freedom of action in relationship to nonhuman natural entities and to nature as a whole" (Callicott 1994, p. 1).

Significantly, Leopold's land ethic is implicitly referred to in Mackin's (1997) call for an ecological approach to communication ethics. "An ecological approach," notes Mackin, "avoids the synecdochic error of identifying semiotic with language" (p. 71). Communication ethics, from an ecological standpoint, nurtures individuals in their quest for a good life because it conceives communication as a system pragmatically interdependent upon and shaping other systems. Mackin notes that communication is a means of building, maintaining, and transforming various communicative systems: communication is an ecosystem, "a system that nurtures and supports" communicative practices (p. 85). Leopold's land ethic is consistent with an ecological approach to communication ethics because it focuses on the multifaceted and systematic interdependency between our rhetorical constructions of nature and humanity.

Sustainable Development and the Ethics of Sustainable (Lifestyle) Advertising

To unpack the ethical issues in sustainable advertising, there must be a focus on the discourse of sustainability. The preferred reading of the discourse of sustainability is that it embraces Leopold's land ethic, because it emphasizes notions of community and stewardship. My alternative reading points out that the discourse of sustainability actually promotes unsustainable (unethical) lifestyle practices (excessive consumption, industry dependence) even though it promotes stewardship and community interrelatedness. Sustainable advertising is constructed to foreground consumers' desires and thereby position the lifestyle as powerful, prestigious, and superior in relation to other lifestyles. In essence, sustainable advertising is monologic and self-directed rather than dialogic and other-directed.

Prior to 1992, a lifestyle based equally on environmental and economic motives seemed impossible. According to Tarla Ray Peterson (1997), environmentalists urged the UN to tighten its position on global environmental regulation, while business and industry petitioned for more access to the earth's natural resources. The United Nations Conference on Environment and Development (UNCED, a.k.a. the "Earth Summit"), held in Rio de Janeiro in the summer of 1992, was the UN's attempt to "bridge" the opposition between environmentalists and industrialists. According to the UN, the preservation/conservation concerns of environmentalists and the economic concerns of the industrialists can embrace the practice of "sustainable development" to protect both the environment and its utility for economic prospects (Peterson 1997).

The focus at UNCED was on the convention's guiding document, the four-hundred-plus-page *Agenda 21*, which outlined "sustainable development" practices. According to *Agenda 21*, sustainable development is needed because "integration of environment and development concerns and greater attention to them will lead to the fulfillment of basic needs, improved living standards for all, better protected and managed ecosystems, and a safer, more prosperous future" (UNCED 1992, p. 12). The intent of sustainable development practices is to improve the quality of human life on earth. By bridging the concerns of both industry and the environmentalists, the discourse of sustainable development promises quality of life or "lifestyle" improvement (Meister & Japp 1998).

The UN vision of sustainable development is found in the World Commission on Environment and Development's *Our Common Future* (WCED 1987), and *Agenda 21*. On the one hand, both the vision and implementation of sustainable development by the UN dictates the necessity of technology so that consumers will not cause environmental harm when their survival is threatened. Technology, according to UN sustainable development discourse, provides the consumer with protection from nature. According to *Agenda 21*, "The central purpose of development is to improve the quality of life on our planet—to enable all of humanity to enjoy long, productive and fulfilling lives. A balanced and healthy environment is equally crucial to allow humanity to achieve a standard of living which provides comfort, security and satisfaction" (quoted in Sitarz 1993, p. 30). Thus, the UN describes sustainable development as a perspective whereby "[e]nvironment and development are not separate challenges; they are inexorably linked. Development cannot subsist upon a deteriorating environmental resource base; the environment cannot be protected when growth leaves out of account the costs of environmental destruction" (WCED 1987, p. 37).

Armed with the ambiguous notion of sustainability, marketplace industries began shaping their products and services in sustainable ways in the mid-1990s. The emphasis was on enhancing the sponsoring companies' image as socially responsible by associating their products and services with environmental issues. While sustainable advertising is certainly a complex issue, it potentially promotes two constructs directly in opposition to Leopold's land ethic: technocentrism (O'Riordan 1976) and human-centeredness (Fox 1990). In the technocentric and anthropocentric vein, nature is "usually regarded as an object of knowledge *constructed* through careful scientific methodology" (Herndl & Brown 1996, p. 11, emphasis added). The emphasis here is on the rhetorical construction of nature and its consistent affiliation with technology. Presently, television mediates Jeep commercials in which slowly panning and close-up shots of dashboards, plush bucket seats, and roof racks gradually morph into rocky landscapes, wild animals, and rugged rivers. Another SUV commercial displays a young, Wall Street–type man coming out of a large glass-and-concrete building onto the chaotic streets of Manhattan. As he enters his parked SUV, he magically morphs into a rugged individualist, "shedding" the skin, clothes, and briefcase of the executive, and "growing" the stereotypical long beard, khaki shorts, and Polartech pullover of the stereotypical environmentalist/recreationist. Other commercials portray cars as revered hunting animals, superiot to the wolves that admire and envy the particular car's speed and traction (Hochman 1997).

Given my claims that green advertising has been redefined as sustainable advertising, and that this discourse rhetorically masks its commitment to industry, I offer the following analysis of automobile sustainable advertisements by the Ford Motor Company. Sustainable advertising rhetorically masks (through the promotion of lifestyle activities) its commitment to consumption behind a quasi reverence for nature. The result is a discourse that falsifies and conceals profit intentions in a stylized vision of social responsibility.

Method

To offset criticisms by environmental groups, the automobile industry is particularly active in promoting sustainable advertising. The automobile industry has created its own "Green Index" recognizing industry leaders for their environmental practices. Completed by important opinion leaders in the automobile industry, the Green Index measures the overall environmental and technology leadership of all automobile manufacturers. The Ford Motor Company was selected as the top company for overall environmental leadership by 35 percent of those respondents selecting an automaker ("Ford Recognized" 2000, n.p.). Important to note here is that Ford incorporates nature imagery and themes in its advertising. But distinct from traditional green advertising, Ford is not specifically addressing environmental themes of community (interrelatedness), stewardship, moderation, and responsibility. What is present is the illusion of such themes, consistent with the discourse of sustainability outlined above.

The texts for this analysis are the images of nature contained in the print advertisements and brochures for Ford's best-selling automobiles (in the two-door, four-door, SUV, minivan, and pickup vehicle types) from 1998 to 2002. Although Ford also owns Lincoln, Mercury, Mazda, Volvo, Jaguar, Land Rover, and Aston Martin, only printed texts promoting Ford Motor Company automobiles marketed only in the United States were included in this study. In all, sixty-four advertisements or brochures were analyzed. Ten texts focus on Ford's two-door Mustang, and ten focus on the four-door Taurus sedan. Sixteen texts for the Explorer SUV, twelve for the Windstar minivan, and sixteen for the Ranger pickup are also included in the collection.

Leopold's land ethic characteristics of community, stewardship, moderation, and responsibility are used to critique the ethics of the advertisements. Thus, the themes associated with a land ethic are compared and contrasted with the printed and visual discourse apparent in the advertisements.

Ford's (Un)sustainable Lifestyle

Ford facilitates a sustainable lifestyle in its advertising, a socially constructed good-life theme that seamlessly juxtapositions nature with technology (as manifested in the Mustang, Taurus, Explorer, Windstar, and Ranger vehicles). In all, the advertisements both reflect and deflect Leopold's land ethic. The ethical components of community, stewardship, moderation, and responsibility are ambiguously present, yet the prescribed reading offers distinct deflections from these environmental ethic themes. In what follows I argue that Ford's sustainable advertising promotes lifestyles opposed to Leopold's vision of sustainability, all the while addressing the major themes of his ethic. I discuss the advertisements with regards to the following unethical themes: nature as marginalized other, denying nature, nature objectified as backdrop, and nature as object of consumption.

Nature as Marginalized Other

Generally the ads for the two-door Mustang and the four-door Taurus use bold urban backdrops such as skylines, office buildings, valet parking lines, hotel and spa facilities, salon storefronts, and even a contemporary glass door-front labeled the "Museum of the Western Civilization." The scenes of the Mustang and Taurus ads marginalize nature by implicitly pointing out the superiority of the "human" or "urban" experience over the natural or agrarian experience. Nature is a place of retreat—a place for unwinding and forgetting the perplexities of urban life. In this way, nature is marginalized in a way that promotes service to the human experience.

With no exception, images of the Mustang or Taurus occupy the foreground, and in most cases handsome heterosexual couples are seen either speeding (accentuated by colorful streaks denoting speed) away from the urban backdrops (office buildings) or getting out of the automobile in front of hotels, spas, and museums. It is important to note that in all the brochures for the Mustang and Taurus, technology is discussed in terms of power (control) and style. For example, in a bold-lettered line of copy, a brochure notes that the V-6 engine of the Mustang "MAKES ITS NAMESAKE CRINGE WITH ENVY." A tagline notes that the Taurus's comfort and style "reinforces its powerful engine and wraps you in security." Generally, the mood communicated in the Mustang and Taurus ads revolves around the notions of power and style. It is a mood of security in both wealth (attainment) and comfort (accessories), a context of "urban sophistication" that appreciates the luxuries of urban life (technology) yet is sympathetic to the simplicities of nature. Nature provides a retreat for the important and profitable life of the urban sophisticate, who when given the chance speeds carefree away from the city and into nature (metaphorically represented by hotels, spas, and museums). A Mustang ad staged on country-club polo grounds (with canopy tents and horse stables in the background) sums up the urban sophisticate's grand lifestyle, stating in bold letters that the setting and the car are "THE ESSENCE OF AMERICA." As such, nature is visually represented as a retreat (a country club or polo club) and technology (wealth, profit) as the means by which to attain the deserved rest that retreating to nature (spas, hotels) provides.

Denying Nature

The most direct association between technology and nature imagery is present in ads for the Ford Explorer. The Explorer ads deny nature's inherent ethical value in favor of moralizing technology. Advertisements for the SUV, in general, are ripe with nature imagery (Meister 1997; Olsen 2002) that, according to Olsen, are "used to demonstrate that the fantasy operating in many SUV advertisements attempts to position the SUV as a purchasable and permanent resolution to the dialectics inherent in our relationship with nature" (p. 175). The mood of the Explorer ads is clearly one of escape. But where the ads for the Mustang and Taurus communicate a mood of retreat from urban life made possible by technology, the mood of Explorer ads implies a primal relationship between humanity and nature. The Explorer ads visually demonstrate how humanity and technology morph back into seemingly natural conditions and settings. The Explorer visually morphs into naturelike images, and this morphing allows potential Explorer owners to become more natural. For example, in several ads the Explorer's metallic high-gloss finish reflects images of soaring eagles, a thundering herd of bison, and a mirrored image of a couple rafting a wild river.

In a Ford "No Boundaries" Explorer ad, technology overpowers the obstacles of nature (mountains, rivers, canyons, boulders). The Ford Explorer provides the technology needed to "go farther" (a popular tagline used in the print ads). The Explorer is the ideal vehicle for the ideal "outfitter," intent on getting "back to nature." The Explorer, which always occupies the foreground, is set against nature's boundaries. Yet these natural boundaries are visually manipulated and reinforced as part of technology.

Another visual reference to nature exists in an Explorer ad in which the open spaces of the prairie and grasslands are juxtaposed with visuals of the Explorer's interior space. The bold headline reads: "AND YOU THOUGHT YOU'D HAVE TO GO TO THE COUNTRY FOR OPEN SPACES." The perceived openness emphasizes security and comfort (images of dashboards with stereo, cruise, and air-conditioning controls) rather than the "wildness" of prairies (snakes, bugs, and extreme weather). Herein, the visual association between the Explorer's space and prairie space is one of limited engagement with the prairie (nature). In the comfort, security, and technology of the Explorer, occupants can enjoy watching nature through tinted-glass windows while sitting in cloth or vinyl seats, and being fanned by air-conditioning. Nature's "wildness" is replaced by the Explorer's good-life technology.

Nature as Objectified Backdrop

In the ads for the Windstar minivan, images of the American family are juxtaposed against images of seemingly "natural" settings. For example, at least three Windstar ads show a variation on the image of a thirtysomething mother securing her children into safety seats inside the Windstar. Examples of the copy associated with these ads include: "Trust the Windstar, because you never know what's out there," "Safety for your family is our No. 1 priority," and "At Ford, we are proud of our Five-Star safety rating." The wholesome family—complete with attractive white parents, two to four children, and golden retriever—projects a mood of love, appreciation, and security. Windstar families appreciate the security that the Windstar provides. Most noteworthy is a line of copy below the appreciative family imagery that reads: "FORD UNDERSTANDS THE NEEDS OF FAMILY," under which a tagline elaborates, "From the Ford Family to Yours the Peace of Mind of a Five-Star Safety Rating."

Images of nature are not prevalent in the Windstar ads. In the ads analyzed for this study, only two Windstar ads clearly use nature imagery. Yet the notions of family and security are overwhelmingly present in all ads studied. The settings for the ads vary and include: shopping mall or supermarket parking lots, soccer practice fields, school and church parking lots, and stadium parking lots (family-friendly tailgate parties). Those Windstar ads incorporating nature show images of the wholesome family camping at a modern campsite. The Windstar is parked on a concrete slab with portable camping supplies adjacent to it. The supplies include a gas grill, a hammock hanging between trees, a portable picnic table, and several outdoor lounge chairs. Family members demonstrate their contentment by sitting patiently at the picnic table as they wait for the father figure to bring them the food prepared on the gas grill. A bold headline states: "ALL THE COMFORTS OF HOME." Nature is seemingly a place that is discomforting (even in modern concrete campsites), yet the Windstar secures the family and comforts like a "home away from home."

Nature as Object of Consumption

Ford Ranger owners are adventure seekers, freely and confidently roaming through and over riverbeds, canyon valleys, cascading waterfalls, and lush forests. Nature is a recreational playground for the Ranger owner; it is depicted as a place for recreational consumption. Several Ranger ads show the pickup pulling boats, and carrying skis, canoes, and motorcycles in its "heavy duty" bed.

In this construction, recreating in nature is a dirty job. The visuals in the Ranger ads support this claim. One ad in particular visually depicts Ranger owners washing the pickup after a weekend of recreation. The Ranger is covered with clumps of wet and dry mud. The pickup's alloy wheels have plant life and earth embedded in the wheel wells. Using a garden hose and buckets of soapy water, a young heterosexual couple sprays the vehicle with water. The bold headline states: "WEEKEND WARRIORS KNOW HOW TO CLEAN UP." Nature seemingly provides the ideal setting for the "weekend warrior's" recreational activities. Another Ranger ad shows a young couple driving through thick mud, marsh, and swamplands. The copy reads: "Let it fly." Mud is no challenge to the powerful Ranger engine and optional four-wheel-drive capacity. "Let nature fly" is seemingly the attitude of the Ranger owner.

Ford provides the confirmation that "sustainability" (balancing technology and environmental concern) is possible and, moreover, ethical. For Mustang and Taurus owners, technology is a means for retreating to the sublime relaxation of nature, while the Explorer and Ranger owners are appropriately outfitted with ample technological power for overcoming nature's obstacles. The family is secure from nature because of the "Five-Star" safety rating of the Windstar. Indeed, these sustainable advertisements reinforce the value of community. Yet the community illustrated is one quite distinct from the interrelatedness theme embodied by Leopold. The manifestations are of elite communities, distinct from the other parts of the larger holistic community of humanity and nature. The community in these advertisements includes only those with the wherewithal to enjoy nature's sublime and artistic qualities—apart from the discomforts of the land. Additionally, the theme of stewardship is merely alluded to in these advertisements. The message promotes a stewardship not of nature, but of technology. Moderation and simplicity themes are present, but only to the extent that nature provides an escape, while responsibility to nature is overshadowed by the responsibility to acquire technology.

Implications and Conclusion

Leopold's land ethic assumes that one must communicate with nature with the same sense of dialogue, integrity, and respect as one would with humans. Sustainable advertising violates these basic premises of ethical communication by denying its inherent value, pretending to dialogue with nature while exerting power, and gratifying the self at the expense of the needs of the other.

In advertising, the aesthetic and sublime imagery of nature provides a compelling scene for marketing products. The regularity of the symbolic representations of nature creates among consumers an unwarranted sense of knowledge about or familiarity with nature (McKibben 1992). Because images of nature are a constant part of the cultural landscape—not only through the images of nature in Ford advertising, but also through the poster and calendar art, cartoons, and picture postcards that are woven into our daily lives—we may come to feel we know nature. DeLuca and Demo (2000) note that visual images of nature "cultivate and propagate an image of sublime nature, but, to be precise, a spectacularly sublime nature reduced to domestic spectacle, a nature both sublime and a source of sustenance for the civilized tourist" (p. 254). Because nature is domesticated, thereby catering to human desires, Brian Tokar (1997) suggests that an environmental backlash is taking shape. Tokar points out that three related phenomena—the absorption of the mainstream environmental movement by the political status quo, the emergence of corporate environmentalism, and the proliferation of "ecological" products in the marketplace—have helped fuel the perception of a declining popular commitment to environmental protection. The perspective of nature that Ford promotes in its print advertisements is indicative of this trend because it uses nature as a billboard for accentuating its products. Sustainable advertising contributes to a sense of environmental engagement, by promoting disengagement with nature. Potentially, consumers become interested in environmental issues because they see how such issues relate to consumption interests. In semiotic terms, the visual sign of nature imagery in advertising becomes arbitrarily "connected, disconnected, and reconnected to commodities [and] needs become insatiable" (Goldman & Papson 1997). As such, a sustainable future relies upon how we see through the advertising and marketing of technology and the comfort it promises for living a good life.

Advertising will continue to project themes contrary to Leopold's land ethic while extolling its virtues. What is disturbing, from an ethical communication standpoint, is how themes related to consumption and technology are redefined to include an environmental ethic. In this way, advertising incorporating nature will continue to propagate the nature/culture dichotomy, defining, shaping, and promoting lifestyles that seemingly encourage environmental awareness while necessitating technological and economic sustainability. Leopold foreshadowed this shift:

> Perhaps the most serious obstacle impeding the evolution of a land ethic is the fact that our educational and economic system is headed away from, rather than toward, an intense consciousness of land. Your true modern is separated from the land by many middlemen, and by innumerable physical gadgets. He has no vital relation to it; to him it is the space between cities where crops grow. Turn him loose for a day on the land, and if the spot does not happen to be a golf links or a "scenic"

area, he is bored stiff…. Synthetic substitutes for wood, leather, wool, and other natural land products suit him better than the originals. In short, land is something he has "outgrown." (1966, pp. 261–62)

Advertising, and its vision of sustainability, facilitates a consumption ethic predicated on technology, rather than a land ethic predicated on interconnectedness with nature. The prominence of lifestyle advertising, like that of the Ford Motor Company, requires consumers to be conscious of the ethical boundaries blurred. If the concealment surfaces in an analysis of print advertisements, there certainly exist more manipulative levels of abstraction in television lifestyle advertising. The motion, sound, music, and context of lifestyle advertising on television provide further "synthetic substitutes" that threaten our connectedness to nature.

References

Adorno, T., & M. Horkheimer. (1972). The culture industry: Enlightenment as mass deception. In S. During (ed.), *The cultural studies reader*, 2nd ed. (pp. 31–41). London: Routledge.

Antczak, F. J. (1991). Discursive community and the problem of perspective in ethical criticism. In K. J. Greenberg (ed.), *Conversations on communication ethics* (pp. 81–88). Norwood, NJ: Ablex.

Attfield, R. (1991). *The ethics of environmental concern*. Athens: University of Georgia Press.

Belk, R.W., & R. W. Pollay. (1985). Images of ourselves: The good life in twentieth century advertising. *Journal of Consumer Research* 11: 887–98.

Bishop, R. (2001). Old dogs, new tricks? An ideological analysis of thematic shifts in television advertising for diet products, 1990–2000. *Journal of Communication Inquiry* 25: 334–53.

Bruner, M., & M. Oelschlaeger. (1994). Rhetoric, environmentalism, and environmental ethics. *Environmental Ethics* 16: 377–96.

Callicott, J. B. (1989). *In defense of the land ethic: Essays in environmental philosophy.* Albany: SUNY Press.

———. (1994). *Earth's insights: A survey of ecological ethics from the Mediterranean Basin to the Australian Outback.* Berkeley: University of California Press.

DeLuca, K. M. (1999). *Image politics: The new rhetoric of environmental activism.* New York: Guilford.

DeLuca, K. M., & A. T. Demo. (2000). Imaging nature: Watkins, Yosemite, and the birth of environmentalism. *Critical Studies in Media Communication* 17: 241–60.

Elkington, J., P. Knight, & J. Hailes. (1991). *The green business guide.* London: Victor Gollancz.

Englis, B. G., & M. Solomon. (1995). To be and not to be: Lifestyle imagery, reference groups, and the clustering of America. *Journal of Advertising* 24: 13–29.

Ferre, F., & P. Hartel. (1994). *Ethics and environmental policy*. Athens: University of Georgia Press.

Ford recognized as top automaker in global survey of environmental leadership. (2000). Dearborn, MI: Ford Motor Company, March 16. Retrieved September 20 at: www.ford.com.

Fox, W. (1990). *Toward a transpersonal ecology: Developing new foundations for environmentalism*. Boston: Shambhala.

Goldman, R., & S. Papson. (1997). *Sign wars: The cluttered landscape of advertising*. New York: Guilford.

Goodpaster, K. (1978). On being morally considerable. *Journal of Philosophy* 75: 306–25.

Herndl, C. G., & S. C. Brown. (1996). *Green culture: Environmental rhetoric in contemporary America*. Madison: University of Wisconsin Press.

Hochman, J. (1997). Green cultural studies: An introductory critique of an emerging discipline. *Mosaic* 30: 81–97.

Japp, P. M., & D. K. Japp (2002). Purification through simplification: Nature, the good life, and consumer culture. In M. Meister and P. M. Japp (eds.), *Enviropop: Studies in environmental rhetoric* (pp. 81-94). Westport, CT: Praeger.

Jhally, S. (1989). *The codes of advertising*. New York: St. Martin's.

Katz, E. (1997). *Nature as subject: Human obligation and natural community*. Lanham, MD: Rowman & Littlefield.

Kilbourne, W. E., S. Banerjee, C. S. Gulas, & E. Iyer. (1995). Green advertising: Salvation or oxymoron? *Journal of Advertising* 24: 7–20.

Kinlaw, D. C. (1993). *Competitive and green: Sustainable performance in the environmental age*. San Diego: Pfeiffer and Company.

Knight, R. L. (1996). Aldo Leopold, the land ethic, and ecosystem management. *Journal of Wildlife Management* 60: 471–75.

Leopold, A. (1966). *A Sand County almanac*. London: Oxford University Press. (Original work published 1949).

Mackin, J. J. (1997). *Community over chaos: An ecological perspective on communication ethics*. Tuscaloosa: University of Alabama Press.

McCloskey, H. J. (1983). *Ecological ethics and politics*. Totowa, NJ: Rowman & Littlefield.

McKerrow, R. E. (1989). Critical rhetoric: Theory and praxis. *Communication Monographs* 56: 91–111.

McKibben, B. (1992). *The age of missing information*. New York: Plume.

Meisner, M. (1995). Resourcist language: The symbolic enslavement of nature. Paper presented at the Conference on Communication and Environment, Chattanooga, TN.

Meister, M. (1997). "Sustainable development" in visual imagery: Rhetorical function in the Jeep Cherokee. *Communication Quarterly* 45: 223–34.

Meister, M., & P. M. Japp. (1998). "Sustainable development" and the "global economy": Rhetorical implications for improving the "quality of life." *Communication Research* 45: 223–34.

Moore, D. J., & P. M. Homer. (2000). Dimensions of temperament: Affect intensity and consumer lifestyles. *Journal of Consumer Psychology* 9: 231–42.

Oelschlaeger, M. (1995). *Postmodern Environmental Ethics*. Albany, NY: SUNY Press.

Olsen, R. K. (2002). Living above it all: The liminal fantasy of sport utility vehicle advertisements. In M. Meister and P. M. Japp (eds.), *Enviropop: Studies in environmental rhetoric and popular culture* (pp. 175–96). Westport, CT: Praeger.

O'Riordan, T. (1976). *Environmentalism*. London: Pion.

Peterson, T. R. (1997). *Sharing the earth: The rhetoric of sustainable development*. Columbia: University of South Carolina Press.

Shaw, B. (1997). A virtue ethics approach to Aldo Leopold's land ethic. *Environmental Ethics* 19: 53–68.

Sitarz, D. (1993). *Agenda 21: The earth summit strategy to save our planet*. Boulder, CO: Earthpress.

Sylvan, R., & D. Bennett. (1994). *The greening of ethics*. Tucson: University of Arizona Press.

Tinic, S. (1997). United colors and united meanings: Bennetton and the commodification of social issues. *Journal of Communication* 47: 3–26.

Tokar, B. (1997). *Earth for sale: Reclaiming ecology in the age of corporate greenwash*. Boston: South End Press.

United Nations Conference on Environment and Development. (1992). *Agenda 21: The United Nations program of action from Rio*. New York: United Nations.

Waiters, E. D., A. J. Treno, & J. W. Grube. (2001). Alcohol advertising and youth: A focus-group analysis of what young people find appealing in alcohol advertising. *Contemporary Drug Problems* 28: 695–730.

World Commission on Environment and Development. (1987). *Our common future*. New York: Oxford University Press.

CHAPTER FIVE

Tragedy and Comedy as Ethical Responses to John Rocker

Jeffery L. Bineham

On December 23, 1999, news services in Atlanta reported the following: "John Rocker went to bed Tuesday night a brash, young baseball star. He awoke Wednesday morning a pariah" (Stinson 1999, December 23).[1] Rocker's status as outcast was precipitated by *Sports Illustrated*'s publication of an article in which Rocker calls a female driver a "stupid bitch," castigates Asian women with "Look at this idiot! I guarantee you she is a Japanese woman" (she wasn't), and ridicules New York for its "Asians and Koreans and Vietnamese and Indians and Russian and Spanish people": "How the hell did they get in this country?" He complains about the presence of "some queer with AIDS" and "some 20-year-old mom with four kids," he calls one Hispanic teammate too old to make a play and another African American teammate "a fat monkey," and he says that his manager lied to the media when he told them that he had instructed Rocker not to provoke fans at Shea Stadium (Pearlman 1999, pp. 60, 62). For the next three months the Atlanta media spewed forth innumerable articles, letters, talk shows, interviews, and editorials about the words Rocker had spoken, how people should interpret them, and the punishments or rewards to which Rocker should be subject. This situation provides a helpful case study for those interested in the kinds of public reactions proffered in response to a violation of social protocol.

We should see the Rocker case, therefore, as representative of the many cases in which public figures make remarks about race or gender that violate societal norms. This analysis should provide insight into how we might understand reactions to former Cincinnati Reds owner Marge Schott's racist comments, former Los Angeles Dodgers executive Al Campanis's statement that African Americans do not have the skills needed to manage a team, or former New York Jets quarterback Joe Namath's repeated efforts to kiss a female television reporter. This analysis should also provide insight into how rhetoric frames cases that involve violations of legal standards, such as the Kobe Bryant rape trial or the Pete Rose gambling fiasco. And if we do not confine the Rocker case to the sports world, this analysis can provide insight into violations within the political arena, such as Jessie Jackson's referent to "Hymie town" or Bill Clinton's sexual escapades while in the White House. Perhaps most important, if the Rocker case contains examples of rhetorical forms that recur over time, then understanding those rhetorical forms positions us to understand future situations of similar ilk.

John Rocker was a pitcher for Atlanta's major league baseball team from 1998 until 2001. He became a nationally known sports figure because of his performances in the 1998 and 1999 postseason series, in which he demonstrated exceptional pitching talent and a propensity to engage in shouting matches with opposing fans. Jeff Pearlman says that during the 1999 series against the New York Mets, "Rocker was a one-man psycho circus. He spit at Mets fans. He gave them the finger" (1999, p. 62). He was traded to Cleveland during the 2001 season, to Texas in 2002, and to Tampa Bay in 2003, where as of this writing he evidently has finished his career. But the particulars of Rocker's career as a baseball player or as a public figure are not as important as what he represents as a rhetorical phenomenon. Rocker the individual will fade from view quickly. When we contextualize Rocker as an example of how rhetoric frames transgressions perpetuated by public figures, however, he can teach us something of lasting value.

This chapter is ostensibly about public responses to Rocker's numerous faux pas. I focus exclusively on those responses published in the *Atlanta Journal and Constitution* (Atlanta's major newspaper) between the publication of the *Sports Illustrated* article and the beginning of the baseball season approximately three months later (by which time the issue had run its media course, although it did surface at several times during the season because of further Rocker blunders). But a theoretical question underlies my interest in this event: How might various publics learn ethical principles from the discourse of popular culture (in this case, the discourse of one popular urban newspaper)? I am interested not only in those principles by which we might discern "right" actions from "wrong" actions, but also and most particularly in those principles by which we judge those who do violate widely recognized social mores. What lessons does the *Atlanta Journal and Constitution* present to its readers about the degree to which responsible social institutions (Major League Baseball, the Atlanta baseball club, the Atlanta community) should sanction or punish John Rocker?

I suggest in this chapter that the judgments urged upon Rocker exemplify tragic and comic ethical responses. The first section of the chapter explains tragedy and comedy as ethical responses articulated in the realm of popular culture. The second section examines how specific discourse from the *Atlanta Journal and Constitution* develops these tragic and comic responses. The chapter's conclusion identifies some implications of these responses and reiterates how tragedy and comedy are instructive concepts whenever we seek to understand public responses to the violation of social norms.

Tragedy, Comedy, and Ethics

Kenneth Burke states that while "all animals communicate in one way or another ... only human animals can tell one another Stories, ranging from the most trivial comments or gossip to Stories about geology, archaeology, celestial mechanics" (1984b, p. 331). Since any story is a type of drama, it makes sense that for Burke "the ultimate metaphor for discussing the universe and man's relations to it must be the poetic or dramatic metaphor" (p. 263). And Burke states that one question lies at the heart of his philosophy of dramatism: "What is involved, when we say what people are doing and why they are doing it?" (1969a, p. xv). This seemingly simple question entails three rather complicated concerns: it calls attention to issues of definition (*what* people are doing), it calls attention to

issues of motive (*why* they are doing it), and it calls attention to issues of language (what is involved when we *say* those definitions
and motives). These issues arise for anyone who attempts to understand a controversial action, but they are especially important for
the critic who wants to understand how the discourses of popular
culture dramatize a problematic situation.

Burke emphasizes that definitions and motives are dependent
upon language. That is, "what people do" and "why they do it" are
functions of the dramas into which we cast those actions and incen-
tives. "For the things that happen to us," he writes (1970, p. 169),
"do not acquire their identity from themselves alone, but also reflect
the character of the way in which we confront them" and dramatize them in story. Tragedy and comedy are two common dramatic
forms by which we make sense out of "what people do" and "why
they do it." As such, tragedy and comedy are symbolic responses to
situations. They encourage particular types of interpretations and,
in so doing, implicitly advocate different standards for action and
judgment. They thus embody different ethics.

In this section of this chapter I examine how the forms of tragedy and comedy provide particular perspectives toward ethical
judgment in society. I proceed in two steps. First, I explain the characteristics of tragedy and comedy to demonstrate how they might
frame situations in ways that contain definitions and motives. Second, I assess how the tragic and comic frames are also statements of
ethical principles. This will prepare us for the chapter's second section, where the Rocker case illustrates how these two frames play
out in the rhetoric of popular culture.

Tragedy and Comedy

Central to Burke's conceptions of tragedy and comedy is the idea
that people are mysterious to one another because, as a general
condition of human existence, they embrace different modes of living (1984b, pp. 276–78). People participate in different professions,
they belong to different social classes, they adopt different beliefs
and values, and they enjoy different hobbies. As active audiences
of popular culture they attune to different media organizations and

to different messages, and even when the same or similar artifacts of popular culture garner the collective attention of a public, that public's subgroups are apt to construct different meanings for those artifacts. As people experience their daily lives amid the ubiquitous influences of popular culture, they construct universes of discourse and meanings that serve to facilitate identification with some collectivities and to establish distinction from other collectivities.

Mystery arises from these differences. For Burke (1969b, p. 115), mystery is a kind of "strangeness" within which the estranged are "in some way capable of communion." Sometimes mystery manifests itself in hostility or division between individuals or social groups. Sometimes mystery is a function of identification with one range of meanings and the consequent though quiet disassociation from another set of meanings. In any case, humans orient themselves to mystery through the creation and maintenance of symbolic hierarchies that provide systems of meanings, practices, and values that enable people to relate to one another. When people identify with a common hierarchy, they transcend some of the mysteries that envelope and divide them. A church is a hierarchy that orders relationships so that its parishioners can transcend mysteries evoked by different political commitments, different employment situations, and different levels of socioeconomic status. A corporation is a hierarchy that orders relationships so that its members can transcend mysteries evoked by different religious beliefs. Any society contains multiple hierarchies. Some of those are embedded in the structures of a given society; they are established conditions of our experience, sets of assumptions into which we are born, and while we might on rare occasions critique those hierarchies, they usually serve as fundamental and unquestioned assumptions. In other cases people consciously select the hierarchies toward which they will direct their allegiances.

When someone violates the standards of a social hierarchy, the members of that hierarchy work to repair the violation through their definitions of the transgression and the imposition of punishment upon the transgressor. The dramatic genres of tragedy and comedy describe two symbolic forms that people use to deal with wrongdoing and thus to repair a hierarchy. These symbolic forms contain different explanations of who the transgressor is, the kind of hierarchy the transgressor has violated, the punishment the transgressor should receive, and the desired result of that punishment.

In tragedy we attribute wrongdoing to an essential character defect. Transgressors are evil people whose actions represent their quintessential nature. In tragedy what one does is a product of who one is, so the essence of tragedy is character. Tragic protagonists act autonomously, unhindered by situational constraints, and antagonists assume "demonic proportions" and appear responsible for all evil in the world (Appel 1997, p. 384). So tragic characters suffer not simply because of their circumstances—"the gods hate them, or they are shipwrecked, or wounded in battle"—but because of actions they have chosen to take as a result of some character flaw or "inadequacy" (Freeman 1999, p. 252).

That flaw is a deficiency in their humanity, and their violation is against eternal principles of justice and virtue. A tragedy is "less satisfactory" to the extent that it emphasizes the personal character of an individual rather than the ethical principle that character represents (Williams 1966, p. 34). Burke (1968) writes that "tragedy is based upon the firm acceptance of an ideology" (p. 162) and that it requires a sense of "intimate participation in processes beyond" oneself (p. 200) and a "calamitous persistence in one's ways" (p. 201). The purveyors of the tragic form, then, describe a human world that is subject to a transcendent moral order. Tragedy emphasizes "crime" against an established ideology that cannot be questioned, because its source is beyond the pale of human communication; it is God or the gods, or some other natural or supernatural arbiter of fundamental principles.

Central to tragedy is the dispensation of the tragic victim. In tragedy wrongdoers are banished and possibly condemned, both to protect society and to separate those whose evil nature we cannot redeem. Such punishment is reasonable within the tragic frame precisely because the dysfunctional person has violated the eternal moral order and because that violation, since it emanates from the person's essence, forecasts the inevitability of future evil actions.

But the tragic victim pays for more than his or her own impiety, for tragedy requires its central villain to act as a scapegoat for the rest of society (Burke 1984a, p. 39). Burke (1984b) states that the scapegoat is a formula whereby the sins of a people "could be transferred to the back of an animal, the animal was then ferociously beaten or slain—and the feeling of relief was apparent to all" (p. 16). As a dramatic frame, tragedy involves the symbolic (though sometimes literal) killing or expulsion of a scapegoat upon whom a society has placed the responsibility for collective impieties. The victim must be identified with those whom it would purify so that it can assume their iniquities, their violations of a hierarchy, and then suffer the symbolic alienation that atones for the impieties of those who attack it (Burke 1969a, p. 406). We burden the scapegoat with our ethical shortcomings and then drive it from our midst because in tragedy the violations that the victim represents are irreparable and call for the destruction rather than the rehabilitation of that victim (Williams 1966). The goat is not simply uneducated or uninformed; the goat suffers from willful disobedience and heresy against the established hierarchy (Duncan 1968). The appeal of tragedy is thus located in guilt and fear. Because we banish or destroy the goat, we disclaim responsibility for its transgression and thereby maintain our purity and save ourselves from punishment.

Burke notes that the scapegoat mechanism is an instance of "trained incapacity" or "rationalization" or "error in interpretation" (1984b, pp. 11, 14, 17). It is, in other words, an inability to see beyond an established ideology. But Burke also suggests that the scapegoat is necessary: "some variant of the scapegoat principle *is* required, as soon as you turn to consider the sacrificial element in ethics" (p. lviii). Tragedy offers a symbolic form that assuages guilt and resolves social tensions. It emphasizes the maintenance of a fixed moral code and each individual's responsibility to adhere to that code. It brooks no violation of communal standards. Tragedy thus often resolves itself in tears and anguish. That resolution results, nonetheless, in an affirmation of the values that bind people together and a condemnation of unethical actions that do violence to relationships and to individuals.

Within the tragic frame, then, the transgressor is evil in nature and has violated an ultimate moral order; the required punishment is sacrifice or banishment, and the desired result of that punishment is purification of the social order. The comic frame explains each of these elements in a significantly different fashion.

Comedy is a matter of ridicule, or of the ridiculous, and it thus requires an object for society to ridicule rather than a victim for society to sacrifice. So while tragedy requires the scapegoat, comedy requires the clown. The clown must be like us in some important ways or we would not recognize him or her as a clown, for that sense of likeness provides the common values by which we deem the clown ridiculous. In tragedy the goat acts in accordance with its role, but in comedy the clown violates the expectations of its role. And those violations provide the grounds by which "we must show that he is *inferior*, either to the ordinary, or at least inferior to what has been thought or claimed about him, by himself or others" (Olson 1968, p. 12). The likeness of the clown to other characters in society draws our attention to shared customs and ideals, and the unlikeness of the clown renders it appropriate for derision and ridicule.

While tragedy attributes wrongdoing to a dysfunctional human nature, comedy attributes wrongdoing to a mistake in judgment. Transgressors are otherwise good characters who do something wrong while in difficult circumstances. Their flaws are of error or ignorance, and their violations are against the social values that bind us as a community rather than against the eternal laws of God or nature. In a comic frame the clown is not evil. Our ridicule of the clown might occur for many reasons, but we never mock the clown because we think it is malevolent. Whatever vices the clown thrives upon, they are products of error or ignorance rather than wickedness, and the clown can function therefore as an example rather than as an enemy (Carlson 1988). Indeed, even though the vices that the clown represents are destructive of social order, comedy emphasizes that those vices are frequently the excesses of virtues. Arrogance might be the excess of pride, for example, or foolishness the excess of courage. In comedy, consequently, we can "correct the abuse in the name of a social norm of conduct" (Duncan 1968, p. 175). Because the clown is not evil, the possibility exists for correction and reconciliation.

Also, because the clown is not evil, that correction can feature dialogue and reason rather than castigation and elimination. Hugh D. Duncan (1968) notes specifically that "the social appeal of comedy is based on belief in reason in society" (p. 60). Within the comic frame, a community does punish and renounce a clown, but that is only temporary, and the community then "uses reason to correct" the vices that caused the castigation, recognizes that all human beings are imperfect (Carlson 1986, p. 448), and ensures that reunion can occur "through dialogue" (Toker 2002, p. 63). The ethical standards of tragedy and comedy differ most significantly on this central point: tragedy features excommunication, while comedy features communication. At worst, that communication shames the clown into conciliation (hence the emphasis on ridicule), but it never condemns the clown as an outcast.

Comedy thus emphasizes instruction rather than sacrifice. Its goal is to dramatize the "quirks and foibles" of human experience (Burke 1984a, p. 42) and to call attention to the fact that we are all fools in need of humane instruction. Comedy thus encourages multiple perspectives and requires a willingness to see beyond established ideologies. Comedy emphasizes "stupidity" rather than crime and requires "fools" rather than villains to do its work. "The progress of humane enlightenment," Burke writes, "can go no further than in picturing people not as *vicious*, but as *mistaken*. When you add that people are *necessarily* mistaken, that *all* people are exposed to situations in which they must act as fools, that *every* insight contains its own special kind of blindness, you complete the comic circle, returning again to the lesson of humility that underlies great tragedy" (p. 41).

Given this emphasis, it is no surprise that comedy is the symbolic form most conducive to social improvement (Toker 2002). The clown represents the vices and errors of the community and serves as the symbolic vehicle by which those impieties are rejected, but society ultimately recognizes the clown's humanity and welcomes it back into the social order (Carlson 1986). The theme of comedy is inclusion, and its end is to reconcile the widest range of characters, to recognize the humanity even of those whose values exist on the margins and are most subject to repudiation. Northrup Frye (1957) calls this comedic theme "grace" (p. 166). Burke sees in it the promise for a lasting society, and Carlson says that it "reduces social tension" and invokes a balanced worldview (Carlson 1988, p. 310). Comedy encourages a hopeful vision for the resolution of social ills and for the restoration of community ties that have been damaged or severed. In comedy wrongdoers are censured and rehabilitated, both to provide restitution to society and to forgive transgressors and restore them to the fold. Since all humans are subject to error, all should be open to the possibility for reconciliation and for the creation of harmonious relationships based on the reclamation of common values. This is comedy's message and the appeal of its symbolic form.

Within the comic frame, then, the transgressor is guilty of error or ignorance and has violated a social compact; the required punishment is instruction or ridicule, and the desired result of that punishment is reconciliation to the social order.

Two weeks before I wrote these words, a fifteen-year-old boy from a small town near where I live appeared in court to face charges that he had taken a handgun to his high school and shot to death two fellow students. No doubt exists that he pulled the trigger. Some, including his lawyer, have raised questions about extenuating circumstances. In his court appearance, the boy, John Jason McLaughlin, was certified to stand trial as an adult, a decision that could result in life imprisonment. The media reported different reactions to the decision. The town's mayor stated that some people believe McLaughlin should face the tougher penalties possible in the adult system. Others prefer a different resolution. "I wish it could be solved in some different way that would promote both justice and healing," the mayor said (Burcum 2004, p. A13).

This case provides a clear illustration of the dramatic frames I have explained above. As tragedy, it looks like this: McLaughlin is an evil person whom we must isolate from society as a punishment for his crime and because no hope of rehabilitation exists. Given that his actions stemmed from his flawed and unchangeable nature, we must protect the public from future evil actions. When we ostracize him, we emphasize that he is not like us, and we thus see his isolation as a movement toward social stability and the common good.

As comedy, the case looks like this: McLaughlin is an otherwise good person whose criminal actions were stupid and wrong. Those actions stemmed from a set of circumstances—he was taunted, bullied, and suffered from mental illness—within which he made horrible choices. While we must hold him accountable for those choices, we recognize that they do not make him a monster, and that the proper response is to provide a means for redemption and rehabilitation. We will censure but not ostracize him, and in so doing we maintain our connection to him and include him within the circle of humanity.

If we opt for the tragic frame, we proclaim our belief that we can be free of the evil that we see in McLaughlin. By isolating him we purify society. If we opt for the comic frame, we admit that within all of us exists the potential to make horrible mistakes. By forgiving McLaughlin we recognize the imperfections of society and we learn from his situation. One thing is clear in a case like this: whenever someone violates the protocols of society, we must render an important decision. The frame we choose reveals more than our attitude toward the perpetrator; it reveals also who we are as a people, for it pronounces a particular set of ethical standards.

Ethics

Because they are dramatic forms, tragedy and comedy are well suited to expression in the rhetoric of popular culture, and they provide a coherent set of principles by which to assess human action. Burke notes that "each of the great poetic forms stresses its own peculiar way of building the mental equipment (meanings, attitudes, character) by which one handles the significant factors of his time" (1984a, p. 34). They provide a common orientation, a system of interpretations about the past, present, and future, and any system of interpretations is essentially a classification of events into "because of," "in spite of," and "regardless of" categories (p. 36). These classifications have a decidedly ethical bent, as illustrated in Burke's own example: one might say that a person was hurt in an accident *because of* his or her wickedness, or *regardless of* his or her wickedness, and that attribution is an assessment of the person's character.

Any symbolic frame contains an implicit "program of socialization" (Burke 1984a, p. 170). That is, when we decide why people act as they act we also decide how we should relate to them. The relationships among characters in dramas and in our lives are products of the formal situations in which we place those characters. Thus, a tragic situation calls forth a particular set of roles, and a comic situation calls forth a different set of roles. So as Burke notes, to characterize a situation as a tragedy requires the identification of an appropriate victim and the identification of characters who will perform the requisite sacrifice (1966, pp. 486–87). The formal properties we attribute to the situation construct a set of expectations for how we will relate to one another as a community. Duncan (1968) develops this same idea when he writes that in both tragedy and comedy the actors voice those virtues that a society's "guardians" hope will elicit loyalty from individuals and the community; the presentation of these symbolic forms thus preserves the polity (p. 98).

While tragedy and comedy are both ethical orientations that revolve around character and community, they are decidedly different orientations in that they encourage community members to practice different types of relationships with one another. Tragedy constructs community upon enduring principles that set forth absolute standards for knowledge, conduct, and governance. It calls for obedience to eternal truths and castigates those who act in ways that separate humans from the gods. Comedy constructs community upon principles that regulate our social relationships with one another. It calls us to communicate with each other, and it censures those who act in ways that separate people from people, social group from social group (Duncan 1968). Tragedy, in other words, deals with comprehensive forces; comedy deals with social forces. And in keeping with these general principles, the central figure in a tragedy is ultimately isolated from society, while the central figure in a comedy is integrated back into society (Frye 1957).

In sum: tragedy and comedy are symbolic forms that evince different ethical principles for the construction of character and community. Tragedy features evil and the scapegoat while comedy features error and the clown; tragedy excommunicates the central character from a community while comedy incorporates the central character into a community; tragedy is about retribution while comedy is about correction. Punishment and rectitude are the bases for an ethic of tragedy, as it renders moral judgment against the wicked in an individual. Instruction and humility are the bases for an ethic of comedy, as it renders social judgment against the absurd in a community. As I will demonstrate in what follows, the Rocker case illustrates how the dramatic forms of tragedy and comedy encourage these different standards for ethical judgment.

Public Responses to John Rocker

Tragic and comic themes appear in works of popular culture just as surely as they do in works of great literature. And while Burke says that literature is equipment for living, in the world of popular culture all types of symbolic action can function as equipment for living. The mainstream press provides a rich source of discourse that people regularly attend to and that they use to construct meanings for their experiences. In the Rocker case specifically, the plethora of newspaper coverage was one source of this equipment, and it provided audiences with clear and different ethical visions. This case is of particular interest because it contains a "double plot" with both tragic and comic characteristics (Burke 1966, pp. 400–1). It thus illustrates some differences between these dramatic forms.

Tragic Responses

A tragic character must be of superior status, and if that status does not derive from moral excellence, as it often does for tragic heroes, it can derive from the character's "worldly rank" (Brereton 1968, p. 37) or from "the situation in which he finds himself" (p. 18). Rocker's position as an athlete, and his central role as the subject of a *Sports Illustrated* feature, provide the symbolic resources required to establish him as a tragic figure. And indeed a tragic theme is evident in many of the responses to Rocker. The responses that develop this theme exhibit two characteristics. First, they present Rocker as representative of society at large. And second, they call for Rocker's sacrifice. These responses thus feature the scapegoat motif.

For Rocker to function as a scapegoat requires that the views featured in the *Sports Illustrated* essay be characteristic of his thinking rather than the result of a misstatement or misunderstanding. Brereton (1968) notes that a tragic character's ignominious act might well be devoid of evil intent or based in ignorance rather than malevolence, but the act will not function tragically unless people attribute it to the character's personality. Predictably, Rocker claims a distinction between what he said and what he believes. His initial public statement reads, "Even though it might appear otherwise from what I said, I am not a racist" (Stinson 1999, December 23). And in an interview Rocker states that "I have been definitely grossly misrepresented," that it "wasn't my intent" to offend anyone, and that we all "say things we really don't mean." When asked whether he is a racist he responds, "Absolutely not. If I were a racist, A, would I want a black guy to come into my house? B, would I invite him to my house? I've done that three times over" ("What Was Said" 2000). Rocker's denials of intent notwithstanding, much of the public discourse explicitly connected Rocker's comments to his character. One essay notes that Rocker "laid open an unseen aspect of his character" that was marked by "deep irascibility" (Stinson 1999, December 24), and another essay quotes an Atlanta community leader as saying that "Rocker deserves to be fired because his comments were not spontaneous. He had plenty of time to think about what he was saying during the 7-hour interview" (Roedemeier 1999). A front-page article asserts that the *Sports Illustrated* interview demonstrates Rocker to be "an angry young man at best, and at worst ... an obscene bigot" (Stinson 1999, December 23). In these accounts, Rocker's mistake was to reveal an unseemly part of his character rather than to misspeak in a fashion that contradicted his character.

Perhaps most notably, baseball commissioner Bud Selig mandated that Rocker undergo a "psychological evaluation" in order to determine "whether Rocker's behavior is rooted in a psychological problem" (Head 2000, January 8). For some this implied an excuse for Rocker's behavior: it resulted from "illness," not from conscious intent. Psychologists such as Alvin Poussaint of Harvard's medical school argued that to recognize racism as a mental illness will lead to "guidelines for recognizing racism in the early stages so we can provide treatment"; but others claimed that such a label enables "racists to escape responsibility for their actions" (Head 2000, January 23). But in either case, grounding Rocker's actions in his psyche attributes an agent-centered motive, and thus sets the stage for the next step in the establishment of Rocker as scapegoat.

Any scapegoat must represent the sins of society, and numerous public statements construct Rocker as that representation. Some comments allude to images typically associated with the world of Huck Finn and Tom Sawyer in order to situate Rocker's words as representative of the South in particular. "Yes, Atlanta is the perfect place for John Rocker. And when his arm gives out he can always go back to Macon ... and spend his days fishing barefoot along the quiet banks of the Ocmulgee River" (Fitzgerald 1999). A letter writer notes that Rocker's remarks "do much more than reveal his own bigotry"; they "will fuel old stereotypes of White Southerners as ignorant racists" (Ross 1999). Another warns that "Atlanta cannot afford to turn its tolerant cheek" to Rocker because he represents the city's "own burden": "our history of racism and the reputation of Southern ignorance." Rocker's words "proved true every redneck stereotype that ever existed" (Hsu 1999). Callers to talk radio shows "commonly branded Rocker as typical of the South" and "said he was indicative of stereotypical Southern attitudes" (Schneider 2000). Rocker thus represents the history and culture of the antebellum South.

The scope of his representation, however, is not limited to the historical. The day after the story broke, an article stated that "Nothing about Rocker's manifesto on diversity should shock or surprise. Ballplayers are just a scratching, spitting reflection of society" (Hummer 1999). One letter states explicitly that Rocker represents the impieties even of those who condemn him. "People around the world have spewed hateful remarks at Rocker for his statements...."

Don't they realize that they are just like John Rocker, filled with the same bigotry and hatred?" (Nagelhout 2000). Another writer connects Rocker's comments to specific political views prevalent "in various parts of the country": the use of "English-only" in public documents and institutions, or opposition to government benefits for illegal immigrants (Holloman 2000). Andrew Young asserts that Rocker stands in for the administrative hierarchy of major league baseball itself, which "drove off its top two black executives recently. They had to pick on Rocker because they couldn't face their own problems" (Rogers 2000, February 2). The most powerful tragedies include a character who represents the broadest cross-section of people and orientations, and in Rocker we have a character who reflects the views of society in general and Southern culture specifically, of those who like him and those who despise him, and of those who hold fairly common views on important political issues in the United States.

Ironically, while many of these statements are in Rocker's defense—they indicate that he simply spoke what others believe but won't say—they set him up to be the sacrificial goat. One letter writer states, "Don't fire Rocker. He only said what a lot of us are thinking" ("The Vent" 2000), and another writes, "Three cheers for John Rocker who tells it like it is" (Oudkirk & Kenyada 1999). A columnist suggests that many of Rocker's critics are not shocked by his words; "they are peeved that he left the shadows to share their thoughts in broad daylight.... At least Rocker isn't a fraud" (Moore 1999). Another column asserts that "John Rocker is society in miniature.... He only spoke the sentiments of many white Americans" (Aniwodi-El 2000). And a letter in response suggests that Rocker "spoke the sentiments of many Americans of color as well" (Palmer 2000). The prevalent theme in this discourse is that Rocker's attitudes are not aberrant; only his willingness to speak them publicly sets him apart.

But rather than work as apologia on Rocker's behalf, this discourse sets the conditions for his symbolic sacrifice, for it frames Rocker to become a scapegoat. And indeed numerous examples carry out the sentence of banishment. One letter writer states that "it would be better to never win another World Series, or even another game, than to allow such a person to remain a member of the Braves" (Upadhyay 1999), and another writes that "failure to punish Rocker upholds his actions" (Charles 2000). The president of an Atlanta group called Concerned Black Clergy states that "John Rocker needs to be traded. Send him to Montreal or wherever, make him a foreigner.... Trade John Rocker and make all of us happy" (Donsky 2000). Columnist Mark Bradley (1999) writes, "John Rocker should have no place on the Atlanta Braves. He has dishonored the organization. He has offended everyone with a functioning mind. He has stamped himself a buffoon. Get rid of him." And Bradley states further that "the SI story wasn't a mistake but a revelation, a deeper glimpse into a troubled heart.... Better to lose with dignity than to win with a lout. Get rid of him."

One characteristic of sports culture is that teammates support one another. As one writer states, team members "will forgive all manner of mayhem and larceny," so the reaction of Rocker's mates was surprising: "Rocker is now a full-blown outcast. A contagion" (Hummer 1999). One teammate stated that "you might as well put him on the trading block, because the respect factor is gone" (Stinson 2000, January 7b). For some community activists in Atlanta, Rocker's punishment should transcend his status as a member of the baseball team. "Trading or suspending him will not be enough ... the activists said. They want him out of baseball for good" (Roedemeier 1999). These statements call clearly for Rocker's tragic excommunication.

Other discourse is even more explicitly tragic, as it links Rocker's banishment to redemption and ethical standards. Michael Langford, a community activist in Atlanta, asserts that Rocker might find "some room for redemption, but not as an Atlanta Brave," and he notes further that Rocker is "a cancer within this organization that must be removed" (Roedemeier 1999). And letter writer Thomas Miller maintains that "major league baseball has a long tradition of being, more than any other professional American sport, the standard of sportsmanship and ethical behavior.... Rocker has made himself an embarrassment to baseball.... There is *no place in major league baseball* for the racism and wholesale discrimination he has exhibited in this article" (1999, emphasis added). Georgia state representative Tyrone Brooks "thinks the Rocker episode has placed Atlanta at a moral crossroads" and that anything short of condemnation communicates that Rocker's comments are acceptable (Schneider 2000). The statements cited thus far combine to play out a tragic response to Rocker. They link him to the community *and* portray him as one who must be punished and then banished from that community. His role as scapegoat provides both a means of redemption and a sense of rectitude for those who attend to the discourse of tragedy.

Comic Responses

A markedly different ethical vision is prescribed in comic responses to Rocker. That vision is evident in the themes that these comic responses develop. First, Rocker is characterized as a fool rather than a villain. He is someone who did something stupid, not someone who is fundamentally flawed. Second, the comic statements issue a call to humility and a willingness to see beyond one's own perspectives. And third, the call for people to identify with Rocker as a fool who can learn new ways results in an emphasis on forgiveness rather than banishment.

Comedy's focus is on extreme characters who invite ridicule. To ridicule someone "we must exhibit the *sheer absurdity of taking him seriously at all*" (Olson 1968, p. 13), and we can do this by a focus on speech that is "unpredictable and outside the expectations of social decorum" or that exhibits "excess or defect" that is "out of proportion, disharmonious, and incongruous" with standard social norms (Charney 1978, pp. 52, 69). A comic fool is one who violates social mores out of ignorance but who with proper teaching can learn to follow those same social mores. Baseball Commissioner Bud Selig made clear that Rocker's comments were a "breach of the social compact" that makes major league baseball "an American institution" with an "important social responsibility" (Rogers 2000, February 1). Rocker describes himself as a fool or a buffoon. In his first interview after the *Sports Illustrated* article, ESPN's Peter Gammons quoted Rocker's most controversial statements to him and asked what he would think about a person who said such things. "I would think this guy is a complete jerk," Rocker said. "I shot my mouth off and said a few things that's absolutely not me" ("What Was Said" 2000). Rocker thus attributes his own statements to the persona of the mouthy buffoon or the obnoxious clown. Indeed, he explained his "fat monkey" reference to a teammate as "clubhouse humor," an explanation that the teammate rejected ("Braves' Simon" 2000). Eddie Perez, a teammate who did accept the "clubhouse humor" explanation, said that he didn't take Rocker's comments seriously because he knew of Rocker's clownish demeanor. "I know how stupid you are, [always] joking around," he told Rocker ("Perez Says He" 2000). Others also describe him in these terms. One fan writes that "the Braves should stick with Rocker" because every team sports its "mavericks," "flakes," and "crazies" who "make amends" for their mistakes and are then restored to the fold (Schwartz 2000).

The fool is redeemable. One *Atlanta Journal and Constitution* columnist writes that while "Rocker is clearly suffering from good, old-fashioned, hayseed ignorance," she will not call him a "dangerous idiot" because "we all make mistakes, tiny or grotesque. And the point of mistakes is to learn from them" (Vixana 2000). A second columnist states, "Contrary to general opinion, Rocker is not stupid. He just did something stupid" (Bisher 2000). The fool is called to humility, to go before his teammates "where damage control would be more humanely administered," where he "eats humble pie" and is thus reunited with rather than excommunicated from the community. Such excommunication would in this vision be counterproductive, because "you don't find the solution in another clubhouse of strangers, staring and wondering what kind of monster have we among us" (Bisher 1999). Rocker should be the foolish example, not the evil goat.

Rocker is an example because his case teaches the moral lesson that people should understand multiple perspectives. An opinion column by Cynthia Tucker (2000) connects Rocker to the lessons of *Star Trek*—that humankind should strive for "harmony" and be "united," that it should "set aside its ages-old history of internecine conflict"—and notes that he illustrates a common human flaw: "our hearts remain gripped by an instinctive fear of the other—anybody who looks different, worships differently or speaks a different language. In our prejudices, we remain our primitive selves." In Rocker, and in historical examples from Northern Ireland, the Middle East, Africa, and the United States, Tucker finds depressing prospects. But "there is still the hope," she says, that humans will "learn to live together in peace." And she offers a reaction to Rocker that characterizes the comic promise of forgiveness and reconciliation. "Here's a new millennium wish in that direction: Live long and prosper, John Rocker." The kind of understanding Tucker envisions requires a comic faith in reason and communication. As the situation played itself out and Rocker was reunited with his teammates, the club hired a diversity expert to conduct mandatory sessions with everyone from minor league rookies to the team's president, Stan Kasten. "We had a lot of dialogue," said Kasten. "We could heed the advice of a person who's been through an experience like this before," said third baseman Chipper Jones. And in a clear statement of the comic perspective, the leader of the sessions remarked, "We assume that most people want to do the right thing and that many are pretty ignorant about how to go about doing that" (Joyner 2000).

One of the most widely quoted essays on the Rocker affair is by former Atlanta mayor and Martin Luther King associate Andrew Young. Young's op-ed piece, titled "Rocker Has Chance for Redemption" (2000), expresses a desire for reunion and issues a call for people to see beyond their own perspectives and to learn from their mistakes. Young asserts that Atlantans should address Rocker's attitudes "with humor, truth and reconciliation" in order to "help one another broaden our perspective and vision and to see our life together with new possibilities." For Young, the Rocker case provides an opportunity to "learn something about dignity and restraint," and not just for Rocker but for the entire community. "Rocker experienced a rage and frustration that were real," Young writes. "He was irrational and explosive and when that happens, all of your deep-seated prejudices and insecurities come to the surface. And let's not kid ourselves, we all have them." So "we should offer Rocker a support system" because he is "young enough to change, young enough to be redeemed, young enough to learn those lessons with help from his teammates and the rest of the Atlanta community." Young offers a clear comic vision based on the values of humility, forgiveness, and education.

Through his essay Young establishes himself as a comic hero, in juxtaposition to Rocker's role as a comic fool. The comic hero, Duncan notes, warns us against the advice of "tragic guardians who act as messengers of the gods to visit doom on those who disobey their commandments" (1968, p. 99). To counter the move toward tragedy, the comic hero exposes the vices of all the dramatic players. In so doing, he or she shows that all are guilty of error and thereby invokes a "principle of social order" (p. 82) that calls the players back into relationship with one another. Young's essay clearly exhibits these characteristics.

Numerous letter writers endorse Young's call. One writes, "We as a community should offer Rocker a face-saving way out of his own ignorance. Certainly then our children might learn … the values of forgiveness, repentance and redemption" (Ajanaku 2000). Another writer agrees with Young and states, "Instead of punishing John Rocker, let's help him enlarge his world" (Parko 2000). And a third, who wrote even before Young, says, "I truly believe that with his re-education and love, [Rocker will] respond in positive ways that will benefit everybody" (Byirt 2000). The president of the Atlanta baseball club, Kasten, characterized Rocker as a "remorseful" player who made "a horrible mistake" and wanted to make amends. "Under those circumstances," Kasten pledged, "I'm not going to abandon a player or an employee or a friend" (Stinson 2000, January 7a). Later Kasten stated that "the object should be to get John to a place where he's accepted by his teammates and by his community" (Rogers 2000, February 1). Consistent with the comic form, these statements call for the clown to be reunited with his community. He is castigated and then welcomed back.

Perhaps most significant, many of the teammates whom Rocker had explicitly criticized or insulted (or at least angered) expressed publicly their forgiveness. Randall Simon, the player Rocker called a "fat monkey," said, "We are all sinners and we all make mistakes sometimes, and we are all forgiven the sins we have done. So why not forgive the man and give him another chance and hope that chance will be appreciated, so he can go about his business and try to treat people better?" (Stinson 2000, March 2). Andres Galarraga and Eddie Perez, both of Hispanic descent, said they accepted Rocker's apology and were willing to forgive him because he deserved "a second chance" ("Perez Says Rocker" 2000) and because they "want the team to be together" ("Perez Says He" 2000). Brian Jordan tied reconciliation to education: "We all make the mistake of, instead of getting to know someone, you judge them first, then get to know them later when it's too late.... It's a shame it had to come down this way, but it's all part of the learning process" (Rogers 2000, March 1). And team owner Ted Turner captured the comic perspective well both in meaning and in pun when he said, "He's just a kid ... I think he was off his rocker when he said those things.... He's apologized. I don't think we ought to hold it against him forever. Let's give him another chance. He didn't commit a crime" (Hyland 2000). Turner's statement frames Rocker as a fool rather than a criminal, affirms that Rocker can learn from his mistake, and advocates forgiveness. These are the prevalent themes of a comic ethical vision.

Implications: Certitude and Tolerance

> Comedy censures those who separate men from each other; tragedy destroys those who separate men from the gods.
>
> —H. D. Duncan

Kenneth Burke states clearly the formula for tragedy. It starts with some "unresolved tension" that exists in a society and reduces that tension to a "personal conflict." It features a character who "carries this conflict to excess," places that character in a situation that exacerbates the conflict, and introduces other characters who "help motivate and accentuate his excesses." Those excesses lead to the character's downfall, and the tragedy then establishes that this downfall will provide "a promise of general peace" (1966, p. 94). The formula for comedy is similar except that the central character's downfall is a precursor to reconciliation, and the promise of peace includes the reconciled clown.

This paper demonstrates the existence of these formulas in public responses to John Rocker. He symbolizes unresolved social tensions, particularly about race, and his comments in *Sports Illustrated* portray those tensions in terms of Rocker's personal conflicts with individual representatives of various ethnic groups. Numerous letters, editorials, and articles published in the *Atlanta Journal and Constitution* accentuate Rocker's excesses, often by featuring his relationships with additional characters, especially his teammates. Tragic responses call for Rocker's downfall and excommunication. Comic responses call for his rehabilitation and reconciliation. Thus, upon the announcement of Rocker's $20,000 fine and twenty-eight day suspension (penalties that an arbitrator reduced significantly), Hank Aaron stated, "A month? Marge Schott lost her (Cincinnati Reds) ballclub for making racial remarks. I think Rocker's extremely lucky. I thought it would be longer"; and Andrew Young stated, "To take a problem child and kick him out is not the answer. I think that the purpose of discipline is to correct and rehabilitate" (Stinson 2000, Feb. 1).

To some, the extent to which this case remained a focus of public discourse is baffling, especially when compared with other more troublesome ethical violations. One commentator asked, "Can anyone explain why this case, involving a young kid who just throws a baseball, has remained in the public eye for weeks—while far more serious examples of noxious speech go virtually unnoticed, uncondemned, and unpunished?" (Matthews 2000). Rocker's status as a celebrity athlete accounts partially for the ongoing notoriety of his plight. But voyeuristic motives do not explain adequately the symbolic resources expended on this situation. Although I doubt that most people who attended to or participated in this rhetorical situation consciously used the concepts of tragedy and comedy to interpret the various responses to Rocker, I am convinced that this case became a phenomenon of popular culture because its audiences realized that it teaches something about ethics. The identification of tragic and comic themes contributes to an understanding of how the discourse of popular culture proffers ethical codes, but beyond that identification, we can draw particular implications from the analysis of this discourse.

Edwin Black's discussion of the second persona and Philip Wander's discussion of the third persona provide a set of concepts that help to explain the ethical functions of discourse about the Rocker episode. Black (1970) notes that we can extract from any discourse "a corresponding form of character" (p. 110) that tells us something not only about the persona of the implied author, but about the persona of the implied audience as well. Because that implied audience represents an ideology, we are able to render ethical judgments of the "potentialities of character" we find in rhetorical discourses (p. 113). Early in this chapter I argued that tragedy and comedy are symbolic forms that evince different ethical principles for the construction of character and community. They urge upon popular audiences a second persona; they call us to embrace a particular type of character and thus to be a particular type of community. Wander's (1984) concept suggests that any discourse also negates a range of personas. The third persona refers to "a being whose presence, though relevant to what is said, is negated through silence" (p. 210), and this persona is also evident in the Rocker situation.

Despite the plethora of tragic and comic responses that revolve around the issue of race, for example, a peculiar silence exists about Rocker's ostensibly homophobic statements. Except for a handful of comments, no one said anything in response to Rocker's comments about AIDS or about gay and lesbian people. The statements issued by Major League Baseball, by Andrew Young, by Rocker's teammates, and the apologies issued by Rocker himself all dealt with the racially charged quotations in the *Sports Illustrated* article. No one directly involved mentioned the homophobia exhibited in Rocker's statements. That silence says something about the kinds of social tensions that attract attention and ethical evaluation in popular culture. It helps to establish the range of topics about which we can still safely deliver words of derision or condemnation.

In addition to the meanings that tragedy and comedy produce about specific issues (race, for example), they produce even more important meanings about the criteria we might use to render ethical judgments in our communities. As the furor over Rocker began to subside, several contributions to the Atlanta newspaper called attention specifically to the ethical codes that had emerged in this case.

One writer described the comic responses to Rocker as a trivialization of "the larger ramifications of his comments" and as a contributing factor to the "cultivation of hate" that "motivates white men to chain and drag black men to their deaths behind their pickup truck" and "justifies police firing 41 rounds of ammo at an unarmed African immigrant." Rocker's apparent reconciliation to the team and to the Atlanta community, he wrote, "speaks volumes about the pervasive nature of racism in America, racism that is validated, sustained and encouraged by indifference" (Mahone 2000). Although the Atlanta baseball team eventually traded Rocker, comedy prevailed as the immediate response to Rocker's faux pas. He was ostracized but then reunited with the team, which restored symbolically the hierarchy of the ball club and of the broader community represented in the discourses that shaped this situation. But that comic principle extracts a cost. As Sam Mahone's essay admonishes, an emphasis on harmony and reconciliation can ignore the individual's responsibility for wrongdoing and create indifference to ethical violations that do real harm to real people. Tragedy, Mahone implies, leaves no doubt about public judgments.

Others saw value in the comic theme. A letter emphasizes that the central challenge of the Rocker case is to recognize one's own propensity for error. "John Rocker's original, unexamined views are only too typical in a society that finds stereotypes much easier to deal with than real individuals who are unlike one's self. As a liberal, I have found myself accusing conservative Christians of embodying intolerance, until I realized that I was doing just what I detested—labeling others" (Miller 2000). Comedy requires one to recognize the darkness in one's own heart, not so that one becomes beholden to guilt or shame, but so that one recognizes the connections among all people and the need for forgiveness and reconciliation. We all play the clown sometimes. But tragedy enables us to direct our attention to the violations of others without recognition of our own complicity in those violations. In Burke's words, "if one can hand over his infirmities to a vessel, or 'cause,' outside the self, one can battle an external enemy instead of battling an enemy within" (1973, p. 203).

The tragic and comic visions are not tied to particular political or religious perspectives. But they do have specific implications for those who embrace the two visions. A tragic vision features a certain moral code and demands that people face the consequences of their actions. It establishes a sense of certitude and hierarchy, and it implies sacrifice or banishment as the means of redemption when a person or a society violates that hierarchical code. A comic vision, however, features tolerance of diverse moral codes and asks that people understand those who do not act in accordance with any one specific code. It establishes a need for multiple perspectives and it implies humility and humane instruction as the means of redemption.

When Joseph Lowery, former president of the Southern Christian Leadership Conference, says that Rocker's punishment is not sufficient and that "the Braves still have to act to show that they have *zero tolerance* for this kind of behavior," he advocates an ethic of tragedy (Payne 2000, emphasis added). When Hosea Williams, a pastor in Atlanta, says that "Jesus could forgive ... his hanging on Calvary ... Martin Luther King Jr. could forgive the Ku Klux Klan.... Why can't we forgive this young man?" he advocates an ethic of comedy (Payne 2000). The choices are both clear and complex. Are we served better by an ethic of certitude that calls us to right behavior and demands consequences for the violation of social mores? Or are we served better by an ethic of tolerance that calls us to humility and acceptance and demands forgiveness for the violation of social mores? Perhaps a recognition of these different ethical visions will enable us to choose the most fitting response for each case in which someone violates the recognized protocols of our society.

Note

1.   I accessed all of the letters, editorials, and articles from the *Atlanta Journal and Constitution* through LexisNexis. Page numbers refer to the print version of the newspaper. As the references section indicates, all of these documents

appeared during the three-month span between late December 1999 and late March 2000, and none of them is more than a single page in length. I have therefore limited the contents of the in-text citations to the author's last name and year, except in those cases where a date is needed to distinguish among multiple entries by the same author.

References

Ajanaku, B. (2000). *Atlanta Journal and Constitution*, January 13, p. 18A.

Aniwodi-El, N. (2000). Rocker as a symbol of society. *Atlanta Journal and Constitution*, February 15, p. 13A.

Appel, E. C. (1997). The rhetoric of Dr. Martin Luther King Jr.: Comedy and context in tragic collision. *Western Journal of Communication* 61: 376–402.

Bisher, F. (1999). Braves only place for closer's rehabilitation. *Atlanta Journal and Constitution*, December 29, p. 2D.

———. (2000). We need a closer look at values. *Atlanta Journal and Constitution*, March 4, p. 3H.

Black, E. (1970). The second persona. *Quarterly Journal of Speech* 56: 109–19.

Bradley, M. (1999). Dump Rocker in a New York minute. *Atlanta Journal and Constitution*, December 23, p. 1F.

Braves' Simon says Rocker "lying." (2000). *Atlanta Journal and Constitution*, January 16, p. 11E.

Brereton, G. (1968). *Principles of tragedy: A rational examination of the tragic concept in life and literature*. Coral Gables, FL: University of Miami Press.

Burcum, J. (2004). Rocori suspect to have adult trial. *Minneapolis Star Tribune*, February 11, pp. A1, A13.

Burke, K. (1966). *Language as symbolic action*. Berkeley: University of California Press.

———. (1968). *Counter-statement*. Berkeley: University of California Press. (Original work published 1931).

———. (1969a). *A grammar of motives*. Berkeley: University of California Press. (Original work published 1945).

———. (1969b). *A rhetoric of motives*. Berkeley: University of California Press. (Original work published 1950).

———. (1970). *The rhetoric of religion*. Berkeley: University of California Press. (Original work published 1961).

———. (1973). *The philosophy of literary form*. Berkeley: University of California Press. (Original work published 1941).

———. (1984a). *Attitudes toward history*. Berkeley: University of California Press. (Original work published 1937).

———. (1984b). *Permanence and change*. Indianapolis: Bobbs-Merrill Educational Pub. (Original work published 1935).

Byirt, E. (2000). *Atlanta Journal and Constitution*, January 16, p. 6D.

Carlson, A. C. (1986). Gandhi and the comic frame: "Ad bellum purificandum." *Quarterly Journal of Speech* 72: 446–55.

———. (1988). Limitations on the comic frame: Some witty American women of the nineteenth century. *Quarterly Journal of Speech* 74: 310–22.

Charles, L. (2000). *Atlanta Journal and Constitution*, January 14, p. 22A.

Charney, M. (1978). *Comedy high and low: An introduction to the experience of comedy*. New York: Oxford University Press.

Donsky, P. (2000). Local group says penalty too lenient. *Atlanta Journal and Constitution*, March 2, p. 3E.

Duncan, H. D. (1968). *Symbols in society*. New York: Oxford University Press.

Fitzgerald, W. (1999). *Atlanta Journal and Constitution*, December 23, p. 2F.

Freeman, C. (1999). *The Greek achievement: The foundation of the western world*. New York: Viking.

Frye, N. (1957). *Anatomy of criticism*. Princeton, NJ: Princeton University Press.

Head, J. (2000). The Rocker controversy. *Atlanta Journal and Constitution*, January 8, p. 2E.

———. (2000). Can racists be called mentally ill? *Atlanta Journal and Constitution*, January 23, p. 1B.

Holloman, C. (2000). *Atlanta Journal and Constitution*, January 12, p. 15A.

Hsu, S. (1999). *Atlanta Journal and Constitution*, December 30, p. 26A.

Hummer, S. (1999). Might be too late for rockhead rehab. *Atlanta Journal and Constitution*, December 24, p. 7C.

Hyland, F. (2000). Turner goes to bat for Rocker. *Atlanta Journal and Constitution*, January 20, p. 1A.

Joyner, T. (2000). Braves training: Sensitivity coach is pitching diversity. *Atlanta Journal and Constitution*, March 16, p. 1A.

Mahone, S. (2000). Racism feeds off indifference. *Atlanta Journal and Constitution*, March 22, p. 15A.

Matthews, R. (2000). The Rocker obsession: Why aren't we outraged at bigotry that really matters? *Atlanta Journal and Constitution*, February 3, p. 14A.

Miller, J. (2000). *Atlanta Journal and Constitution*, March 20, p. 13A.

Miller, T. (1999). *Atlanta Journal and Constitution*, December 23, p. 2F.

Moore, T. (1999). Words tore asunder already thin team ties. *Atlanta Journal and Constitution*, December 29, p. 2D.

Nagelhout, S. (2000). *Atlanta Journal and Constitution*, January 8, p. 10A.

Olson, E. (1968). *The theory of comedy*. Bloomington: Indiana University Press.

Oudkirk, F., & R. Kenyada. (1999). *Atlanta Journal and Constitution*, December 26, p. 2G.

Palmer, K. (2000). *Atlanta Journal and Constitution*, February 22, p. 9A.

Parko, J. (2000). *Atlanta Journal and Constitution*, January 14, p. 22A.

Payne, D. (2000). Civil rights leaders differ on Rocker suspension. *Atlanta Journal and Constitution*, February 1, p. 5E.

Pearlman, J. (1999). At full blast. *Sports Illustrated*, December 27, 60–64.

Perez says he has accepted Rocker apology. (2000). *Atlanta Journal and Constitution*, January 30, p. 8G.

Perez says Rocker needs punishment. (2000). *Atlanta Journal and Constitution*, January 23, p. 9E.

Roedemeier, C. (1999). Minority and gay activists call for braves to fire Rocker. Associated Press, December 23. Available at: www.accessatlanta.com.

Rogers, C. (2000). Players union files grievance to overturn Rocker suspension. *Atlanta Journal and Constitution*, February 1, p. 1A.

———. (2000). Rocker issue hangs in air. *Atlanta Journal and Constitution*, February 2, p. 1C.

———. (2000). Sensitivity training gets warm response in camp. *Atlanta Journal and Constitution*, March 1, p. 3C.

Ross, E. W. (1999). *Atlanta Journal and Constitution*, December 26, p. 2G.

Schneider, C. (2000). How has John Rocker changed us? *Atlanta Journal and Constitution*, January 23, p. 1D.

Schwartz, J. (2000). *Atlanta Journal and Constitution*, January 16, p. 2E.

Stinson, T. (1999). Rocky day. *Atlanta Journal and Constitution*, December 23, p. 1A.

———. (1999). The two faces of John Rocker. *Atlanta Journal and Constitution*, December 24, p. 1C.

———. (2000). Rocker may get new chance. *Atlanta Journal and Constitution*, January 7a, p. 1A.

———. (2000). Rocker's future remains a question mark. *Atlanta Journal and Constitution*, January 7b, p. 1A.

———. (2000). Braves: Rocker must pay the price. *Austin American Statesman*, February 1, p. C1.

Toker, C. W. (2002). Debating "what ought to be": The comic frame and public moral argument. *Western Journal of Communication* 66: 53–83.

Tucker, C. (2000). New millennium: Divided world defies my childhood dreams. *Atlanta Journal and Constitution*, January 5, p. 10A.

Upadhyay, M. (1999). *Atlanta Journal and Constitution*, December 23, p. 2F.

The vent. (2000). *Atlanta Journal and Constitution*, January 13. Available at: www.accessatlanta.com.

Vixana. (2000). Ignorance: A founding tradition. *Atlanta Journal and Constitution*, January 8. Available at: www.accessatlanta.com.

Wander, P. (1984). The third persona: An ideological turn in rhetorical theory. *Central States Speech Journal* 35: 197–216.

What was said. (2000). *Atlanta Journal and Constitution*, January 13, p. 3E.

Williams, R. (1966). *Modern tragedy*. Stanford, CA: Stanford University Press.

Young, A. (2000). Rocker has chance for redemption. *Atlanta Journal and Constitution*, January 11, p. 11A.

CHAPTER SIX

Is There More to Ethics than the Prime Directive? Personal Integrity in *Star Trek: The Next Generation* and *Star Trek: Voyager*

Paula S. Tompkins

For almost forty years, with five television series, ten movies, web-sites, conventions, fan clubs, and more, *Star Trek* has explored society's tensions by going to outer space.[1] Although originating with Gene Roddenberry, the *Trek* universe is a cultural and rhetorical product of professional writers and fans, who write for fan-zines and list-servs or attend *Trek* conventions (see Anijar 2000; Barrett & Barrett 2001; Pounds 1999; Tulloch & Jenkins 1995; Wagner & Lundeen 1998). Seemingly an "acquired taste," the *Trek* television series exhibits an important element of the formula for serial television drama—character and relational development over time. Episodes of serial dramas are constructions of ongoing experiences in the lives of characters in serious personal, social, or political situations, rather than "snapshots" to be rearranged at will by viewers. The special appeal of *Trek* as science fiction is that it takes place in a future where taken-for-granted assumptions do not apply. Despite its "foreignness," *Trek* presents a familiar narrative of utopian hope, depicting the human capacity to address seemingly intractable problems.

> Foremost among the tenets of Roddenberry's vision is humanism—a compassion for our species and a faith in its ultimate wisdom and capacity for self-reliance. Bolstering this central premise are an optimistic view of the human future; an emphasis on the imperatives of freedom, growth,

and change; a tolerance of diversity; a central role for the emotions of friendship and loyalty; an opposition to prejudice or tradition-for-its-own-sake; and a visceral rejection of organized religion and divine authority. While some persons involved in the production of *Trek* may have had misgivings about various aspects of this vision on philosophical or artistic grounds, most admit that it has provided the unifying, hopeful vision that makes *Trek* so beloved and so durable. (Wagner & Lundeen, 1998, p. 8) [2]

Exploration of contemporary issues is a key feature of *Trek*. *The Original Series* (*TOS*) explores social and political issues such as the Cold War ("Balance of Terror," #9, 12/15/66)[3] and racism, as in the oft-cited first interracial kiss on television ("Plato's Stepchildren," #67, 11/22/1968) and the episode-as-parable "Let That Be Your Last Battlefield" (#70, 1/10/69). *The Next Generation* (*TNG*) marks a narrative shift from social and political to more individualistic issues, often focusing on personal integrity (Pounds 1996, p. 106). *TNG* explores how individual crew members maintain their integrity when facing competing demands, whether from different species, coworkers, or family. Viewers, facing competing demands from community, work, and family, watch the crew figure out how to balance similar demands. In *Voyager*, the crew searches for a way home through uncharted space, as viewers experienced the end of what some call the most violent century in human history. As they face the unknown, viewers watch *Voyager*'s captain strive to care with integrity for her crew's survival.

As *TNG* and *Voyager* continue to play in the digital afterlife, viewers will watch characters struggle to maintain their personal integrity. As relatively enduring artifacts of popular culture that engage viewers in explorations of ethical problems, these television serial dramas warrant critical study of their contribution to our public conversation about integrity. In analyzing these depictions, I will, first, discuss integrity as an ethical concept and, second, explore the distinctive narrative depictions of integrity presented in each series. The narrative depiction of personal integrity in *TNG* is that of casuistic moral reasoning, while *Voyager* depicts issues of personal integrity through the ethics of care.

Integrity

Stephen L. Carter (1996) claims that "integrity is like the weather: everybody talks about it but nobody knows what to do about it. Integrity is that stuff we always say we want more of" (p. 6). We expect integrity in ourselves and others because it creates a basis for trust. Integrity is a quality of character or personal virtue, comprising part of an individual's ethical identity. It integrates an individual's actions and understanding of her life into a whole. "The notion of integrity is inseparable from the idea of a kind of wholeness of self or of a moral identity, which can be forfeited or violated by certain actions" (Diamond 2001, p. 864). The simplest, and sometimes simplistic, concept of integrity is consistency in following a principle. While consistency is part of integrity, consistent adherence to an *unethical* principle is not, for this would grant integrity to, for example, an unrepentant racist (see Carter 1996). The notion of a moral temptation clarifies our understanding of integrity as consistency. When tempted to do something we know is wrong, the decision is clear; the ethical challenge is finding the courage to act upon our decision. Integrity requires acting upon principles recognized by others as ethical.

> Moral integrity ... requires that an individual refuse to abandon important moral principles even when it is advantageous to do so, and that the content of these principles be such that reasonable people would recognize them as moral. Moral steadfastness on behalf of manifestly sound moral principles entitles one to the esteem of others as an honorable person who maintains a high degree of consistency between principle and behavior when faced with the temptation to do otherwise. (Forest 1994, p. 441)

Integrity is based on an integrated understanding of an individual's character and action as virtue. Alasdair MacIntyre (1984) argues that reintegration of character and action as virtue is best accomplished in narrative or story. Integrity as narrative helps compensate for simplistic notions of integrity as consistency. Stories of individual acts of integrity could illustrate an ethical principle, contributing to public discussions of ethics; yet they can also be separated from more complex and nuanced life stories of integrity. The latter explore lifelong questions that give unity and meaning to an individual life.

"A person's life, to be of genuine moral significance, must be one in which a set of virtues, firmly held and consistently acted upon, unifies the various roles that the individual occupies, and confers upon that individual a corresponding set of obligations. Such a life requires integrity ... which is intelligible only in relation to a more universal good" (Forest 1994, p. 442).

One challenge to the integrity of one's life is an ethical dilemma, where differing principles have equivalent claims for primacy. The challenge is deciding which should be primary, or creating a new framework for ethical action that incorporates both. This view of integrity recognizes that two individuals may act with integrity and follow very different courses of action or the same course of action for different reasons. The challenge of an ethical dilemma to one's integrity is not moral steadfastness, but understanding the complexity of a situation and discerning an ethical course of action.

Stories provide a vehicle for exploring integrity. As they are retold and compared, stories of individual acts of integrity raise consciousness and encourage public conversation about integrity. The story of a life of integrity explores how a principle gives a life meaning and the challenges of ethical commitment. Stories are valuable in studying how integrity does or does not develop in real people and relationships, and also in fictional characters and relationships across a broad range of situations. Television dramas such as *TNG*, *Voyager*, *The West Wing*, and *Law & Order* provide viewers with important texts for investigating what integrity means, for television serial dramas present the story of a life of integrity as a character develops by facing temptations and dilemmas. Serial television dramas also can reinforce integrity's public nature. Without communicating the reasons for ethical action, the good of integral acts is circumscribed to the situation in which the acts occur. There can be no stories of integrity when integrity is silent, no opportunity for others to judge if the principles or action are ethical. When integrity is silent, public discussion of ethics suffers.

Ultimately, the challenge of integrity is acting. Action is the sine qua non of drama. Acting with integrity, however, often focuses on a particular action—compromise. "Like fire, compromise is both necessary and dangerous to human life. Were we never to accept

political compromise on matters of ethical conviction, we would
cut ourselves off from large numbers of our fellow humans; were
we always to accept it, we would become alienated from ourselves"
(Benjamin 1990, p. 3). The danger compromise poses to our integrity is losing our sense of self. When we compromise too much, the
story of our life makes little sense. But without compromise, we
isolate ourselves from others. With zealous consistency to the same
ethical values, our life story may lose its relevance as it avoids experiences that challenge those values. We risk becoming less humane,
perhaps less human. The challenge of integrity is maintaining personal integrity with humanity, of discerning when to compromise
and when to hold fast.

   As *TNG* and *Voyager* increasingly focus on personal rather than
political and social themes, narrative explorations of communicating
and acting with integrity become more prominent. In *TNG* the crew
faces the challenges of integrity in problems arising from maintaining diplomatic relations between competing and warring species,
exploration, and balancing their personal and professional lives.
Individual episodes illustrate a form of moral reasoning known as
casuistry, in which general principles are applied to specific cases.
In *Voyager* the struggle to survive challenges the integrity of the
crew and particularly its captain, who is responsible for stranding
the crew in uncharted space. *Voyager* explores the tensions of integrity within an ethics of care, whether the captain and crew can care
with integrity in their struggle to survive.

TNG and the Search for Personal Integrity

TNG, originally running from 1987 to 1993, takes place approximately seventy years after the events of *TOS*. The interplanetary
government, the Federation, negotiated peace with its enemies (Ro-
mulans) or brought them into the Federation (Klingons). The mission of Starfleet's flagship *Enterprise* is twofold—diplomacy and
exploration. While the crew is comprised mostly of humans from
Earth, it includes a few of the diverse species in the Federation—a
telepath Betazoid ship's counselor, an android science officer, and
a Klingon chief of security.[4] The narrative conceit that the Federa-

tion has solved poverty, racism, and more frees the crew to address ethical questions in a "pure" form. Typical problems are temporary, whether running out of fuel for the engine or infighting within the Federation. This helps structure the ethical problem of each episode as a variation of a "paradigm" or prototypical ethical case that characters explore using casuistic reasoning.

> Casuists believe that we should resolve the ethical questions of a particular moral problem by considering different but related cases that involve greater complexity. The goal is to identify the relevant similarities and differences among cases in order to determine the proper moral rule to apply to a given problem. Casuists start with a simple maxim or rule, called a dictum. A dictum might be a rule such as "Do not lie" or "Obey your parents." Next they present a paradigm case, a clear example of a situation in which the maxim should be followed. The casuists changes the case little by little to consider whether the maxim still holds. In this way, casuists can refine the rules or principles that best apply to the moral problem at hand. (Duval 1999, p. 31)

Casuists reason by analogy, comparing the facts of an actual situation to the paradigm case (Jonsen & Toulmin 1988). Difficulties may arise with the discovery of additional facts that distinguish the actual case from the paradigm, or the possibility of applying more than one paradigm, perhaps in conflicting ways, or the unique social or cultural history of the case may create exceptions to the paradigm. Exceptions may create precedents, modifying the recommended ethical course of action, as occurs in common law. "Proponents of casuistry hold it to be a good way to approach moral problems because it actively seeks to account for the subtleties of moral issues" (Duval 1999, p. 31). Some critics argue that casuistic reasoning is misguided, starting us down a slippery slope to justify inconsistent or unethical action, imperiling our integrity. Others question the ethicality or relevance of the principles themselves.

The Prime Directive of noninterference with less-developed species is the most widely recognized principle of *Trek*; however, it provides little guidance for interacting with peer species and extreme situations—for example, genocide. Since not following the Prime Directive is a source of dramatic tension in the series, characters reason using principles of the *Trek* vision (tolerance, honor, respect for the individual, freedom, individualism, and rational decision making) when facing many ethical problems. Because respecting cultural differences is critical to maintaining diplomatic relations, recurring ethical tensions between tolerance or respect for differences and principles (for example, justice, preserving life, privacy, or truthfulness) is a recurring source of dramatic tension in the series. As each episode unfolds, the viewers watch a narrative struggle between different ethical principles as crew members search for a path of action with integrity until a decision maker or sequence of events crystallizes a principled course of action at the dramatic climax of an episode. The *Trek* vision of humanism, with its emphasis on the individual, provides a guide to ethical decision making, but not an overriding principle. Respect, toleration, and noninterference are principles episodes repeatedly depict; however, some episodes raise questions about the limits of tolerance and respect for cultural difference, prominently raising questions about the nature of integrity in decision making. I will present an analysis of two such episodes that explore the same act and that present two different courses of ethical action—support of and opposition to a ritual suicide.

Integrity and ritual suicide. "Half a Life" (#196, 5/6/1991) and "Ethics" (#216, 3/02/92) explore the tensions between tolerance of cultural differences and prohibitions against killing in the case of ritual suicide. They present two different outcomes of ethical reasoning, support and opposition. I chose these episodes for two reasons. First, they illustrate the criticism that casuistic ethical reasoning lacks integrity because it encourages inconsistency. Second, they explore tolerance of an act for which Americans have little tolerance—ritual suicide. For Americans the presumption against suicide is strong. In the Christian tradition, taking one's life imperils one's immortal soul. More secular and popular views of suicide see it as a moral or mental weakness, an act of despair, even selfishness. American viewers are not predisposed to consider ritual suicide a morally reasonable act or understand why someone would consider it. Thus, the episodes present a significant test for the principle of tolerance for both the fictional crew and the viewers.

In "Half a Life" and "Ethics," crew members learn that someone for whom some of them care is preparing to commit ritual suicide. In the culture of each individual, suicide is honorable and an
expected course of action in their circumstances. The narrative and
rhetorical challenge of each episode is to convince the audience that
(1) a choice of ritual suicide is ethically justifiable for the respective
cultures and (2) the course of action taken by certain members of
the crew exhibits personal integrity—in one episode interpersonal
support that results in a successful ritual suicide and in the other
persuasion that helps prevent the suicide.

In "Half a Life," an alien scientist, Timicin, fails in his latest ex-
periment to save the dying sun of his planet. He also has begun to fall
in love with the mother of a crew member, Lwaxana Troi. Cultural
tradition, however, dictates that in four days at his sixtieth birthday
he must return home for his "Resolution"—a celebration of his life
during which he says good-bye to those he loves and then commits
suicide. Realizing he is close to a breakthrough in his effort to save
his planet's sun and at Lwaxana's urging, Timicin asks the captain
for asylum, which the captain grants, almost provoking a war with
Timicin's home planet. As his realization grows that his people will
turn their backs on him and his research if he does not complete his
Resolution, Timicin is visited by his beloved daughter. She clearly
communicates that by forgoing his Resolution he is abandoning
his culture and would lose the integrity of his life, the values and
principles that give the story of his life meaning. Although he has
come to understand from conversations with Lwaxana that his life
still has value and that he could finish his work to save his dying
planet's sun, ultimately his work would be meaningless because
it would never reach and help his people—"I am a man without
a world. I can't go home." Thus, Timicin decides to return home
for his final Resolution, accompanied and supported by Lwaxana,
the person who initially awakened in him the desire to continue
his life.

There is no question about the cultural correctness of ritual suicide for Timicin. Dialogue between Timicin and Lwaxana reveals
the careful reasoning and ethical principles on which the Resolution
is based. The narrative also makes clear in conversations between

Lwaxana and her daughter, the ship's counselor, that Lwaxana's, and by implication the audience's, disagreement with Timicin is based on a different set of cultural values. It is only our point of view that the Resolution is, in Lwaxana's words, "a barbaric act of murder." The narrative underscores the significance of this cultural difference, with a potential war the cost of interfering with this ritual. Only noninterference and honoring the cultural practices of Timicin's world ultimately prevent this harm.

The second *TNG* episode about ritual suicide, "Ethics," presents a different narrative of moral reasoning and a different outcome. The Klingon head of *Enterprise* security, Lieutenant Worf, has injured his spine, making him a paraplegic. There is little medical or psychological study of Klingons in his condition, for once a Klingon cannot live a warrior's life the honorable course of action is to commit ritual suicide. In a parallel storyline a visiting neurogeneticist has developed an experimental and highly dangerous surgical procedure for transplanting humanoid spinal cords that might restore Worf to his former mobility. The *Enterprise*'s doctor is unwilling to even tell Worf of the procedure, because it could kill him. With current medical technology he could live a healthy and productive live, but a life not valued in Klingon culture. The captain points out to the doctor that it is intolerant and culturally insensitive to Worf and his Klingon heritage to deny him the opportunity to make his own decision about the operation. In addition, suggesting the operation may be the only way to convince Worf not to commit suicide, since he is uninterested in what he considers the doctor's halfway measures. With Klingon honor at stake and without the surgery, suicide is his only option. Even the need to raise his young son is insufficient to change his mind. While denying that Worf's request would not provoke a diplomatic incident, it does test Worf's personal relationships among the crew, by testing their tolerance of and sensitivity to his culture. Worf asks his closest friend on board, First Officer William Riker, to assist in the suicide. Riker refuses, arguing that committing suicide in this situation would be an act of cowardice. Worf decides not to commit suicide and undergoes the experimental surgery, which successfully replaces his spine.

Casuistry and Cultural Difference

As ethical cases the episodes "Half a Life" and "Ethics" share important similarities. Both explore tensions between the principles not to
kill, tolerance, and respect for cultural differences. In both, the individuals contemplating suicide conclude that they can no longer live
a meaningful life according to their cultural standards—Timicin's
life's work would be ignored, and Worf would not live a warrior's
life of honor. Both have relationships with others who want each to
live and tell him so, despite concerns about cultural sensitivity and
tolerance. There also are important factual differences. Although
each has a relationship with a child, Timicin's daughter is a grown
woman, while Worf's son is a young boy who would have difficulty
fitting into Klingon culture without his father's help. Choosing life,
Timicin would be cut off by his people and family, while Worf could
raise his son as a disabled Klingon or as a Klingon warrior, if the
surgery is successful. Diplomatic relations are a factor in Timicin's
case; they are not in Worf's case.

Another critical difference is in conversations in which personal
friends present arguments against ritual suicide. Each conversation
is an example of casuistic reasoning in which the arguer presents
examples for drawing analogies to Timicin's and Worf's situations
to convince each that ritual suicide is wrong. The effectiveness of
the analogies, however, depends upon the quality of the arguer's
knowledge about Timicin's and Worf's cultures. As Lwaxana tries
to persuade Timicin, she learns that she and the Federation are ignorant of his culture, for Timicin's people chose to isolate themselves
from other species. As she presents each example in her argument,
Timicin responds with examples that reveal his people's thought-
fulness, care, and concern for families and the elderly. Lwaxana's
claims are not convincing enough to outweigh the principles of
tolerance and respect for another culture's values. Her charge that
his culture is heartless because it kills vital people, like Timicin,
who have something yet to contribute, is less convincing, as viewers learn that his culture chooses not to warehouse their elderly in
institutions, letting them wait alone to die. Instead, each has a death
with dignity, allowing them to say good-bye to families and friends

when they are in full command of their mental faculties. They are remembered as strong and vital individuals, rather than frail and confused shadows of their former selves. Even Timicin's explanation of why age sixty was chosen for the Resolution illustrates a different cultural perspective on "heartlessness," which is what he asserts would be the burden placed on families if they had to individually decide when their loved one would die in the Resolution ritual. The death of a loved one is painful enough, without the additional burden of personally deciding when the Resolution should occur. For each example that Lwaxana claims is analogous to his situation, Timicin presents a powerful counterexample supporting the Resolution. Her arguments against ritual suicide are unconvincing because they are not responsive to his cultural values. The values of tolerance and respect for Timicin's culture established in this conversation prevail in the casuistic argument of the plot, culminating in Lwaxana's support of Timicin at his Resolution.

The conversation in which Riker presents arguments to Worf against ritual suicide proceeds differently, not only because of their friendship, but also because of Riker's familiarity with Klingon culture (see "A Matter of Honor," #134, 2/06/1989). Worf asks Riker for help performing the ceremony of ritual suicide, ostensibly because friends have helped him perform Klingon rituals in the past. Riker considers this request, but ultimately rejects it, telling Worf, "I've been studying this ritual of yours, and you know what I've decided? I think it's despicable. The casual disregard for life. The way it tries to cloak suicide in some glorious notion of honor. I may have to respect your beliefs, but I don't have to like them." After Worf states that he doesn't expect Riker to understand his tradition and that asking is not easy, Riker recalls fellow crew members who died in the line of duty and how each fought to live. When Worf responds that he does not welcome death, Riker queries, "Are you sure? Because I get the sense that you're feeling pretty noble about this whole thing. 'Look at me. Aren't I courageous? Aren't I an honorable Klingon?' Let me remind you of something, a Klingon does not put his desires above those of his family."

Riker appears steadfast in opposing this suicide and insensitive to Klingon culture. His reasoning and communication, however, are more subtle. He honors Klingon traditions in the confrontational tone of a fellow warrior and his argument justifying his disagreement with Worf. He uses the analogy of fellow crew members who, as *warriors*, died struggling to live to argue that in *this situation* suicide would be a dishonorable act of cowardice. Riker turns on its head the Klingon value of courage expressed in the maxim "Today is a good day to die," arguing by analogy that for Worf the courageous and honorable act is to live. Riker will not help his friend commit a dishonorable act of cowardice. This is a powerful argument, because it employs Worf's cultural values and because Riker's use of them is credible. Riker also conveniently discovered in his research of the ritual that a Klingon son, not a friend, must help his father in the suicide. Affirming Klingon values, he states, "I'm sorry, Mr. Worf. I can't help you. There's only one person on this ship who can." In the end Worf chooses to have the experimental surgery that miraculously restores his full mobility. He returns to duty and remains father to his son, keeping the group of central characters in *TNG* intact. As narrative, the casuistic argument of this episode makes a claim about communication—disagreement with the actions of someone from another culture must be based upon knowledge and respect of that culture. The ship's doctor unsuccessfully argued against ritual suicide based upon her values as a doctor, while Riker's arguments using Klingon values were more convincing.

Thus, we have two narratives of ritual suicide with fundamentally different outcomes. One person dies; another lives. Both narratives apply the same principles—prohibitions against killing, personal integrity, tolerance and cultural sensitivity—important ethical principles that the characters and viewers struggle to weigh and balance. Superficially, the episodes reveal an inconsistency in the *Trek* vision, with Lwaxana's reluctant support of Timicin and Riker's denial of Worf's request. Which character lacks integrity? The moral reasoning processes differ in regards to Lwaxana's and Riker's familiarity with Timicin's and Worf's cultures, respectively. Each episode depicts disagreement and argument across cultural boundaries as a difficult process that often fails because of a lack of sensitivity toward and knowledge of the culture of those with whom we disagree. The narrative argument of each episode claims that when arguing against another culture's practices, integrity is not simply a matter of consistency but requires the integrity of discernment. To discern with integrity, we must understand the cultural values and principles of those with whom we disagree and consider them in our thinking and communication. The narratives of these episodes pose questions for viewers about the nature of integrity as discernment—is integrity as discernment a commitment to a principle that gives our life meaning, must our integrity be responsive to others, or must it do both? The narratives of these episodes argue it must do both.

Voyager and Caring with Integrity

Between 1993 and 1998, fans went somewhere they had not gone before, on a mission with a female captain, Catherine Janeway, whose decision making is informed by a relatively unfamiliar ethical principle—care. Far from the Federation and often any Federation communication signal, Janeway works to get her crew home through uncharted space. *Voyager* explores how an ethic of care could be practiced.

Although caring is familiar, an ethic of care is not. Care, only recently accepted as an ethical principle (Timmons 2002, p. 224), was first posited by Carol Gilligan (1982) in her criticism of Kohlberg's theory of moral development, which contends that an individual's capacity for moral reasoning progresses through stages of development organized by the principle of justice (Duska & Whelan 1975). In the preconventional stages of Kohlberg's framework, individuals reason to avoid punishment or gain reward, at mid-range stages reasoning incorporates conventional standards of morality either as models of the good girl/good boy or the rule of law, while reasoning at the postconventional stages employs abstract principles of justice such as human rights. Gilligan argues that according to Kohlberg, women she studied would be classified as "good girls," rarely rising above conventional moral reasoning. Most women reasoned with an alternative principle, care. Because they were concerned for the individual as a person and were interested in the interdependency and particularity of a relationship, Kohlberg's framework labels them as ethically less developed than the men in the study.

Ethicists and feminist theorists have begun to explore an ethics of care (see Held 1995; Noddings 1984; Nussbaum 2000). Care brings together our intellect, in its capacity to recognize when those we care about are in need and knowing in general what is good for them in certain circumstances, and emotions that arise from relational closeness, such as joy in the successes and unhappiness in the failures of those about whom we care (Timmons 2002, pp. 227–29). Care requires us to put aside self-interest, which may lead to a danger of care—sacrificing or losing one's self in relationships of abuse, martyrdom, or oppression (Noddings 1984; Tronto 1989). Sensitivity to how power and authority are exercised is one of many complexities of moral reasoning using care. In fact, reasoning with care is untidy, resistant to rules and abstractions, for reasoning with care is grounded in the particulars of persons, relationships, and situations. Caring in one relationship may be uncaring in another, raising questions of fairness and justice, as when we care for more than one person or when caring for one person harms or puts another at a disadvantage. In fact, some consider care unethical because "rule-governed behavior is so often associated with moral life [and] ... that if we are bound to follow the rules then we are bound to act impartially, not giving special favors to those nearest us. Another problem with caring from a moral point of view, then, is that we might, because of our caring relationship, provide special treatment to those closest to us and ignore others more deserving of care" (Tronto 1989, p. 111).

Discerning the needs of those we care about is not a clear-cut endeavor. It requires being open and receptive listeners, a challenge in itself, as well as being open and receptive to the potential for what those we care about can become. This means discerning the difference between articulated and unarticulated needs and between real and perceived needs. Such discernment employs a complex combination of receptiveness, insight, humility, and willingness to act, for care, ultimately, is a practice. An irony of caring is that those for whom we care may tell us that our caring lacks integrity, as when we look to the future while those we care about focus on the demands of the immediate situation.[5] Yet this, too, cannot be generalized into a rule, for care reminds us that if we lose sight of the particular individual before us and stop listening, we may misunderstand their actual needs and individual potential.

The complexity of an ethics of care and the importance of discernment in acts of caring indicate that caring with integrity is complicated. Consistency or steadfastness would result in caring without integrity, because it ignores the particulars and differences between individuals, relationships, and situations. The concept of integrity as discernment would facilitate understanding dilemmas faced by a caregiver—distinguishing between real and perceived needs, balancing needs of more than one individual, or balancing competing obligations of justice, honesty, or other ethical principles with care. Thus, an integrity of discernment is more appropriate for assessing the integrity of care than an integrity of steadfastness.

A Captain Who Cares

Care is established as a primary theme of *Voyager* in the opening episodes, "Caretaker Parts I & II" (#101 & #102, 1/16/1995). On a mission to capture a rebel ship, *Voyager* and the ship are brought seventy thousand light years away, to the uncharted Delta Quadrant, by a powerful being called the Caretaker. The Caretaker's imminent death threatens his life's work, care of the Occampa, a species whose survival was threatened by actions of the Caretaker's species. The Caretaker used the power source that protects the Occampa to bring *Voyager* and the rebel ship to the Delta Quadrant in a search for a species with whom he could procreate, to create an offspring to continue his life's work. Like an overprotective parent, the Caretaker's ministrations are so complete that the Occampa depend on him for everything, including protection from other violent species that want the power source. The Caretaker dies before he can protect the Occampa by destroying the power source, leaving Janeway with a decision—to use the power source to send *Voyager* and the rebel ship home, which would make the Occampa immediately vulnerable to attack, or destroy the power source to secure their short-term protection, giving them time to learn to live without the Caretaker. To protect the Occampa would violate the Prime Directive and would leave *Voyager* stranded. Janeway chooses to save the Occampa, arguing that she will not trade lives for convenience.

Janeway's decision creates a new mission, to survive in unchart- ed space and search for a way home. Survival becomes her first duty, and requires that she meet the needs and nurture relation- ships within this new crew of former adversaries.[6] Although every- one must learn to care for each other to survive, as captain, Janeway is the most powerful caregiver, like a parent of an extended and diverse family. When Janeway cares, she does not always employ rules and abstract principles, such as justice and fairness. If she does, they are not always applied consistently. Before the second episode is over, Janeway violates Starfleet regulations, promoting some members of the rebel crew and a convicted felon to leadership positions with authority over original *Voyager* officers. Although justified for the crew's survival, her actions open her to charges of inconsistency and unfairness. For some, the reality of survival in a hostile environment changes the ethical landscape, justifying typically unjust behavior. For others, no special circumstance can justify violating the principle of justice. Insofar as Janeway brings her crew home by the end of the series, *Voyager*'s narrative arguably endorses her application of care. A careful examination of the series reveals a more nuanced depiction of care that explores the integrity of care as discernment.

Voyager's exploration of care requires viewers to follow the story of relationships through multiple episodes and seasons. The most systematic exploration of care is in the relationship between Janeway and Seven-of-Nine, a former member of a collectivist, machine-enhanced species called the Borg. The Borg explore space to assimilate new species into the Collective, transforming every species into functionally equivalent, machine-enhanced drones. On board, in a temporary alliance to combat an even more dangerous species, Seven tries to assimilate the crew ("Scorpion Part I," #168, 5/21/1997; "Scorpion Part II," #169, 9/3/1997). The crew severs Seven's connection to the Collective, stranding her. Recognizing that she is human and feeling responsible for her plight, Janeway decides to keep Seven on board to nurture her humanity and indi- viduality, to care for her. Seven, however, is uninterested, instead demanding that she be allowed to return to the perfection of the Collective. Janeway sees the potential for humanity in Seven if she becomes an individual and learns to exercise her freedom of choice. This means refusing Seven's demand to return to the Collective, an inconsistency Seven points out to Janeway. Caring for Seven is like caring for a child, as Janeway nurtures Seven's human intellect and emotions suppressed by Borg implants. To help Seven understand herself as a human being, Janeway tells Seven her birth name and information about her parents, information that Seven initially considers irrelevant ("The Gift," #170, 9/10/1997). As the series progresses, viewers watch Janeway encourage Seven's development as an individual, often with a child's awkwardness, and, an integral crew member.

Inconsistencies in Janeway's interactions with Seven are part of a pattern of caring. As when judging the integrity of parental care, it is often too simplistic to judge Janeway's care for Seven in a single act or episode. Rather, the test of Janeway's care is whether Seven becomes capable of forming and sustaining her own caring relationships. Seven meets this test in a storyline in which she nurtures four Borg children rescued by *Voyager* ("Collective," #235, 2/16/2000; "Ashes to Ashes," #238, 3/01/2000; "Child's Play," #239, 3/8/2000; "Imperfection," #248, 10/11/2000) and which culminates in Seven developing a relationship of mutual care and affection with one of the children.

Ending here points to the conclusion that *Voyager* presents a narrative of caring with integrity. Like parents, caregivers may appear inconsistent when we view care episodically, but the life story of the relationship reveals the integrity of their care. The series finale, "Endgame Parts I and II" (#271 & #272, 5/23/2001), however, depicts caring that lacks integrity, specifically the potential of care to harm others, raising questions of justice and whether there are limits to care. As the series ends, we see Admiral Janeway on the sixteenth anniversary of *Voyager*'s arrival home. She regrets how life turned out for some crew members, holding herself responsible, especially for those to whom she was closest. A longtime friend suffers from a degenerative neurological disorder that could have been cured if he had received treatment years before *Voyager*'s return to Earth. Another died of a broken heart from the loss of his wife, Seven, who died on a mission before *Voyager*'s arrival. The admiral believes these outcomes and the deaths of twenty-two others could have been avoided if she had taken a shortcut home, conduits in space used by the Borg to attack and assimilate species. The admiral has found a way to go back in time to a critical point where *Voyager* passes this shortcut. She reasons that if *Voyager* used one of these conduits, all crew members would arrive home alive.

Admiral Janeway violates Starfleet regulations, deceives trusting friends, steals a Federation starship, and lies to steal technology for what she claims is a secret diplomatic mission to present to her younger self the plan to use the Borg conduits, all in an effort to care. Yet the plan puts the *Voyager* crew at risk of never arriving home and killing everyone on board. Like a parent, the admiral perceives an obligation to care for those with whom she has developed especially close relationships and for whom she believes her care was insufficient. Her decision to change the course of history is based upon her understanding of the needs of individuals who are themselves unaware of these needs, for they are either dead or mentally incompetent. To care, Admiral Janeway willingly breaks rules and violates ethical principles to which she typically adheres, while also putting others at risk of needlessly dying. Despite the success of her plan and subsequent happy ending, the finale episodes hardly present a model of the integrity of care as discernment. The admiral is like the Caretaker in the episodes that began the series, caring as a parent willing to do anything to protect her children from the vagaries of life, to the point harming others. The essence of Captain Janeway's advice to the Caretaker could be given to Admiral Janeway:

> Janeway: Did you ever consider allowing the Occampa to care for themselves?
>
> Caretaker: They're children!
>
> Janeway: Children have to grow up.... Most of the species we've encountered have overcome all kinds of adversity without a caretaker. It's the challenge of surviving on their own that helps them to evolve. Maybe your children will do better than they think. ("Caretaker Part II" #102, 1/16/1995)

The admiral and the Caretaker are so committed to caring that they dismiss questions of justice, honesty, and the needs of others, so they willingly break rules, violate ethical principles, and risk harming the innocent.

The admiral's caring lacks the integrity of discernment in two ways. First, in caring for some she is willing to sacrifice others, like parents willing to sacrifice others to protect their child. She did not act on the discernment that surviving crew members had equally or even more legitimate needs than those with whom she had special relationships. Second, the admiral's caring did not help those she cared for meet the challenges of life. When care focuses on ensuring the immediate or short-term success of those we care for, we may undermine instead of nurture human qualities such as perseverance, self-discipline, and self-motivation. When those we care for fail, as they inevitably will, they may be unprepared because only a portion of the person they could become had been nurtured. Caring too much can produce an irony of caring, that sometimes our acts of care are harmful to those for whom we care. Caring with the integrity of discernment requires the discipline to acknowledge this irony when it arises and, then, to limit appropriately our acts of care.

TNG, *Voyager*, and Personal Integrity

This chapter has analyzed *TNG* and *Voyager* as popular culture explorations of the complexity of personal integrity. Arguably, the struggle to understand and act with integrity is an important quality of American society at the close of the twentieth and the beginning of the twenty-first centuries. Each series contributes a distinctive narrative approach to our public conversation about ethics that explores the complexity of integrity as discernment. *TNG* explores integrity as balancing competing demands, especially demands that test one's tolerance and sensitivity to other cultures, while *Voyager* explores the nature of integrity in caring relationships. In *TNG* the casuistic narrative structure of each episode encourages viewers to balance and weigh competing demands, cultures, ethical principles, and viewpoints along with the characters. This

narrative structure fits well the generic constraints of the serial television drama, with each episode producing a sense of closure as it
presents a structurally complete narrative exploration of an ethical
problem. The narrative approach of *Voyager*, however, is to explore
integrity by presenting the life stories of caring relationships. Care
is depicted as a lifelong endeavor that encompasses multiple and
sometimes superficially inconsistent acts of caring. This narrative
structure requires more sustained attention and reflection by viewers, to think back on previous episodes to make sense of the story
of a caring relationship, such as Janeway's relationship with Seven.
Ongoing narratives of the life story of a caring relationship do not
easily fit into the generic constraints of a one-hour television episode. Viewers often must have viewed previous *Voyager* episodes,
sometimes from previous seasons, and recall them to follow the
narrative argument. Those unwilling to make this effort may find
Voyager unfocused and the narrative unsatisfying. Adding to the
confusion is the ethic of care, a principle that not only avoids rules,
but may accept inconsistency of a caregiver if it meets the needs of
those cared for. Thus, it is not surprising that some find Janeway
impulsive (Gregory 2000, p. 91) or acting like Plato's philosopher-
king (Barad 2000). Finally, the happy ending of the series finale, in
which *Voyager* successfully takes the shortcut back to Earth, side-
steps questions of justice and care raised by the plot. Perhaps at *Trek*
marathons it would be easier to follow *Voyager*'s exploration of the
integrity of care.

As artifacts of popular culture that continue in the digital afterlife, these *Trek* series contribute to our society's conversation about
ethics and integrity, and encourage viewers to participate in that
conversation. Characters in *TNG* and *Voyager* struggle to discern
what it means to act with integrity—to balance the competing demands of our busy lives, to interact with people who are culturally different, and to care. Like *Trek* characters, we strive to act with
integrity, humanity, care, and concern, or at least not make things
worse. Part of the enduring appeal of *TNG* and *Voyager* are their
claims that while we are imperfect and may fail in our search for
personal integrity, our struggle is a worthy one and that our acts of
integrity, however small and fragile, do matter.

Notes

1. One author notes that those who do not find American cultural values appealing may find *Trek* "stupid" or uninteresting (Collins 1996, p. 137).
2. *Deep Space Nine* (*DS9*) downplays exploration, with an African American single father in charge of a frontier space station. *DS9* has the most extensive explorations of religion and violence in a *Trek* television series (see Barrett & Barrett 2001). The most recent *Trek* series, *Enterprise*, takes place before the interplanetary government known as the Federation was established.
3. Textual references will refer to specific episodes by episode title, series episode number, and original airdate. This information and plot summaries of episodes are available at Paramount Pictures' official *Star Trek* website, www. startrek.com.
4. Wagner & Lundeen (1998) argue that *Trek* explores what it means to be human by juxtaposing humans/humanoids with nonhumanoid characters such as the android Data (*TNG*), software-based life forms such as the Doctor (*Voyager*), and the fluidic life form Odo (*Deep Space Nine*). Scholars have criticized *Trek*'s depictions of gender (see Roberts 1999) and race in this exploration of what it means to be human/humanoid (see Bernardi 1998; Pounds 1999). Barrett and Barrett (2001) argue that *DS9* and *Voyager* use a postmodern style to explore what it means to be human, while *TNG* is modern.
5. Even Noddings (1984), who endorses relational "engrossment," states that receptivity to those we care about "need not lead to permissiveness nor to abdication of responsibility for conduct or achievement" (pp. 59–60).
6. One criticism of the series is that it does not adequately explore the difficulties of uniting the adversarial crews.

References

Anijar, K. (2000). *Teaching toward the 24th century: Star Trek as social curriculum*. New York: Falmer.

Barad, J. (2000). *The ethics of Star Trek*. New York: Harper.

Barrett, M., & D. Barrett. (2001). *Star Trek: The human frontier*. New York: Routledge.

Benjamin, M. (1990). *Splitting the difference: Compromise and integrity and ethics and politics*. Lawrence: Kansas University Press.

Bernardi, D. L. (1998). *Star Trek and history: Race-ing toward a white future*. New Brunswick, NJ: Rutgers University Press.

Carter, S. L. (1996). *Integrity*. New York: HarperCollins.

Collins, S. F. (1996). Trilateralism and hegemony in *Star Trek: The Next Generation*. In T. Harrison, S. Projanski, K. A. Ono, & E. R. Helford (eds.), *Enterprise zones: Critical positions on Star Trek* (pp. 137–56). Boulder, CO: Westview.

Diamond, C. (2001). Integrity. In L. C. Becker & C. B. Becker (eds.), *Encyclopedia of ethics*, vol. 2 (pp. 863–66). New York: Routledge.

Duska, R., & M. Whelan. (1975). *Moral development: A guide to Piaget and Kohlberg*. New York: Paulist.

Duval, S. R. (ed). (1999). *Facts on file: Encyclopedia of ethics*. New York: Book Builders.

Forest, B. (1994). Integrity. In J. K. Roth (ed.), *Ethics*, vol. 2 (pp. 441–42). Englewood Cliffs, NJ: Salem.

Gilligan, C. (1982). *In a different voice: Psychological theory and women's development*. Cambridge, MA: Harvard University Press.

Gregory, D. (2000). *Star Trek: Parallel narratives*. New York: St. Martin's.

Held, V. (1995). *Justice and care: Essential readings in feminist ethics*. Boulder, CO: Westview.

Jonsen, A. R., & S. Toulmin. (1988). *The abuse of casuistry: A history of moral reasoning*. Berkeley: University of California Press.

MacIntyre, A. (1984). *After virtue: A study in moral theory*, 2nd ed. Notre Dame, IN: Notre Dame University Press.

Noddings, N. (1984). *Caring: A feminine approach to ethics and moral education*. Berkeley: University of California Press.

Nussbaum, M. C. (2000). *Woman and human development: The capabilities approach*. New York: Cambridge University Press.

Paramount Pictures. (2003). *Startrek.com*. Retrieved November 24. Available at: www.startrek.com/startrek/view/index.

Pounds, M. C. (1999). *Race in space: The representation of ethnicity in "Star Trek" and "Star Trek: The Next Generation."* Lanham, MD: Scarecrow.

Roberts, R. (1999). *Sexual generations: "Star Trek: The Next Generation" and gender*. Urbana, IL: Chicago University Press.

Timmons, M. (2002). *Moral theory: An introduction*. New York: Rowman & Littlefield.

Tronto, J. (1989). Women and caring: What can feminists learn about morality from caring: In V. Held (ed.), *Justice and care: Essential readings in feminist ethics* (pp. 101–115). Boulder, CO: Westview Press.

Tulloch, J., & H. Jenkins. (1995). *Science fiction audiences: Watching Doctor Who and Star Trek*. New York: Routledge.

Wagner, J., & J. Lundeen. (1998). *Deep space and sacred time: "Star Trek" in the American mythos*. Westport, CN: Praeger.

CHAPTER SEVEN

Public and Relational Communication Ethics in Political Communication: Integrity, Secrecy, and Dialogue in *The Contender*

Jon A. Hess and Joy Piazza

There is no denying the omnipresence of media in the twenty-first century. One form of media that is particularly influential is film. Unlike print forms of entertainment, in which age and reading ability dictate accessibility, movies are accessible to virtually everyone. And, regardless of the producer's purpose for making the film, all movies provide an insight into our culture and the individuals who reside within it. Some movies are produced solely for entertainment value, but others seek to convey some type of message or to stimulate thought on the part of the viewer (Good & Dillon 2002; Kupfer 1999; Lipkin 2002). All movies have ethical content, but for some the ethical content is not the focus of the film, while for others, directing viewers' thoughts toward particular moral issues is the primary purpose of the movie. Sometimes filmmakers seek to raise questions about cultural, social, and political practices; sometimes they seek to move viewers to consider points of view that perhaps they have not previously encountered or thought about. When they do, these goals are communicated through visual images and character dialogue situated in various realistic or metaphorical sites of our social and political culture.

Movies that invite viewers to consider communication issues in the American context include: *All the President's Men* (1976), *Wall Street* (1987), *Philadelphia* (1993), *Sling Blade* (1996), *The Apostle* (1997), *The Truman Show* (1998), *The Contender* (2000), *Artificial Intel-*

ligence (2001), and *Chicago* (2002). Each of these films, in its own way, depicts powerful social and interpersonal communication issues. Because these films are a form of mass speech and expose large numbers of people to their messages, it is important to consider what they have to say about communication ethics (Valenti 2000).

Aristotle considered politics to be that "master science of the good," because it is through politics that we work for the good of all people (1962, p. 4). Although our connotations of the term *politics* have become considerably more negative over the years, there is no denying the importance of politics and government when considering ethics. For this reason, a movie focusing on politics is especially appropriate for an examination of ethics in popular film. *The Contender* (DreamWorks, 2000) is a good film to analyze not only because of its topic, but also because the writer-director Rod Lurie did an excellent job of demonstrating that making ethical communicative choices is an inherently complex and difficult task. The ethics and communication issues raised through this film are also applicable to our everyday interaction vis-à-vis the choices we make for ourselves and the judgments we make about others. On both personal and public levels, this film is provocative for its presentation of the tension between an individual's goals and motivations, and the communicative choices one makes while seeking to protect those interests.

Like *All the President's Men*, *The Contender* was produced on the heels of a political scandal. Whereas the specific issues in Watergate were different from the issues in the Clinton-Lewinsky scandal, both scandals share fundamental communication issues surrounding integrity, secrecy, and deception among government leaders, both in public and interpersonal communication. *The Contender* is a fictional political drama about the events that unfold as the president attempts to fill the vacant position after the untimely death of the vice president. The main characters in the movie are the Democrat president, Jackson Evans (played by Jeff Bridges); the Republican-turned-Democrat senator and vice-presidential nominee Laine Hanson (Joan Allen, who was nominated for an Academy Award for her performance in this movie); Shelly Runyon, a ruthless Republican congressman determined to destroy Hanson's confirmation (Gary Oldman); Democrat congressman Reginald Webster (Christian Slater); and Virginia governor Jack Hathaway (William L. Peterson).

The film begins with a tragic accident in which a car goes careening off a bridge just above where Hathaway is giving an interview to a reporter while in a fishing boat. Hathaway dives into the water attempting to rescue the woman inside the car, but his efforts are to no avail and she dies. After this incident the audience learns that the sudden death of the vice president has required President Jackson Evans to select a replacement. Instead of selecting Hathaway, whose popularity is soaring after his heroic rescue attempt, Evans makes a radical choice when he chooses Senator Laine Hanson to become the nation's first female vice president.

Hathaway's friend and supporter Shelly Runyon is a powerful congressman who is the head of Hanson's confirmation hearing. Firmly against Hanson's nomination and preferring Hathaway instead, Congressman Runyon secretly gathers a team to destroy Hanson personally and professionally. Photographs emerge on the Internet allegedly depicting Hanson having sex with two men during her freshman year in college as part of a sorority initiation. Depositions are taken from people who claim to have been witnesses, and the nightly news airs interviews with others who claim to have attended or participated in the initiation. Runyon slyly finds ways to insert references to the website photographs during Hanson's confirmation hearing. Hanson refuses to respond to the allegations, even to Evans, taking the position that her private life is not the public's business and challenging the public-private double standard that female political candidates face during their bids for higher-level political offices. Hanson handles the scandal with dignity and resoluteness. She never plays victim, but rather portrays a model of an individual who stands by her principles, even "when it's not convenient."

Meanwhile, an FBI agent investigates the circumstances surrounding the automobile accident that Hathaway witnessed, and finds that Hathaway paid the woman to drive off the bridge so that he could save her during his news interview. As Runyon's campaign to destroy Hanson approaches success, Evans is in jeopardy of losing his legacy—what he calls his "swan song." Evans meets with Runyon to negotiate a deal whereby he cunningly induces Runyon to agree to publicly back Hathaway's nomination, agreeing because "his fall is your fall." Runyon acts as agreed, telling the media that he would stake his career on Hathaway's smooth confirmation. Evans then exposes Hathaway's criminal behavior, ruining Runyon's credibility and clearing the way for Hanson's confirmation.

The Contender offers insight into some of the constructs most central to communication ethics. In this chapter, we examine three of these constructs: integrity, secrecy and deception, and dialogue. We begin with integrity. It is the foundation of all virtue, because ethical values can hardly be said to exist if people do not adhere to those values with some consistency. Second, we examine secrecy and deception. There is probably no issue in communication ethics more widely discussed than complete and truthful disclosure of information. These issues—integrity, secrecy, and deception—are major themes in *The Contender*, so it is natural that we direct our attention to them in our analysis. The final construct we examine in this chapter is the dialogic ethic. Whereas the other concepts are salient due to their centrality in the movie, this theory is salient due to the complete *absence* of dialogue depicted in the film. The presentation of a world in which dialogue has almost completely ceased to exist allows viewers to confront the question of how feasible dialogue is in certain situations and what the consequences are of abandoning it altogether.

Integrity

The most salient ethical issue addressed in *The Contender* is integrity. Ostensibly, the theme of the movie was Senator Laine Hanson's struggle to maintain her integrity in the face of immoral opposition. Hanson felt that there should not be a double standard as to what questions are asked of men and women, specifically as pertaining to a person's sexual history. The charges levied against Hanson, that she had been involved in a sexual orgy as part of a sorority initiation rite during her freshman year in college, were charges that she believed a man would not be asked to answer. Thus, the movie is about her quest to adhere to her principle of equality by not answering these charges in the face of great risk to her career and reputation.

The ideal of integrity is not only a central focus in *The Contender*; it also turns out to be an essential starting point for discussion of ethics because of its nature and importance. Integrity is not an ethical system itself, but rather it is the adherence to whatever ethical beliefs people value most highly. Different people may hold different beliefs, but as long as each person adheres to what he or she most highly values, they maintain their personal integrity. Without faithfulness to some value system, though, all other ethical issues become meaningless. It is pointless for a person to contemplate ethical values if that person is not prepared to consistently abide by the values he or she feels is most justified.

Stephen Carter (1996) defines integrity as the act of doing three moral tasks: (1) discerning right from wrong, (2) acting on that discernment, even at personal risk, and (3) telling others what principles one is adhering to. In his description of integrity, Carter suggests several qualities of integrity that makes it admirable. Among these, steadfastness and risk are particularly notable. Risk is an essential quality of integrity because it shows people what values are most important. Only when people must make choices, accepting some conditions and sacrificing others, do we see which values are most strongly held. Thus, it is when people expose themselves to significant risk that we know which principles are truly essential to their character. As Carter notes, "we can never really know whether we are acting from deep and steadfast principles until those principles are tested" (p. 23). Steadfastness is important because once people take a risk and make a stand, they are likely to encounter criticism and opposition. In order to maintain their integrity, people need to stand firm to their principles under such challenges.

Integrity of Senator Laine Hanson

Integrity exemplified by Hanson. The Contender makes no mention of the discernment process Senator Laine Hanson goes through to arrive at her decision; instead it focuses on her actions in adhering to it, on the costs she bears, and on her messages to others about this decision. Hanson refuses to deny the charges of sexual impropriety not only to the public, but also to the president and his aides, who are her support team. When confronted by Kermit Newman (who is implied to be Evans's chief of staff), Hanson defends her choice not to answer as simply being beneath her dignity. This course of action shows integrity not only in her consistent adherence to her principles (she refuses to answer both to her enemies and her allies), but also integrity due to the risk involved. Were the president to withdraw his support, Hanson would not only lose her nomination but also her reputation, because such a withdrawal would be seen by the public as a concession of guilt. Hanson's actions force the president to make a choice—support her whether or not the charges are true, or replace her with someone who would not risk smudging the administration's reputation.

Senator Hanson's integrity is shown in the movie in several other ways. First, when Chief of Staff Newman suggests fighting the attack by finding salacious information about Runyon, she objects, saying, "If we do that, we're no better than he is." Second, Hanson's multiple refusals to refute the charges show steadfastness. Third, Hanson explicitly identifies the role risk plays in integrity when she says, "Principles only mean something if you only stick by them when they're *in*convenient." Finally, if the dialogue was insufficient to make the point, the movie producers add some other signals as well. In the climactic conversation between Senator Hanson and President Evans, when she finally reveals the truth to him (as personal friends rather than as the president and appointee), the producers introduce the music under the voice track just as she begins telling him about her moral views—starting with her view that this personal, private encounter was not his or anyone else's business. This production cue directs viewers' attention to her integrity as the central element in this ordeal.

Shortcomings in Laine Hanson's integrity. If the viewer watches this movie and concludes that Senator Hanson is indeed the moral star of the movie, we ask them to watch it again. Although Hanson's integrity is the thematic centerpiece of the movie, we argue that another character, Representative Reginald Webster, may better embody integrity. Despite the movie's celebration of Hanson's integrity, a closer inspection shows several potential shortfalls in her integrity.

The first potential shortcoming of Senator Hanson's integrity can be seen not in her actions, but in the overarching storyline of the movie. The movie's vindication of Hanson's integrity stems from the results of her choice. Hanson stands by her principle and eventually triumphs by achieving a victory over Congressman Runyon in the hearings, and doing so without compromising on the values she so strongly holds. This outcome sounds good, but the viewer cannot escape the fact that her victory is not achieved because of her integrity, or even in spite of it, but because of President Evans's unscrupulous manipulation of Runyon. As the movie develops, it is clear that Hanson's integrity would have caused her defeat if Evans had not stooped to Runyon's level. In fact, viewers are forewarned of this fact by Chief of Staff Newman's response to Hanson's objections earlier in the film. When she protests that his tactic of finding something harmful in Runyon's past would be no better than he (Runyon) is, Newman responds, "We *are* no better than he is."

A second potential weakness in Senator Hanson's integrity lies in her moral reasoning. Although the film does not show her process of moral discernment, it does show her steadfastness being tested. And, while she does indeed stand firm, the matter of whether she exhibits sound moral judgment in her discernment is open for discussion. Later in the chapter, we will examine some support for her position based on the theories of Sissela Bok. At this point, we will address some possible weaknesses in her moral discernment. Hanson's unyielding devotion to one good (equality) is countered by the fact that she might be shortchanging other goods that are being compromised (for example, setting a moral exemplar), which she seems unwilling to consider. This unwillingness to contemplate is a serious moral deficiency, because without adequate discernment a person risks adhering to a fallible position. Carter (1996) notes this when he writes, "If we refuse to take the time for discernment, a discernment that might challenge cherished beliefs, then it is hard to see how we can ever construct a politics of integrity" (p. 28).

It is also unclear why Hanson does not object to answering the question of whether she has ever committed adultery. Although adultery is different from collegiate premarital sexual encounters, Hanson does not explain why this question is acceptable to answer, leaving the audience to wonder why one incident in her sexual history should be open to public discussion whereas the other incident should not. This contrast creates confusion about Hanson's moral stance on the boundaries between acceptable and unacceptable questions, and makes her discernment appear potentially flawed.

Integrity of Representative Reginald Webster

The character who we believe may best embody the ideal of integrity is Reginald Webster, the newly elected congressman from Delaware. Although Webster's integrity is more subtle than Senator Hanson's prominently portrayed integrity, he displays some aspects of integrity that seem superior to Hanson's adherence to virtue.

Webster's own integrity is depicted in the film starting with his first attempt to get onto the committee hearing Hanson's confirmation. When asking to be on the committee, Webster first tells Congressman Runyon, "I believe you'll find me industrious and hardworking." The following exchange then occurs:

> Congressman Runyon: I take it you have a predisposition ... about the confirmation, I mean?
>
> Congressman Webster: Uh, no. Actually I'm one hundred percent objective.

Although Runyon chastises Webster for such a stance (saying that his constituents want him for his opinions and philosophy, his "subjectivity"), the point about Webster's character is made clear for the audience. When Webster approaches Runyon later and again requests membership in the committee, he says it is because he feels Hanson's policies belong in the Republican party.

Although Webster's integrity could be criticized for his seeking membership on a committee in order to sack someone, this stance can be partially defended in that Webster does examine the facts and makes a decision based on his principles and what he thinks is best for the public, not because of a personal vendetta. Furthermore, Webster is exhibiting integrity in taking risk, as he stands a lot to lose by going against his own party. The other way Webster can be vindicated is to say that his initial actions constitute a moral lapse. But, because he begins from a fallible position, his eventual conversion to the other perspective shows that he is remaining vigilant in looking for the truth. Ultimately, there is some element of truth to both these positions. The best description is to say that Webster is not completely integral in his reasons for trying to get onto the committee, but he does have some justification and in his actions on the committee he eventually corrects for the shortcomings he initially showed.

Webster's integrity is also shown in several key dialogues. In one of these, the president asks him to support Senator Hanson's nomination as a personal favor. Webster responds that he will not do that, saying, "I am nothing if I do not follow my heart, sir." Later, when Webster finds that Runyon has been feeding false rumors to the press, the two have the following exchange:

> Congressman Runyon: I, uh, think I have some self-righteous indignation coming my way.

> Congressman Webster (rolls his eyes): Well, is there any truth whatsoever to this story?

Then, Webster does something no one else in the movie does—he tries to talk to all parties, in an attempt to find the truth and to do what is most right. In so doing, he visits Hanson in an attempt to discuss the moral issue of setting the sexual standard for America's girls. Instead of engaging in this moral discussion, Hanson abruptly ends the conversation. In this scene, the viewer sees Webster reflecting on the moral questions while Hanson refuses to do so.

If these scenes were not enough, the filmmakers add other clues about Webster's integrity. As he waits to speak to the president, the movie allocates over a minute to a scene showing him admiring portraits of great presidents, suggesting that he admires their virtues as well. Second, when Webster gives the president the affidavits that prove Hanson's innocence in the sexual scandal, President Evans says of him, "He may not know his right from his left, but apparently he does know right from wrong."

In the end, we judge Webster as showing greater integrity than Hanson, not on account of what values each adhere to, but because of how both go about enacting their integrity. Hanson's integrity is in her faithfulness to gender equality; Webster's integrity emerges from his commitment to finding the truth and making a choice that is best for the greater good. Both values are worthy. And both characters take risks in their actions—Hanson risks losing her nomination, and Webster risks loss of support, first by going against his party and then later by changing sides. However, where the two characters diverge in the level of integrity they show is in Webster's vigilance for the truth and in his ongoing attentiveness to moral issues. When he becomes suspicious of Runyon's tactics, he begins to investigate the allegations on his own. And, whereas the process of discernment seems to end for Hanson once she arrives upon her stance, Webster continues to ask and reflect on the emerging moral dimensions as the events continue to unfold.

The Contender's depiction of integrity suggests some implications for our understanding of integrity. For instance, the movie shows the importance that discernment and steadfastness play. Carter (1996) treats discernment and steadfastness as parts of a sequential process (with discernment culminating in the decision that is upheld through steadfast commitment), but the movie reveals the fact that while discernment must take place before steadfastness can begin, discernment should not be abandoned once an initial decision is reached. Instead, steadfastness should be added to ongoing discernment. Hanson's discernment is limited to her initial decision, and she seems unwilling to reconsider the issue in light of other aspects of the issue that she may not have thought about initially. Webster, on the other hand, shows integrity by keeping active in his discernment process, such that he can change his position— *without* changing his principles—when new information comes to light. Steadfastness is indeed to be admired, as Carter notes, but we should add the caveat that blind adherence is not equivalent to steadfastness, and it is not to be admired. Integrity is an ongoing process, and it is premature to complete one's discernment before the situation has fully played itself out.

Secrecy and Deception

In Senator Hanson's quest to preserve her integrity, the issue at stake is when it is appropriate to disclose certain personal information versus when such information ought to remain secret. Thus, the moral conflicts in this movie revolve around matters of secrecy and deception. The most central issue of secrecy is Hanson's refusal to respond to charges of sexual debauchery during her freshman year in college. In addition to Hanson, however, many other characters in the movie also deal with issues of secrecy and deception. Foremost among these other characters is President Evans, who makes choices of disclosure and deceit related to Governor Hathaway's plot and Congressman Runyon's campaign to thwart Hanson's nomination.

Moral reflection on secrecy and deception in *The Contender* forces the viewer to confront several difficult issues. For Hanson, the movie leads the viewer to wrestle with two central issues. The first of these is the question of when silence is deception. This is the issue that Congressman Webster raises with Hanson when he expresses concerns that she is setting the moral standard for the nation's girls. The second is a multifaceted issue related to the construction of one's identity. To what degree should an individual be able to control her or his own identity? How can we determine the legitimacy of requests (or demands) for openness of personal disclosure?

In her analysis of secrets, Sissela Bok (1983) lays out a theoretical foundation that provides a good starting point in addressing these issues. First, Bok establishes the point that secrets are not always intended to deceive, nor always interpreted as deception. For example, voting is often done by secret ballot. This practice is not done to deceive, but simply to protect privacy. Second, Bok establishes two key principles that underlie all other judgments about secrecy: (1) equality of secrecy and (2) partial individual control over disclosure of personal matters. Bok's argument about equality of secrecy is that "whatever control over secrecy and openness we conclude is legitimate for some individuals should, in the absence of special considerations, be legitimate for all" (p. 27). This argument is essentially a requirement of impartiality, found in almost every major ethical perspective (for example, Kant 1997; Rawls 1971).

Bok's second principle asserts that people should be allowed a degree of personal autonomy in control over secrecy to protect their identity, because secrecy protects our vulnerability, our sense of uniqueness from others, and our sense of possibilities for the future self. In her words,

> Human beings can be subjected to every scrutiny, and reveal much about themselves; but they can never be entirely understood, simultaneously exposed from every perspective, completely transparent either to themselves or to other persons. They are not only unique, but also unfathomable. The experience of such uniqueness and depth underlies self-respect and what social theorists have called the sense of the sacredness of the self. (1983, p. 21)

Secrecy in order to protect sacredness of self helps us understand why a right to privacy is so important to many Americans. It is why the argument in defense of the Patriot Act that includes the question "If you have nothing to hide, why does it matter whether someone is monitoring your e-mails, reading your mail, or tapping your telephone?" has yet to be universally persuasive.

Based on these two principles of individual control over disclosure, Bok (1983) proposes the following question, which is essential to answer: "What considerations override these presumptions?" (p. 28, emphasis removed). That is, under what circumstances should some people be forced to disclose information that others are not, and when should people have to give up sacredness of self? In Bok's eyes, each situation must be judged on its own merits; there are no blanket rules for secrecy and disclosure that can be applied to all cases at all times. In light of this foundation, Senator Hanson's refusal to disclose secrets of her sexual history invites a challenging ethical analysis.

Secrecy of Senator Laine Hanson

Senator Hanson's silence and thus refusal explain or defend herself against the allegations about her moral character invites the audience to interrogate the tension between the public's right to know and personal privacy for political candidates, particularly at the executive level. The first issue is whether her secrecy constitutes an act of deception.

Silence as deception. The issue of secrecy as deception is a significant issue. As this chapter was being written, Americans were debating whether the Bush administration used secrecy as a means to deceive the public into believing that Iraq represented a greater security threat than it really did (allegations were also surfacing that the president and his administration had also simply lied about certain facts, but that is a separate issue that is not germane to the present discussion). Of particular interest was a memo from the CIA to the president, which was heavily censored before being released to the public. The publicly released document "was stripped of dissenting opinions, warnings of insufficient information and doubts about ... Saddam Hussein's intentions" (Landay 2004, p. A1). In instances like this one, the use of secrecy as a means of deception is clearly at the fore.

Not all secrets involve deception, but deception inevitably involves secrecy. Indubitably this begs the question, When is secrecy deceptive? Bok argues that, in the case of those with government power, secrets are deceptive when concealment is motivated by a desire to shelter information from open discussion and debate. Thus, the Bush administration's use of secrecy seems likely to be an instance in which secrecy is used as a means of deception.

The questions for viewers of *The Contender*, then, are whether Senator Hanson's secrecy is deceptive, and under what circumstances secrecy is a means of deception. The best response in the case of Hanson is to say that her secrecy, while not done for the purpose of deception (as was President Evans's secrecy toward Congressman Runyon about Governor Hathaway's guilt), is still misleading. Near the end of the film, Evans tells Hanson he will call a press conference to present evidence that the sexual allegations are unfounded, and she asks him not to do so. "You would sacrifice your reputation?" Evans asks, to which Hanson replies, "Yes, I would. I really would." In this exchange, the movie makes it clear that Hanson's silence does indeed lead people to accept a false claim about her past behaviors.

Legitimacy of requests for openness. The second major issue that Senator Hanson's silence invokes is how to determine whether or not a request for disclosure is appropriate. For answers to this question, we turn to Bok's two principles—equality and individual control. Hanson uses both arguments. When Congressman Webster attempts to privately discuss the issue with Hanson, she justifies her silence with the principle of equality before abruptly ending the conversation: "If I were a man, nobody would care how many sexual partners I had when I was in college. And if it's not relevant for a man it's not relevant for a woman." To President Evans, Hanson begins her argument with the principle of limited individual control by suggesting that this just is not appropriate material for conversation:

> President Evans: K [Chief of Staff Kermit Newman] told me about your little sexual romp in college.... Were you married at the time?
>
> Senator Hanson: I was a freshman in— You know sir, I'm just not going to comment. The whole thing is beneath me and it's beneath the process.

Based on this reasoning, not only is Hanson's refusal to speak to the matter ethical, but also it is essential to her well-being. Her silence can be defended as an ethical choice in order to protect her identity, because protecting one's identity is a legitimate pursuit. We could even take this argument a step further and suggest that her silence seems to be an ethical choice that serves both fundamental individual human needs and the greater good for women in society. This idea is exemplified in an exchange between Senator Hanson and the wife of Congressman Shelly Runyon. Mrs. Runyon approaches Hanson with some damaging information about Shelly. In explaining her rationale for offering harmful information about her husband, Mrs. Runyon tells Hanson, "In this business with so much at stake, it's not enough to believe in yourself, you have to be right. This [attack on you] is an ideological rape, of all women." To this comment, Hanson replies, "Well, then I'll survive it for all of us."

If equality and individual control were all there were to the judgment, this matter would be simple enough. However, the question is much more difficult. Bok describes this right as "limited," to acknowledge the fact that there are times when someone's right to protect identity is overridden by larger concerns. Larry J. Sabato, Mark Stencel, and S. Robert Lichter (2000) offer some factors to clarify the limits to secrecy of a public official's sexual activities. Among the factors they identify as supporting the legitimacy of a request include sexual activity that impacts an official's public role (for example, sexual relations with a staff member or lobbyist), sexual activity where conflict of interest exists or where there is coercion, or sexual activity that is compulsive and indiscreet (and therefore potentially dangerous). In contrast, they specify that sexual activity can be legitimately kept secret if it does not fit these categories, or if it is from a person's distant past (more than a decade ago).

Because these are abstract categories, it can be difficult to know exactly how to categorize some of Senator Hanson's behaviors. So, these additional criteria require further discussion. But, in general, we can view the allegations against Hanson as targeting behavior that was noncompulsive, unrelated to her role as a public official (especially since she was not a public official at the time), and past the statute of limitations. The problem for Hanson is that the allegations are that she participated in sexual activity that was indiscreet, at least by some standards. Nonetheless, Hanson seems to fare pretty well by these standards.

The complicating factor is that as the first woman to serve at the highest office of government, Hanson will not only be a policymaker but also a role model. Here is where her moral justification for not taking a stand becomes more problematic. Hanson argues, with some merit, that her refusal to answer to the charges is the most moral way to respond. Critics, however, could respond—also with merit—that her silence creates some harm because it would be interpreted as a confession. This is the concern of Congressman Webster:

> Congressman Webster: I just feel like there should be some back and forth between us; you and the committee.

> Senator Hanson: I'll give you back and forth: on social security, relations with Israel, the Dow Jones, the census, almost everything, but not this. Not my personal life. It's just nobody's business.

> Congressman Webster: Well that's not what the people will tell you. They'll tell you it is their business. They'll tell you that you're setting the standards of morality for their children, especially their girls.

When looking at all the facts, Senator Hanson's position based on equality and control over identity seems reasonably sound. Yet, we argue that her position was not completely morally praiseworthy. Why do we criticize the moral soundness of her action? We suggest two points. First, her claim that standards of privacy are unequal for men and women is debatable. The Clinton-Lewinsky scandal, which was mentioned in this film, was a recent case in which a male political figure was asked questions about his sexual history. Just as Clinton was asked, so too is Senator Hanson asked to confirm or deny the moral charges against her. Thus, her presumption about the status of equality in her historical moment is suspect.

Second, what appears as steadfastness on the part of Senator Hanson could be evaluated as moral blindness (or at least short-sightedness). In *The Contender*, viewers are never given a sense that Hanson has considered options other than flat refusal to discuss. If it were the case that the only two available options were to answer the charges or remain silent, then we would be content with what she does if we agree that her choice was based on sound reasons. However, in seeing only these two choices, Hanson creates a false dichotomy. One option would have been for Hanson to have made a statement about the moral reasons why she felt that the question was inappropriate to answer and that her lack of response should be considered neither an acceptance nor a denial of the information being circulated in the press. In doing so, she would have retained the secrecy about her sexual past, but also possibly mitigated the negative impact that Webster and others were concerned her silence was having on the sexual morals she was presenting to girls by making her principles clear. Furthermore, while not a certain outcome, it is possible that such a response could even be a catalyst for a public discussion over whether there is a sexual double standard in political inquiry.

We suggest that the choice Senator Hanson makes is of positive moral quality, but that it does not maximize possible ethical quality in her actions. Vernon Jensen (1985) posits that ethics are better judged as a matter of degree, rather than dichotomous right/wrong positions. For ease of discussion, he suggests using a continuum, with the low end reflecting behavior that is of extremely low ethical quality, the midpoint representing ethically neutral behavior, and the high end signifying behavior that is of extremely high ethical quality. One advantage to this conceptualization is that it prevents philosophers from being satisfied with one ethical behavior when another choice that is of higher ethical quality is readily available.

If we adopt Jensen's stance, we can easily evaluate Senator Hanson's communication. It is clear that her actions are of positive ethical quality, thus meriting a score above the scale's midpoint. But it is also the case that her choice is not the *best* option that she has available, particularly in light of her reluctance to share her moral reasons with many parties involved, such as President Evans, Representative Webster, and the American public. Thus, we suggest that while Hanson's actions are indeed of positive ethical quality, they are deficient in the sense that they are not as positive as they could have been.

Secrecy of President Jackson Evans

Secrecy and deception are relevant to an analysis of the communicative choices made by Jackson Evans as well. Early in the film President Evans seems preoccupied not with important matters of the state, but rather with the petty pleasures that power in high places provides. He enjoys demanding exotic foods from his cooking staff, bowling, and trying to catch his staff unprepared for an unusual request. But as his character unfolds, the audience is shown a man who is determined to win, who is shrewd and cunning, and who has a loyal right-hand man to facilitate his success. The appearance of absorption with petty pleasures is a ruse in service of his strategy to have his term in office end with a "swan song." Because his vice president has passed away while in office, leaving the position vacant and in need of an appointment, he has a unique opportunity to appoint a woman to serve in the highest executive office of government in the history of the country. His challenge is to win a confirmation from the head of the hearing committee, a man who is not only on the other side of the ideological aisle from Evans, but who was Evans's losing opponent in his campaign for president. Both Evans and Congressman Runyon are shrewd competitors, who use secrecy and deception to win their game, yet Evans's strategies seem more acceptable.

Beginning with his meeting with Governor Hathaway just after the tragic accident, subtle cues in the film (such as Evans's nonverbal behaviors) suggest inauthenticity from the president's gestures of sympathy and condolence, almost as if he knows something is suspicious about the incident. Late in the film, the plot suggests that the likely reason Evans never pushed Hanson to abandon her silence was that he had an ace in the hole—the truth about Hathaway.

Ends and means. This reading of the text seems to forgive President Evans for what is recognizably ruthlessness, because the film suggests that Hathaway and Runyon are immoral, and Hanson is upright. But does Evans's behavior stand up to basic tests of ethics? After all, his goals were to win, "to beat Shelly at his own game," and to end his administration with a claim to fame—hardly moral goals. When Governor Jack Hathaway learns that he will not be the vice-presidential nominee, this latter motivation is made clear. Hathaway asks Chief of Staff Newman, "I don't understand ... can't you do something?" to which Newman replies, "I've tried, but he's already made up his mind. Filling the slot may well be his swan song."

The issue of whether the good ends justify the use of bad means is an ancient question in ethics. In general, ethicists tend to be negative about the possibility of good ends justifying otherwise immoral means, pointing out such problems as the fact that the means is just as important as the end and that actions often have consequences other than those intended (Johannesen 2002). However, the issue is not as simple as it might appear. First, some people argue that under extreme circumstances we may need to make exceptions to the usual principles (see, for example, Bok 1978). Furthermore, when inspected more closely, the idea of ends justifying means relates to the issue of utilitarianism (Mill 1947). The difference between these two perspectives is that utilitarianism seeks to determine whether the means are acceptable based on the outcomes, whereas the means-ends approach seeks to excuse an admittedly bad means because of its morally desirable outcome. But how can a utilitarian thinker judge the means other than by their outcomes? From a utilitarian perspective, the moral quality of the means is a blank slate until the ends determine it, and so in a sense, when reasoned from this theory the ends always justify the means (whatever they are).

One answer to the question of whether good ends justify bad means is presented by Warren Bovée (1991). He argues that good ends can justify bad means, but rarely. To determine whether the ends justify the means, he suggests six questions. These questions involve matters of what the good is, the likelihood of the evil means achieving it, and the other available options. In the competition over Hanson's nomination between President Evans and Congressman Runyon, both Evans and Runyon use secrecy and deception in seeking their ends. Yet the viewer is led to see Evans's actions as less vile than Runyon's. Why is this? Although Runyon argues that he wants to block Hanson's confirmation because he does not see the promise of greatness in her, the film portrays him as simply being a misogynist, thus undermining any claims to righteous motivation. Evans, on the other hand, warrants a mixed evaluation. The film makes it clear that his motivation is to leave a legacy, and so that cause is self-serving. But virtually every ethical theory accepted today would reject the idea that women are categorically unfit for the presidency, and thus Evans's attempt to rectify this glaring inequity meets moral acclaim, as long as the woman he nominates is fit for office.

Where the two characters' courses of action more strongly separate, however, is in availability of other choices. Runyon makes no attempt at morally commendable strategies, but jumps directly to deceit and treachery, whereas Evans only resorts to such tactics when all other possibilities are exhausted. It is worth noting here that strategizing for such contingencies, as Evans is clearly doing throughout the movie, is not the same thing as actually doing the behaviors when other choices are still available. Furthermore, the position Evans finds himself in when he resorts to manipulation was created by Runyon's treachery. This action is different from resorting to foul tactics when it becomes apparent that one is losing a fair fight; in this case Evans is defending himself with the same tactics his attacker is using against him. Thus, even though both parties use deceptive tactics, viewers can tolerate Evans's actions better than Runyon's.

Dialogic Ethic

One ethical theory that is conspicuous by its absence in the characters' interactions is the dialogic ethic. The dialogic ethic is an ethic for interpersonal interactions, especially under circumstances in which persuasion is important. It is one of the few theories specifically designed for communication in personal relationships, and seems like an ideal fit for guiding relationships among political leaders because of the centrality of persuasion in such relations.

As delineated by Paul W. Keller and Charles T. Brown (1968), the dialogic ethic calls for people to discuss issues in a spirit of dialogue. Key elements of dialogue include presenting oneself in the most genuine manner possible, showing the other unconditional positive regard, being fully present in the interaction, showing empathetic understanding of the other person's perspective, and similar behaviors (Johannesen 1971). Furthermore, Keller and Brown assert that communicators need to recognize their mutual influence on each other, and treat each other with the greatest of respect. In their view, communication is ethical to the degree that it enhances the other person's self-determination, and unethical to the degree that it develops hostility toward the other or attempts to subjugate the other. Communication that opposes these goals is described as monologic, because it stifles dissent and tries to subjugate the other person.

Lest the reader quickly dismiss this theory as being an unrealistic relic of the 1960s, two reminders are in order. First, the theory's impact has been significant, and dialogue continues to be an important area of interest in philosophy of communication (see, for example, Anderson, Baxter, & Cissna 2004; Arnett & Arneson 1999;

Cissna & Anderson 1998). Second, while many of the ideas in the theory seem naïve and idealistic, Keller (1981) argues that ethical theories should be ideals people strive toward, not realistic reflections of what we most commonly do.

The interactions depicted in *The Contender* show a cast of characters who almost universally abandon any pretense of engaging each other in a spirit of dialogue. President Evans's dealings with Governor Hathaway are set against a backdrop of the secret investigation he is conducting of Hathaway's role in the fatal accident, Congressman Runyon deems Senator Hanson unfit for service as vice president before he ever interacts with her, Hanson walks out on lunch with Runyon after a brief skirmish, and Runyon's wife secretly gives Hanson information she can use to publicly embarrass her husband without giving him a chance to learn about or respond to the issue. When Congressman Webster tries to initiate dialogue with Hanson about her ethical choices, she demeans him, saying, "You know what? You're young. That's okay, it's okay. You're young. And, um, I'm just gonna choose to be amused by your naïveté, give you the benefit of the doubt, and spell it out for you even more clearly."

Furthermore, the movie makes it clear that these characters see their interactions as confrontational, not mutually cooperative, as the dialogic ethic suggests. Evans says, "I'll die before Shelly Runyon checkmates me!" indicating that he sees the essence of their relationship as a match against each other. Runyon, for his part, states that politics and war are "one and the same," and therefore the interpersonal dimensions of their interactions are like combat. In *The Contender*, it is clear that these characters live in a world defined by survival of the fittest, where even one's allies are sharks (a metaphor that is instantiated in the movie).

One liability of using the dialogic ethic is that both parties must be able to trust each other to participate fully and honestly, because a person communicating dialogically with someone who is monologic will be taken advantage of (Keller 1981). Clearly, that assumption of dialogue is not a safe one to make in the realm of political dealings. The word *politics* has taken on a connotation of self-interest, dirty deals, and disloyalty, a sharp contrast with Aristotle's notion of politics as the "master science of the good," as noted at the beginning of this chapter. It is hopeful to many people that their own workplaces involve a greater degree of dialogic interaction with at least some of their coworkers than that portrayed in *The Contender*, and that their personal relationships involve even more.

The question for ethicists is, Should we advocate dialogue as an ideal form of involvement in political professional relationships, or is such a stance unrealistic? If it is unrealistic, should we still seek it as an ideal that we strive to work toward, or do we abandon it altogether, as nice but impossible? Although the movie does not make an explicit or intentional statement about this matter, the characterization it gives of political dealings paints a picture of dialogue as impossible, and thus not wise to strive for. In fact, the movie's portrayal of President Evans as an admirable figure, in spite of (maybe even because of) his manipulation of Congressman Runyon, may even lead to the interpretation that a spirit of dialogue will leave a person weak and vulnerable.

The challenge to this interpretation is that Representative Webster does act dialogically in several cases—talking to Runyon about the false rumors, attempting to discuss the moral issues with Senator Hanson, and sharing the results of his investigation with both Runyon and Evans. What is interesting is that while Webster is portrayed as a good person, it is Hanson's character that is of greater focus, yet it is Webster's approach that allowed Hanson to succeed. So, despite the general rejection of dialogue in the movie, viewers could still see the dialogic ethic as viable, even if only in limited ways.

Ultimately, this balance may be what the film best portrays—the idea that blind adherence to dialogue leaves a person vulnerable, but that, strategically used, dialogue can be beneficial. Should dialogue be relegated to a cautious maneuver, situated in otherwise strategic relations? That issue is left for viewers to decide. In our view, it may be wise to suggest that even if dialogue cannot become the dominant mode of communication, people should strive to interact in that manner wherever possible, and seek to inject some element of dialogue into even the most stubborn and resistant pockets of today's culture.

Conclusion

One reason this film lends itself so nicely to an analysis of communication and ethics is that the characters deal with the same type of challenges that real people face when making communicative decisions and ethical evaluations about the communication of others. *The Contender* shows us that moral judgments require deep investigations rather than surface treatment, that things are not always as they appear, and that, in fact, no one is a completely virtuous moral agent. Humans are flawed and ethical evaluations are not appropriately made by drawing a line in the sand where right is clearly on one side and wrong clearly on the other. Complex interrelationships require investigation of the moral facts and an evaluation of relative good and relative bad contained within.

The Contender proves to be a good tool for exploring the intricacies of many ethical theories. When we start trying to understand these ideals in light of what is portrayed in the movie, we must confront subtle nuances that we might miss if just reading about or describing the theory. For instance, the contrast between Hanson's and Webster's renditions of integrity bring to light issues of discernment, steadfastness, and integrity as a *process* that would otherwise go unnoticed in a simple description of integrity. The uses of secrecy in the movie show how secrecy can be used for both morally praiseworthy and morally questionable ends. And, the role that monologue and dialogue play in the film invites viewers to consider difficult issues of how people should relate to each other interpersonally. Through the examination of the ethical theories discussed in this chapter, the reader should gain insight not only into the ethical elements of this film, but also, more important, into the ethical issues all people face in everyday interactions.

References

Anderson, R., L. A. Baxter, & K. N. Cissna. (2004). *Dialogue: Theorizing difference in communication studies.* Thousand Oaks, CA: Sage.

Aristotle. (1962). *Nicomachean ethics* (M. Ostwald, trans.). Indianapolis, IN: Bobbs-Merrill. (Original work published in antiquity).

Arnett, R. C., & P. Arneson. (1999). *Dialogic civility in a cynical age: Community, hope, and interpersonal relationships.* Albany: SUNY Press.

Bok, S. (1978). *Lying: Moral choice in public and private life.* New York: Vintage.

———. (1983). *Secrets: On the ethics of concealment and revelation.* New York: Vintage.

Bovée, W. G. (1991). The end can justify the means—but rarely. *Journal of Mass Media Ethics* 6: 135–45.

Carter, S. (1996). *Integrity.* New York: Harper Perennial.

Cissna, K. N., & R. Anderson. (1998). Theorizing about dialogic moments: The Buber-Rogers position and postmodern themes. *Communication Theory* 8: 63–104.

Good, H., & M. J. Dillon. (2002). *Media ethics goes to the movies.* Westport, CT: Praeger.

Jensen, J. V. (1985). Teaching ethics in speech communication. *Communication Education* 34: 324–30.

Johannesen, R. L. (1971). The emerging concept of communication as dialogue. *Quarterly Journal of Speech* 57: 373–82.

———. (2002). *Ethics in human communication,* 5th ed. Prospect Heights, IL: Waveland.

Kant, I. (1997). *Groundwork of the metaphysics of morals* (M. Gregor, trans.). Cambridge, MA: Cambridge University Press. (Original work published in 1785).

Keller, P. W. (1981). Interpersonal dissent and the ethics of dialogue. *Communication* 6: 287–303.

Keller, P. W., & C. T. Brown. (1968). An interpersonal ethic for communication. *Journal of Communication* 18(1): 73–81.

Kupfer, J. H. (1999). *Visions of virtue in popular film.* Boulder, CO: Westview.

Landay, J. S. (2004). Two intelligence documents differ. *Kansas City Star,* February 10, pp. A1, A4.

Lipkin, S. N. (2002). *Real emotional logic: Film and television docudrama as persuasive practice.* Carbondale: Southern Illinois University Press.

Mill, J. S. (1947). *On liberty.* Arlington Heights, IL: Harlan Davidson. (Original work published in 1859).

Rawls, J. (1971). *A theory of justice.* Cambridge, MA: Harvard University Press.

Sabato, L. J., M. Stencel, & S. R. Lichter. (2000). *Peepshow: Media and politics in an age of scandal.* Lanham, MD: Rowman & Littlefield.

Valenti, F. M. (2000). *More than a movie: Ethics in entertainment.* Boulder, CO: Westview.

CHAPTER EIGHT ————————————————

"In the End, It's All Made Up": The Ethics of Fanfiction and Real Person Fiction

Jennifer McGee

> (Aragorn comes back to Helm's Deep after everyone thought he had died. Legolas comes up to him and gives him a long look.)
>
> Legolas: You're late. You look terrible. (Aragorn grins. Legolas hands Aragorn the Evenstar of Arwen. Aragorn's bloodstained hand closes over it.)
>
> Aragorn (softly): Thank you.
>
> —Scene from the movie *The Lord of the Rings: The Two Towers*, directed by Peter Jackson

Movies like the recent *Lord of the Rings* trilogy, books like the *Harry Potter* series, television shows like *Friends*—all of these are carefully crafted to tell interesting or amusing stories and feature characters audiences can enjoy, understand, and even come to care about. When audiences become "fans" of a media artifact, they enter into a relationship with the characters they enjoy, a relationship encouraged by the creators of the artifact. The fact that this relationship is of necessity a one-way relationship (I can worry about Frodo's safety and wonder about his motives, but he can never do the same for me) does not make it any less meaningful for the fan, or less valuable to the creator. This chapter is an exploration of one activity fans use to connect with the objects of their enthusiasm, that of writing fanfiction.

Fanfiction is any story created by a fan about a movie, book, television show, or other media artifact. Fanfiction stories are non-canonical, where the canon is the body of information considered to be officially correct about a show, book, or movie. These stories can range from explaining canon (Why does Jean Grey of the X-Men choose Scott Summers over Logan?), filling in gaps in canon (What happened during Arwen's voyage to Gondor to meet Aragorn in *Return of the King*?), expanding canon forward or backward in time (How did Lily and James, Harry Potter's parents, meet and fall in love?), altering canon into "alternate universe" stories (How would *Attack of the Clones* have been different if Qui-Gon Jinn had lived?), or creating crossovers between artifacts (Mulder from *The X-Files* finds himself on Jack Sparrow's ship from *Pirates of the Caribbean*), among other forms.

Fanfiction has a long history. Some of the first fanfiction seems to have been written by fans of Sherlock Holmes in the 1930s (Ecks n.d.). However, organized and large-scale fanfiction writing didn't come into being until the age of television, when fans of *Star Trek* began to meet and share stories about their favorite characters. Media fandom grew in scope through the 1960s, 1970s, and 1980s, gaining adherents from new shows (*Starsky and Hutch, Man from U.N.C.L.E., Blake's 7*, and others, in addition to *Star Trek*). Fans usually distributed fiction through the postal system, mailing them to a designated editor, who then photocopied them and sent them to other members of the mailing list. Although some of the creators of the original characters expressed their dislike of fanfiction, the genre remained mostly private and obscure.

In the early 1990s, fandom became a popular topic of academic writing, as researchers became interested in the ways people interacted with the media. Fans, with their more intense relationship to the media artifacts, and their articulate discussions of the media, became the topic of research in books like Henry Jenkins's *Textual Poachers* (1992) and Camille Bacon-Smith's *Enterprising Women* (1992). At the same time, the explosion of the Internet, especially the World Wide Web, moved fandom and fanfiction into entirely new realms. Suddenly fanfiction of every type and quality was readily available to anyone with a computer and Internet connection. Fans of shows and books both popular and obscure found easy access to other fans and an eager audience for their fiction. A quick look at the popular site Fanfiction.net as of late 2003 reveals a sprawling, vigorous world of fanfiction, from the well known (1,900 *Matrix* fanfics, 25,000 *Lord of the Rings* fanfics, a staggering 106,000 *Harry Potter* fanfics) to the unusual (4 *Casablanca* fanfics, 30 *Iron Chef* fanfics, 190 *Lord of the Flies* fanfics).

The Internet has created new trends in fanfiction that Jenkins and Bacon-Smith did not have the opportunity to discuss, and new ethical problems to consider. To discuss the ethics of fanfiction in the early twenty-first century, I first explain the basic ethical dilemmas of fanfiction and the parasocial relationships it is born from. Then I look at two genres of fanfiction that raise especially difficult ethical issues: slash stories that pair up characters into homosexual relationships, and real person fiction, which features real actors and musicians rather than imaginary characters. These two types of stories, and the debates they prompt about ethics, raise questions about the ethical responsibilities of fan writers, the shifting limits of permissible behavior, and the increasingly muddled distinctions between real people and fictional characters.

Parasocial Relationships, Identification, and Fanfiction

Legolas, son of Thranduil, lay on his back and studied the clouds as they scurried across the sky. He was awaiting the arrival of his closest friend and confidante, Aragorn of Arathorn. The two had been friends for years, ever since, Aragorn was but a young lad of sixteen summers. Eighteen years later, the bonds of friendship held for them both—stronger than ever. Legolas smiled absently as he remembered some of the scrapes that he and his friend had gotten into over the span of their association—the most recent being that of the quest of the ring and the battles that were faced then. It was two years since Sauron had been defeated and Legolas would be the first to admit that he was BORED! The ensuing years had been peaceful and quiet, and while that was good, the elven prince knew that he had warrior blood in his veins and that he was actually spoiling for a fight.

—From Tribalbutterfly's story "Onward to Adventure"

Parasocial Relationships and Identification

The relationships people feel they share with television and movie characters or celebrities are called parasocial relationships. The term was first used in 1956 to explain the connection many television viewers felt to television characters (Horton & Wohl 1956). Such relationships are by their very nature unidirectional—the fan feels a connection with the character, but the character can feel nothing similar in return. Because they are unidirectional, such relationships are often dismissed as merely "imaginary" by researchers. For example, A. A. Berger (1996) describes the illusion television gives a viewer "of actually being *with* other people. That is why people often have parasocial relationships with television performers, that is, they feel (or more precisely, they have the illusion) that they 'know them' intimately.... The medium provides people who watch it with a spurious kind of companionship, a (visually speaking) virtual community of sorts" (p. 114). Another book, about the social lives of the elderly, rejects parasocial relations as entirely unmeaningful: "parasocial integration is a symbolic alternative to actual participation in core social relationships, obligations, and responsibilities.... One can admire and cheer, if one so chooses, but real life is still with real people and real relationships in real places" (Tomer 2001, p. 277).

Putting aside the fact that parasocial relationships are often used as a means to interact with actual people (whether "water-cooler discussion" about *Friends* or conventions where *Star Trek* fans meet, party, and fall in love), such dismissive comments ignore the reality that relationships with media-created characters can be deeply meaningful to the fan. In the documentary *Trekkies*, for example, James Doohan (Scotty) speaks with tears in his eyes of how he encouraged a depressed young woman to hold on to life by encouraging her to come to the conventions where he was appearing (Nygard 1997). The actual relationship between Doohan and the woman was negligible; combined with the parasocial relationship between her and the character of Scotty, it may have saved her life. Nearly all of us are invested in parasocial relationships with characters or celebrities to some extent; even Joshua Meyrowitz, in

No Sense of Place (1985), writing about the dangers of such relationships, notes that "an awareness of the para-social mechanism is not enough to permit escape from its 'magic'; the death of John Lennon, for example, was strangely painful to me and my university colleagues who had 'known' him and grown up 'with' him" (p. 120).

Thus, the fan finds herself[1] caring about a character, but aware that this relationship between them is a one-way relationship only. One very common way of trying to express and experience this relationship is through writing fanfiction. Fanfiction is valuable and meaningful to the fan because it creates *identification* between the fan and the character. Identification, as explained by Kenneth Burke in *A Rhetoric of Motives* (1969), is the feeling that an audience and speaker share important things in common. Explaining the way identification works between two people, Burke says, "A is not identical with his [or her] colleague, B. But insofar as their interests are joined, A is *identified* with B. Or he may *identify himself* with B even when their interests are not joined, if he assumes that they are, or is persuaded to believe so" (p. 20).

Burke's model of identification is that of a speaker and an audience in which the speaker mentions things held in common with the audience: "I grew up on a farm," says the political candidate speaking to farmers in Iowa. In the case of fanfiction, however, the fan is attempting to create identification by re-creating the character in an image that humanizes and gives identifying detail to the character. For example, in the course of "Onward to Adventure," the story cited at the beginning of this section, Legolas expresses his restlessness, his admiration for his friend, his envy of Aragorn's happy marriage, and his hope that someday he might also find someone with which to share his life. Although it's impossible to be sure, it seems unlikely Tolkien's original vision of Legolas included such details. Even the Peter Jackson movie versions of the series, which generally humanize Tolkien's characters, do not go into a great deal of depth. What are Aragorn and Legolas thinking in the scene quoted at the beginning of this essay, as they meet again? The fan can only guess, and fanfiction allows her to create characters that feel and think in ways she recognizes and can connect with. In Burke's image of identification, the speaker uses rhetoric to explain similarities, whether real, false, or spurious, between the speaker and the audience. In fanfiction, the writer uses rhetoric to *create* those similarities that allow identification between the fan and the character.

Fanfiction and the Ethics of Dialogue

The fan yearns for a truer connection or identification between herself and the favorite character, for what Richard L. Johannesen, in his *Ethics in Human Communication* (1990), calls a "dialogic relationship." Various ethics theorists, most famously Martin Buber, have detailed the differences between communication as a dialogue and communication as a monologue, concluding that the former is a more ethical way of approaching relationships. A dialogue features several key ethical components. In a dialogue, participants strive for: authenticity, honest self-presentation without facades and false images; inclusion, trying to see the world from the other's perspective; confirmation, valuing and affirming the other as a human being; presentness, giving attention and concentration to the communication; a spirit of mutual equality, avoiding manipulation or exploitation; and a supportive climate, encouraging the other in free expression and listening without inflexible judgments (Johannesen 1990, pp. 62–64).

In short, the dialogical relationship is one that aims to treat what one is communicating with as a person rather than as an object. Objects are to be used for one's own ends; persons are to be cherished and communicated with. "Objects can be *talked about*.... But only persons can be *talked with*. Only persons can engage in mutually responsive communication" (Johannesen 1990, p. 66). Fanfiction, in its attempt to identify with a fictional character, strives to *talk with* that character rather than just *talk about* him or her. It yearns for intimate identification, the dialogue that is born of a "drive for contact ... aim[ed] at reciprocity, at 'tenderness'" (Buber 1970, p. 79).

This desire for dialogue is what drives the fanfiction writer, and ethical justifications for fanfiction rely a great deal on this ideal of dialogue, the dream of making the character more real to the fan. When characters have been created as extremely stoic or inexpressive, fans often resort to extreme measures to make the character more open to dialogue and identification. Thus, the popularity of what are called hurt/comfort stories, in which a character is badly hurt (either physically or emotionally) and usually is comforted by another character who empathizes with the other's pain. Whether the preferred character is being hurt or feeling for another person being hurt, he or she is being driven by the plot to express vulnerability, fear, compassion, tenderness, trust—all the things that humanize a character and create identification between the fan and the character. For example, in the *Star Trek* episode "Operation: Annihilate," Spock loses his sight for a while, but bears it with typical Vulcan stoniness. However, a fanfiction called "And in the Darkness Bind You ..." details how Spock might have really been feeling under his emotionless facade: "I rise, turn to follow [Kirk]—And fall, as I become entangled with his chair, which is not where I had expected it to be. He is on his knees beside me almost as I hit the floor. When I come to rest, I simply lean my cheek on one upraised knee, not trying to rise. Suddenly I am utterly discouraged, disillusioned" (Greywolf the Wanderer 1999). This Spock—blinded, discouraged, and despairing—is one with whom a fan can empathize and identify. Hurt/comfort, angst, and torture stories have large followings of fans who understand perfectly well that they are using pain as a plot device to re-create a character in a way that encourages identification and dialogue. As one writer puts it, "There [is] always this overwhelming desire to strip our heroes' feelings bare, to lay it all open for us to see ... to see them hurting, crying, sobbing, clinging to each other for support; to see them break down and show their emotions to the world, cracking the tough facade, stop the teasing, the banter, the macho behavior, and bring out the agony" (Pahati 2002). As dialogical theorists point out, when there are "tough facades," authenticity and dialogue are impossible.

This ethic of dialogue also explains the antipathy of most fanfiction writers and readers to so-called Mary Sue fanfiction. Mary Sue stories are stories in which a thinly veiled, highly idealized version of the author is inserted into the story and interacts with the characters, of course winning their respect and love with her bravery, intelligence, loyalty, and stunning beauty in the process.[2] Sometimes the Mary Sue character is from within the story's boundaries, like Nirnaeth, the young elf seeking sanctuary in Legolas's kingdom in "Night's Dawn": "Her hair was the color of autumn leaves—red, gold, brown, and silver—and it fell straight, almost to her shoulders. She had large eyes, the colors of a deepest sapphire and violet; an unusual color, even for elves. Her skin was lightly tanned from working under the sun. And she had the most beautiful smile; a smile that stole the breath from any who was unprepared for it" (Any Other 2004). Often the Mary Sue is from our world, pulled into the world of the other characters; the number of young human women who have fallen into the Council of Elrond and joined the Fellowship of the Ring (winning the heart of Aragorn/Legolas/ Frodo in the process) is nearly innumerable.

Mary Sues are perhaps the most reviled kind of fanfiction, yet most writers will admit to writing stories with Mary Sue characters at some point in their writing career. The reason they are both tempting to write and hated by other readers lies in the lure of identification and dialogue. A Mary Sue character is the writer's attempt to literally put herself in dialogue with the desired characters, to make that identification clear and concrete. In "Someone Else to Love," for example, a mysterious stranger called Tatiana meets the emotionally scarred X-Man Wolverine in a bar and immediately gets through his defenses: "The stranger's eyes narrowed for a moment, then widened in understanding. 'You came here to forget,' she whispered. He looked at her sharply and hesitantly nodded.... The woman bit her lip before continuing. 'So did I.' Her last statement jolted Wolverine to the core.... He gave a low grunt and a slight nod of acknowledgement" (Laney 2004). Thus, the Mary Sue character gets to actually have the dialogue the fan yearns for.

Such characters are an ethical violation of the fanfiction community's mores because although they give the author a direct dose of dialogue, they deny it to the other readers. Laney's Wolverine identifies directly with her character Tatiana, rather than being open to dialogue in a wider sense. A Mary Sue story leaves no space for the reader to imagine a dialogue between herself and the character; the dialogue is happening without her. It's not surprising, then, that Mary Sue stories are so commonly written and so intensely disliked at the same time, as they turn the possibility of dialogue back into a monologue with the Mary Sue character denying the reader any connection with the other characters.

Most creators of books or movies see general fanfiction as valuable, or at worst a necessary evil, an inevitable result of popularity. Some, however, do not. Perhaps most famously, Anne Rice, creator of *The Vampire Chronicles*, has objected vigorously to fanfiction of any sort based on her books. In 2000, Rice issued a statement on her web page stating, "I do not allow fan fiction. The characters are copyrighted. It upsets me terribly to even think about fan fiction with my characters. I advise my readers to write your own original stories with your own characters. It is absolutely essential that you respect my wishes" (cited in Where n.d.). Unlike many other primary creators who have made such statements, Rice backed up her words with harsh legal action, which many in the fanfiction community have characterized as "harassing." Anne Rice fanfiction has gone deeply "underground" as of this writing, although it is highly unlikely it has ceased to exist as Rice would like it to.

When called upon to ethically justify what are technically violations of copyright, most fans have little difficulty explaining the reasons for their actions. Put simply, the most common ethical justification is that of love. When a movie, book, or television show is interesting and involving to its fans, they want to take an active role in imagining and connecting with that world and the people in it. By writing about the characters, especially their inner lives, fans feel like they are making the characters more real. Indeed, the world of "fanon" (as opposed to "canon") features characters much more detailed and often more interesting than in the original. For example, Harry Potter's nemesis, Draco Malfoy, usually appears in fanfiction as a conflicted, complicated character rather than the rather simple bully he is in the books. Jenkins (1992) compares this process to the story of *The Velveteen Rabbit*, in which a boy's love for an object makes it "real." Speaking of a group of fans of *Star Trek*, he says, "Much like the Velveteen Rabbit, *Star Trek* was transformed by these young women's interaction with it. Perhaps, the newness of the individual stories were worn away, the aura of the unique text was eroded, yet, the program gained resonance, accrued signifi-

cance, through their social interactions and their reactive rework-
ings" (p. 52). Fans love their fandoms so passionately that they see
them as truly "real," and through their work make them more so
to each other.

Slash and Fan Identification

> Legolas bent down lightly and pulled Aragorn so close their lips touched.
> The elf's lips were thinner than a woman's but surprisingly as soft. Like
> the rose petals in spring and the tender leaves in summer. There was an
> alluring scent of leaves and flowers crushed together on the elf's body as
> the elf pushed his tongue against Aragorn's lips, seeking entrance. With
> a gentle push, Legolas' tongue playfully entered Aragorn's warm mouth
> just as Aragorn pulled the elf's lithe body onto his lap.
>
> —From Ice and Fire Vanessa's story "Moonlight by the River"

The first subcategory of fanfiction that pushes ethical boundaries
is that of slash. Slash stories are basically stories that show love or
sex between same-sex characters who, in canon, are not homosexual. The term *slash* comes from the punctuation used to divide the
names of the couple being paired up: Kirk/Spock, Harry/Draco,
Cyclops/Wolverine, and so on. Kirk and Spock from the original
Star Trek series were probably the first pair to be "slashed," but
now slash is one of the most popular genres of fanfiction writing. The majority of fanfiction writers are female, but among slash
writers, the proportion is even higher: there are almost no male
slash writers.[3]

Why has slash become such a dominant form of fanfiction writing? The first reason rests on simple issues of identification. Of
course, love affairs are a common way to show a character made
open to dialogue, whether they are wracked by joy, anxiety, or suffering. In addition, a love affair between two favorite male characters creates tighter identification all around, because the pair and
the writer/reader now share a very important thing in common. A
Pirates of the Caribbean story in which Will Turner feels tenderness
and passion for Elizabeth Swan means that Will has an object of desire that a heterosexual female writer might not identify with. But

if Will Turner and Jack Sparrow lust after each other, each of them shares something essential with a straight female author or reader: Jack thinks Will is hot, Will thinks Jack is hot, and the writer gets to agree with them both.

More complicated reasons for the appeal of slash lie in the desire of the writer to create a dialogue with the characters that is her own, shaped and created by her rather than dictated to her by the creators of her favorite show, book, or movie. By finding bits of subtext that can be used to support a relationship between two same-sex characters, the fanfiction writer makes the story her own. For example, Aragorn and Arwen are clearly dictated by the book and movie of *Lord of the Rings* to be the correct romantic pairing, despite the characters' lack of time together on-screen (a lack even more apparent in the books, where Arwen gets about five lines of dialogue, most of them not even with Aragorn). The writer who insists that Legolas and Aragorn, or Sam and Frodo, are a more appropriate and evocative pairing is taking the story into her own hands and engaging the story more directly, making it more real and meaningful to her. As one fanfiction writer puts it:

> The classic model of consumption is that we are given these narratives, pay our money to experience them, and are expected to be passive receptors. Read your books, watch your tv, but don't dare engage your brain. Fanfic rejects that model—fanfic writers take our mass culture, including books, intervene in it and create from it—it's a matter of engaging with culture rather than letting yourself passively be subjected to it. (KannaOphelia 2002)

Most fans prefer to write stories in which there is an established "subtext" that points to a relationship between two characters. For example, Qui-Gon Jinn and Obi-Wan Kenobi, in *Star Wars: The Phantom Menace*, clearly care a great deal about each other. They understand each other without speaking, protect each other, and grieve when one dies. It takes only a small leap of the imagination to portray them as in love with each other. As another fanfiction writer puts it,

> Tolkein [sic] might be happy to stop spinning in his grave long enough to kill anyone who dared suggest that any of his characters were queer,

but when ... Frodo looks into Sam's eyes, tells Sam that he couldn't have gotten far without him, dubs him "Samwise the Brave" and Sam is both touched and shy and blushy about it ... well you tell me how that scene would read to you if we did a search and replace and changed one of those names to "Samantha." (The Brat Queen 2003)

By doing the extra emotional work to find a plausible pairing, explain it, and write about it eloquently, the fanfiction writer engages her fandom directly in dialogue and enters into a more intimate relationship with the world and its characters.

By such passionate involvement, the fan comes to see the characters and world as much more concretely "real" (in the sense of Jenkins's Velveteen Rabbit analogy). Ethical justifications for writing slash or other adult fanfictions often rest on the feeling that the characters are real, with wants and desires that the fanfiction writer has an ethical duty to respond to. Writers often preface their stories with comments that reveal this belief. One *Lord of the Rings* writer, for example, explains that her story "turned out just a bit smuttier than I expected, for a bit, because Merry didn't behave :)" (Shirasade 2004). Another says that the characters aren't hers, "I just like making them do stuff, and they don't seem to mind" (Razzle 2004). Some people write stories because the characters even seem real enough to nag them into writing them: one author, posting a *Harry Potter* story in which Peter Pettigrew/Wormtail is in love with Severus Snape, sighs in an author's note: "Peter is one messed up guy, and it was terrifying to have him babbling on and on in my head. I only pray that he will leave now that I have posted this story" (RaspberryPele 2002). Fans see their characters as real, which causes them to write fanfiction that makes them more detailed and interesting, increasing that sense of realness and intensifying the identification between fans and characters.

The Final Frontier: Real Person Slash

Orlando lifted his head and raised a hand to the back of Viggo's neck pulling him gently but firmly down in to the inevitable kiss. But not the swift and showy assault that Orlando bestowed liberally on all his friends, it was a real kiss, a searching and sensuous kiss, a kiss that intensified as his tongue insinuated itself between Viggo's lips. And as their tongues duelled together Viggo wondered why the whole room wasn't bursting into flames around them. Eventually Viggo needed to breathe and he broke away panting. Orlando smiled and brushed a thumb across his kiss swollen mouth. "I've wanted to do that properly for so long."

—From Artemis Allen's story "And I Need You Now Tonight"

Actors Viggo Mortensen and Orlando Bloom—Aragorn and Legolas from *Lord of the Rings*—passionately in love? Probably only in the hotly controversial fanfiction genre known as RPS—real person slash. RPF (real person fiction) and RPS are very recent developments in the fanfiction community and as such are still the subject of intense debate. The most common subjects for RPS at the moment are "boy bands," like N'Sync and the Backstreet Boys, and the actors in the *Lord of the Rings* movie trilogy. However, there are RPS stories about many actors and most singers, including the members of Korn, Metallica, Good Charlotte, and (perhaps most deliciously) Eminem.

RPS has been roundly denounced in the fanfiction community as most likely illegal and almost certainly unethical, but it continues to grow dramatically in popularity, steadily winning converts among the general community. When called upon to defend their subject matter, RPS writers tend to come up with two main responses (beyond the rather self-evident "They're two great-looking guys and I like writing stories about them together").

The first is a continuation of the main reason behind slash: people love movie stars and singers in the same way they love characters, and writing stories about them is a way of connecting and communicating with them. One online essay defending RPF references Henry Jenkins specifically, noting his argument that

> the television shows and movies are our modern-day mythos—since we live in a world that in many ways has been stripped of mythos … we are left only with logos, and to fill that void, people have begun to create new mythoi … and as such, the ficcers have the right to use them as they see fit. They become public domain because they fill a psychological need for the mythos within our cultural heritage. And if that is the case—then aren't our celebrities our new gods, and therefore, don't we have the right to use our gods as we need them? (Joudama 2003)

The author concludes that stories about celebrities exist "because we love our gods. And this is our worship," capturing the sense of identification to the point of near-religious communion for which many writers seem to be aiming.

The desire for dialogue has been oddly thwarted by many recent shows and movies, and RPS seems to be a new kind of attempt at dialogue. Writing slash stories about characters was subversive and liberating because it gave the author or reader a chance to create a personal connection with a fandom from the subtext they had worked to uncover and piece together. Lately, however, many books, television shows, and movies include deliberate "winks" and references to slash. For example, Xena and Gabrielle's relationship in *Xena: Warrior Princess* became more and more overtly romantic in response to fans' slash fiction, and Buffy's relationship with rival vampire slayer Faith included some deliberate slash-friendly overtones. The less well-known *Due South* has had episodes putting the nominally straight but much-slashed heroes into "romantic" situations. Ironically, these slash-friendly tendencies can be frustrating to the fan: they deny the fan the intimate, subversive pleasure of discovering and embellishing that subtext herself. In "Why Subtext Is Better than Text" (2004), Janis Cortese details this reaction: "Don't turn subtext into text, for pete's sake! *I'll* do that. As a fanfiction writer, that's my damned job…. Slash, het, whatever. I want control. Subtext gives it to me. Making the subtext into *text* takes it away." Writing fiction about actors and singers may be the next logical step in the fans' attempt to create identification and appropriate popular culture for themselves.

One of the most common defenses of RPF is that the "people" being written about are not really people at all. Instead, RPF writers argue, they are carefully constructed personas, created for the consumption of the public in the same way entirely fictional characters are. Real-person stories "break the rules" by refusing to consume those personas in the way intended by Paramount, Warner Bros., or Disney—but since the personas themselves are created to be a commodity, it is not unethical to use them as such. What appears to be a "real person" is instead usually a "carefully crafted fairytale to meet with public standards" (Theoria 2001). The created nature of these personas is especially clear in some cases, like Eminem (see Dan T. Molden's chapter in this volume), the Spice Girls, or the Backstreet Boys. In the case of people like Viggo Mortensen or Johnny Depp, it is less clear, but is still strongly asserted by writers of real-person fanfiction. As one RPF fan explained in a message board conversation on the topic,

> Very few people put out their real self for public consumption, even non-celebs. People create FICTIONAL fronts for themselves. Celebs do this a great deal more than any one else. They might pretend to be more outgoing, more lively, more potty mouthed. Some celebs play up aspects that fans enjoy like the boys from *Lord of the Rings* who play up their relationship for fans. This is FICTIONAL. The PERSONA is fiction. Yes, the person is real, but the PERSONA is not. As such, when fans are writing about these people, they are writing FICTION about FICTIONAL personas. Anyone who thinks celebs put out their real selves for their camera are sadly niave [*sic*]. (PurplePopple 2003)

So what are commonly thought to be "real people" are actually merely manufactured characters available to do with as the fan pleases. Ironically, in the final analysis "real people" are less real than the characters they play. People write fiction about "Aragorn" from *The Lord of the Rings* because the books and movies make him a complicated, interesting, nuanced character whom they want to engage in dialogue. On the other hand, people write fiction about "Viggo Mortensen" because he remains forever a cipher, a set of publicity stills assembled to create a persona. As far as fanfiction is concerned, Aragorn can be more meaningfully real than Viggo Mortensen.

Many fans, of course, do not agree with this assessment; for example, another participant in the conversation about RPS argued back that in real-person stories "You take a real person and turn them into a character. They have the right not to have this done to them. You take that right away from them. Once you use that real person's name, etc., etc., you're turning them into the character" (Ginmar 2003). People arguing against RPF often basically make the point that it is a violation of the ethics of dialogue to treat another person as an object, that to treat Elijah Wood or Justin Timberlake as puppets and make them act out your fantasies in a story denies them their personhood. RPF writers seem to agree with that ethic in theory, but they maintain that the "personhood" of the people involved is questionable at best and therefore they merit less ethical consideration. Thus, the "reality" of celebrities becomes a site of ethical debate.

Conclusion

Fanfiction writers are driven by an ethic of dialogue and identification. In their search to connect to the "realness" they sense in characters they love, they write stories that open those characters to the possibility of dialogue. Characters seen as stoic or opaque—Spock from *Star Trek*, Avon from *Blake's 7*, Snape from *Harry Potter*, Legolas from *Lord of the Rings*—are especially popular, as fans enjoy finding ways to evoke emotion and thus communication with these characters. In the quest to transform a fandom and make it one's own, many fans deliberately try to alter the story enough to personalize it and mark it as "theirs" rather than a mass product. Some fans create "fanon," or alternate readings of characters. As mentioned before, fanon's Draco Malfoy tends to be extremely witty and smart, and often is a sensitive boy who feels pressured by his father to join Voldemort's army—all of which are rather large departures from Rowling's actual books. Fanon's Legolas is usually a childhood friend of Aragorn's and is often portrayed as abused by his father, neither of which are facts from Tolkien's books. By deepening the characters, adding conflicts and relationships, fans "use" characters like the Velveteen Rabbit was used, making them feel more real and personal. Some primary creators object to this practice as a violation of their ownership of the characters. Fan writers respond that such deep and realistic characters are no longer appropriate to be "owned"—they have become real to the fans and thus are fair game for dialogue-creating activities.

Slash is a continuation of this tendency, creating intense relationships where most readers would see simple friendships in canon. The slash writer adds passion and conflict that the actual text does not explicitly include—but usually does not explicitly rule out, either.[4] By weaving together aspects of subtext, fan writers and readers enrich and deepen the world of their fandoms and their relationships with the world and its characters. Slash is a subversive pleasure that creates a special dialogue between fans and the fandoms.

RPF, and especially RPS, takes this process of identification a step further, by calling into question the reality of the celebrities themselves. Leaving the media text behind, RPF writers turn "reality" into the text for their stories. "Characters" like Britney Spears and Orlando Bloom are as fair game as Legolas or Luke Skywalker. Created as commodities for fan consumption, actor and singer personas are free for "poaching"—Jenkins's famous term for fan activity that reappropriates media images for fan use. Many fans disagree about whether writing RPF is ethical; however, its existence and the debates over it call into sharp relief ethical questions about the limits of dialogue and identification, as well as the nebulous nature of celebrity "reality." Well-loved, fan-detailed, and deepened characters meet the glossy PR-made facades of celebrities in an ethical gray area where the former often end up seeming more authentic and real than the latter. As one fan writer puts it, capturing the ambiguity of these different "characters," RPS is acceptable because celebrities aren't really "Real People": "in the end, it's all made up. And our fictional people are often real people, too, just made up" (Amber 2003).

Her conflation of fictional and real people raises some serious ethical issues: For example, what does it take to move a "real" person into the realms of the fictional? Highly sculpted personas like the members of the Backstreet Boys fall well into the fictional. However, other celebrities, like Orlando Bloom, are considered "fictional" simply because they have a public persona. The problem is, everyone has many "public personas" they present to the world—we attempt to show a face to the public that is perhaps more outgoing, more brave, more witty than we feel we truly are. How fictional does this make all of us? Is identification and dialogue easier with characters in books and movies than it is with the actual physical people in our lives, because we can create the former in any way we please and thus be sure we are seeing the "real" them? If the answer is "yes," the ethical challenge of the twenty-first century may be to find ways to make dialogue between real people as meaningful as that between real and fictional people.

Notes

1. Of course, there are fans of both sexes. However, writers of fanfiction are mainly female, and writers of the genres discussed in this paper are almost overwhelmingly female—about 97 percent, according to one survey (Rushlight 2003)—so the female pronoun seems most appropriate.
2. The name is derived from a parody story in which the perfect heroine was named Mary Sue.
3. The vast majority of slash stories link two men, but there is also a genre called femslash featuring female couples. The demographics of femslash are a little more complicated than regular slash; stories are written by straight and lesbian women and sometimes straight men. Because the audiences are so different for femslash, this paper focuses on the generally more homogenous—though by no means monolithic—group of slash writers.
4. An apocryphal story about Leonard Nimoy (Spock from *Star Trek*) has him respond to a fan asking if Spock and Kirk had a romantic relationship, "I don't know. I wasn't there" (Truckle 2003).

References

Allen, A. (n.d.). And I need you now tonight. Retrieved February 11, 2004, from Characters in Bloom, www.charactersinbloom.com/Fics/ArtemisAllen/artemisallen_andineedyounowtonight1.htm.

Amber. (2003). I know, surprised me too. Message posted to Burning Roma, October 27, www.tuginternet.com/burningroma/archives/000963.html.

Any Other. (2004). Night's dawn. Retrieved March 6, from Fanfiction.net, March 2, www.fanfiction.net/read.php?storyid=1756276.

Bacon-Smith, C. (1992). *Enterprising women: Television fandom and the creation of popular myth*. Philadelphia: University of Pennsylvania Press.

Berger, A. A. (1996). *Narratives in popular culture, media, and everyday life*. London: Sage.

The Brat Queen. (2003). *What is slash?* Retrieved March 7, 2004, from The Fanfic Symposium, http://trickster.org/symposium/symp139.html.

Buber, M. (1970). *I and thou* (Walter Kaufmann, trans.). New York: Scribners. (Original work published 1922).

Burke, K. (1969). *A rhetoric of motives*. Berkeley: University of California Press.

Cortese, J. (2004). Why subtext is better than text. Retrieved March 8, from the Fanfic Symposium, February 3, www.trickster.org/symposium/symp141. html.

Ecks, M. (n.d.). History: When did fan fiction truly start? Retrieved December 15, 2003, from Writer's University, www.writersu.com/WU/modules.php?name=News&file=article&sid=74.

Ginmar. (2003). Re: And for those who don't separate ... message posted to Fan-Domination.net, February 11, http://pub29.ezboard.com/ffandominationnet-frm23.showMessageRange?topicID=1.topic&start=101&stop=120.

Greywolf the Wanderer (1999). And in the darkness bind you ... Retrieved February 13, 2004, from Trekiverse.org, December 25, www.trekiverse.org/star-trek/startrek/adult/tos/AndInTheDarknessBindYou.

Horton, D., & R. Wohl. (1956). Mass communication and para-social interaction. *Psychiatry* 19: 215–29.

Ice and Fire Vanessa. (2003). Moonlight by the river. Retrieved February 11, 2004, from Fanfiction.net, December 19, www.fanfiction.net/read.php?story id=1646939& chapter=1.

Jackson, P. (writer/director). (2002). *The Lord of the Rings: The Two Towers* [Motion picture]. New Zealand: New Line Cinema.

Jenkins, H. (1992). *Textual poachers: Television fans and participatory culture*. New York: Routledge, Chapman and Hall.

Johannesen, R. L. (1990). *Ethics in human communication*, 3rd ed. Prospect Heights, IL: Waveland.

Joudama. (2003). Because we love our gods: Mythoi, logoi, and real person slash. Retrieved March 8, 2004, from The Fanfic Symposium, April 3, www.trickster. org/symposium/symp114.html.

KannaOphelia. (2002). R_E_S_P_E_C_T? Message posted to FanDomination.net, October 16, http://pub29.ezboard.com/ffandominationnetfrm23.showMessa geRange?topicID=1.topic&start=21&stop=40.

Laney, D. (2004). Someone else to love. Retrieved March 6, from Fanfiction.net, February 26, www.fanfiction.net/read.php?storyid=1750466.

Meyrowitz, J. (1985). *No sense of place: The impact of electronic media on social behavior*. Oxford: Oxford University Press.

Nygard, R. (director). (1997). *Trekkies*. [Motion picture]. United States: NEO Motion Pictures.

Pahati, O. J. (2002). Sexing up the boy bands. Retrieved March 4, 2004, from Alter-net.org, April 10, www.alternet.org/story.html?StoryID=12823.

PurplePopple. (2003). Writing fiction. Message posted to Fandomination.net, February 11, http://pub29.ezboard.com/ffandominationnetfrm23.showMessage Range?topicID=1.topic&start=81&stop=100.

RaspberryPele. (2002). The red watercolor stain. Retrieved March 9, 2004, from Fanfiction.net, April 21, www.fanfiction.net/read.php?storyid=732810.

Razzle. (2004). The only one. Retrieved March 6, from Livejournal.com, February 7, www.livejournal.com/users/razzleslash/55057.html#cutid1.

Rushlight. (2003). Slash survey results. Message posted to Livejournal.com, October 14, www.livejournal.com/users/rushlight75/38193.html.

Shirasade. (2004). Here comes the bride. Retrieved March 6, from Livejournal.com, January 20, www.livejournal.com/users/shirasade_fic/47110.html# cutid.

Theoria. (2001). Duty of every writer. Retrieved March 9, 2004, from The Fanfic Symposium, August 27, www.trickster.org/symposium/symp80.html.

Tomer, A. (2001). *Death attitudes and the older adult*. New York: Brunner-Routledge.

Tribalbutterfly. (2004). Onward to adventure. Retrieved February 11, from Fanfiction.net, January 8, www.fanfiction.net/read.php?storyid=1677849& chapter=1.

Truckle. (2003). LotR slash: The actor's perspective. Message posted to Barbelith Underground, February 2, www.barbelith.com/topic.php?id=10934.

Where has Anne Rice fanfic gone? (n.d.). Retrieved July 6, 2003, from Croatoan Fanfic, www. angelfire.com/rant/croatoan.

Eminem and the Rhetoric of "Real": The Implications of "Keeping It Real" on Ethics and Credibility

Dan T. Molden

> The fuckin' world's so fucked up, the country's fucked up. But the fire-men, you actually see them produce. You see them put out a fire. You see them come out with babies in their hands. You see them give mouth-to-mouth when a guy's dying. You can't get around that shit. That's real. To me, that's what I want to be.
>
> I worked in a bank. You know, it's just paper. It's not real. Nine to five and it's shit. You're looking at numbers. But I can look back and say, "I helped put out a fire. I helped save somebody." It shows something I did on this earth.
>
> —Tom Patrick, in Studs Terkel's *Working*

I want to begin this essay with the suggestion—no, make that the assertion—that the word *real* might well be considered one of the god terms of the late twentieth and early twenty-first century. A god term is a sort of organizing principle around which the rest of our world begins to take shape. As Richard Weaver (1953) explains it, "by 'god term' we mean that expression about which all other expressions are ranked as subordinate and serving dominations and powers" (p. 212). In essence, I am asserting that *being real* and *keeping it real* are phrases that begin to help us understand the rest of our language, the rest of our communication, the rest of our experiences.

Now, claiming god-term status for any word is a fairly weighty assertion to make. *Real* is certainly an oft-heard term. We are now

confronted by *reality television* and *real Florida oranges* in addition
to *the real Slim Shady*. My assertion is made especially problematic
when one considers that this chapter is intended to be about ethics. Ethics and values are usually considered as somewhat separate.
Richard L. Johannesen (1990) argues:

> Ethical judgments focus more precisely on degrees of rightness or wrong-
> ness in human behavior. In condemning someone for being inefficient,
> conformist, extravagant, lazy, or late, we probably would not also be
> claiming that they are unethical. However, standards such as honesty,
> promise-keeping, truthfulness, fairness, and humaneness usually are
> used in making ethical judgments of rightness and wrongness in human
> behavior. (p. 1)

That is to say that ethics are more or less about what thoughts, actions, and so on are considered right or wrong, and values are more
or less about what things are considered good or bad. Simply put,
a good sandwich is not necessarily an ethical sandwich and a bad
sandwich is not necessarily an unethical one. The most common
use of the word *real*, obviously, would seem to be connected more
clearly with values than with ethics. Promoting the interactions of
avowedly "real" people in a "reality"-based television program
(while engaging for a moment in the fascinating thought that actors
are somehow not really people—or perhaps that nonactors have no
ability to perform rather than behave) would seem to argue that a
particular program is good television rather than right television. I
wish to assert here, as well, that the term *real* has come to encompass both value and ethics. It has come to mean both that which is
good and that which is right.

    In order to consider *real* and its potential status as a god word,
it might serve to begin by considering a specific example. As he has
made something of a point of using the term himself, Eminem seems
a good place to start. After considering who Eminem is and to what
extent he is "real," we can then consider what "real" means, what
might make people "real," and what consequences being "real" or
trying to "keep it real" have for communicators and for ethics. Specifically, what options and constraints does "real" present to communicators, and to what extent does "real" function as designator
for credibility and a standard for ethics?

The Real Marshall Mathers

I will have to return to my assertions about the god-term status of the word *real* at the end of this chapter, but for now I want to consider the meanings of the term *real* and its connection to popular culture, specifically the rap artist known as Eminem. Marshall Bruce Mathers III was born in Kansas City, Missouri, on October 17, 1972. As a child, he moved frequently between the Kansas City area and the Detroit area in Michigan. He eventually dropped out of high school and began working a variety of jobs, mostly at restaurants. He had decided to try and make a career out of rapping, something he had done since his early teenage years. He started performing under the stage name of M&M, which quickly changed to Eminem. He signed to record for a small label called FBT Productions in 1992. His first album, *Infinite*, was not well received by critics—somewhat ironically, it was seen as too much of an imitation of other rap artists.

Two years after the release of *Infinite*, Eminem released the album *The Slim Shady EP* and was signed by former NWA rapper Dr. Dre to the Aftermath label. His first chart hit came two years later with the release of the similarly titled *The Slim Shady LP*. He has released two additional albums, *The Marshall Mathers LP* and *The Eminem Show*. Each of these albums was, at one point, the top-selling album in the United States, and *The Marshall Mathers LP* was the second best-selling album in the United States in 2000 (Rock on the Net n.d.).

In the years following the release of *The Slim Shady EP*, according to the ARC Weekly Top 40 (www.rockonthenet.com / charts / arc. htm)—a list that combines weekly sales, radio play, and video play of songs—Eminem went from the number-eighty-three-ranked singles artist of the year (in 1999) to the number-nine singles artist (in 2002). He also starred in an animation, *The Slim Shady Show* (2001), and a movie, *8 Mile* (2003). At the same time as he was experiencing that success, however, he also pled guilty to charges resulting from a fight at a bar involving carrying a gun and hitting another person with the gun, was sued by both his mother and his wife for defamation, divorced his wife, and had his performances around the world protested (and well attended).

Eminem has also won a number of awards, beginning with Best New Artist at the MTV Video Music Awards in 1999 and including eight more MTV VMA Awards and nine Grammy awards. One award he did not win, however, was for Best Song Written for a Motion Picture, Television, or Other Visual Media for a song he performed in the movie *8 Mile*. As reported by Edna Gunderson (2004) in *USA Today*, "*A Mighty Wind*, the theme to Christopher Guest's mockumentary, beat Eminem's eminently classier *Lose Yourself* for best song from a movie. *Wind* is an amusing ditty from a clever reenactment of the folk era, but even cast member Eugene Levy seemed confused by the song's win, stating the obvious: 'The songs aren't real'" (p. D2).

Whether Eminem manages to maintain his current position in popular culture or not, the fact remains that in the first part of the twenty-first century, his position as a popular culture icon offers a unique opportunity to examine the intersection of credibility and persona. Eminem is in a position where his words are seen as indicative of the current state of the United States. Andrew O'Hagan (2003) claims, for example, that Eminem has "turned his social station into a platform, and made his native experience, his amazing journey out, part of a riveting and demanding investigation into the mental condition of America."

Now, of course, any one person's life might seem worthy or unworthy of investigation on its own merit, but whether or not a rap artist or other popular culture figure can really provide us with a way to investigate the condition of a whole people is another question. I must, myself, "keep it real" by admitting that this chapter is not exactly about Eminem the rap artist. It is, rather, more clearly about Eminem the communicator and about that "platform" from which his "native" (read: "real") experiences are seen and understood. That is to say, I am not going to focus on his lyrics but on how the lyrics and the rest of the communication by and about Eminem help audiences to get some sense of what it means to be a "real" person.

Real Music

The word *real* has any number of meanings, of course. Raymond Williams (1976) noted the two most common historical meanings of real in his discussion of the term *realism*:

> **Real**, from the beginning, has had this shifting double sense.... Its earliest English uses, from C16, were in matters of law and property, to denote something actually existing.... The sense of something actually existing was transferred to general use, from C16, in an implicit or explicit contrast with something *imaginary*.... But at the same time there was an important sense of **real** as contrasted not with imaginary but with *apparent*. (p. 216)

So, then, we might take the word *real* to mean "existing" as opposed to "imaginary," or we might take it to mean "actual" as opposed to "apparent." Thus, a real horse is opposed to an imaginary unicorn on the one hand, and a real computer is opposed to the cardboard kind one might see in a furniture store, on the other.

I want to return briefly to the comments made by Eugene Levy and Edna Gunderson about the song "A Mighty Wind." Both people agreed that this particular song was not "real." Did that seem odd to you? While it may be "obvious" to them (and perhaps to you) that the songs in *A Mighty Wind* aren't real, is it also obvious what "real" means in this context? Did Gunderson and Levy mean to imply that the song "A Mighty Wind" does not really exist? That would seem a very difficult assertion to defend. "A Mighty Wind" exists just as much as "Lose Yourself" exists, in any meaningful sense. They can both be purchased, listened to, even belittled. It seems quite a stretch of the imagination to insist that one of these songs exists in a strong sense more than the other.

Did they mean, then, to imply that it is not actually a song—merely something that has the illusion of being a song? Possibly. Gunderson's use of "ditty" might well be construed as something of a backhanded compliment. Nonetheless, a ditty is still a song. Both songs, again, seem to share all the same components that might go to make up a song. In what sense could a song only appear to be a song without actually being a song?

So what could possibly serve to make one of these songs more "real" than the other? One quite plausible answer is to stop thinking about the songs themselves and consider instead the people who made the songs. Eminem, the creative force behind "Lose Yourself" is a rap artist, a musician, if you will. Christopher Guest, Eugene Levy, and Michael McKean, the creative forces behind "A

Mighty Wind," are actors, not musicians (despite the fact that both Guest and McKean are also part of another famous movie band, Spinal Tap). Perhaps only musicians can make "real" music (and to be fair, as Eminem acted in *8 Mile*, perhaps only actors can make "real" movies).

This answer might be pointing us in a more useful direction. We are, after all, living in an age in which, as Richard Dyer (1991) notes, "the truth of social affairs has become rooted not in the general criteria governing social behavior itself but in the performers themselves" (p. 133). That is to say, it is not what people do (when they sing, write, act, and so on) that counts; it is who the people are (as a singer, writer, actor) that counts.

Real People

Dyer (1991) continues his discussion of the changing societal attitudes toward well-known performers by noting that the public focus had shifted away from some assessment of talent or skill and moved toward the "realness" of the persona for the person:

> The criteria governing performances have shifted from whether the performance is well done to whether it is truthful, that is, true to the "true" personality of the performer. Even truth is a peculiar criterion—we no longer ask if someone performs well or according to certain moral precepts but whether what they perform is truthful, with the referent of truthfulness not being falsifiable statements but the person's "person." (p. 133)

In other words, what matters is not the truthfulness of the world described by the song, but rather how well the song fits the "real" personality of the performer. I suppose, then, that the answer might be that Eminem was performing a song that, while written for a movie, was true to his person as well as his persona. Levy and company, on the other hand, were merely singing a song that fit a role—and were not, in that sense, connected to either their persons or their personas (as actors) but only to their roles in a movie.

This gets to be a fairly dangerous game, of course. There is a fairly old commercial for a lollipop with a candy center in which an owl asks those gathered around how many licks it would take to reach the candy center. The answer is always shrouded in mystery and doubt, however, because no one can quite seem to make it to the center. In the same way, the current idea of being "real" or "keeping it real" is problematic because of the difficulty in getting to the center or "real" part of a person.

Take, for example, Eminem. Here is an artist who has, at least in his first albums, made something of a career out of making it hard to find the center of his personality or persona. He portrays himself as a variety of different characters ranging from Marshall Mathers (his birth name), Eminem (the name he uses as a performer), and Slim Shady (the name he uses to describe his alter ego), even going so far as to name his first three major-label albums after these three characters. And yet, despite all of this identity switching, he is often noted for his "realness."

So what is it that makes a persona real? Dyer (1991) continues his discussion of stars and stardom by noting that there is a large vocabulary in English devoted to explaining the "realness" of the persona/person: "There is a whole litany in the fan literature surrounding stars in which certain adjectives endlessly recur—sincere, immediate, spontaneous, real, direct, genuine, and so on. All of these words can be seen as relating to a general notion of 'authenticity.' It is these qualities that we demand of a star if we accept her or him in the spirit in which she or he is offered" (p. 133).

Indeed, within the world of music generally and rap music specifically, authenticity or "realness" is a prime concern. Within the broader music community, Eric Boehlert (2000) tried to find the reason why music critics were essentially ignoring the protests about Eminem's lyrics in the rejection of "unreal" or "poser" bands: "Fed up with watching boy bands and girl pop posers win over the hearts of consumers, critics welcomed the chance to bond with fans of some tougher sounds." As for the rap music community, Eva Neuberg (2000), in a review of *The Marshall Mathers LP* for the *New York Press*, notes, "'Realness' is the commodity in rap these days." In fact, realness is such a commodity that to be found lacking is, in a real sense, to lose not only your chance for success but also the success you have already gained. *Contactmusic News* recalls the story of Vanilla Ice, a formerly successful musician whose fame came to an end quite suddenly: "[Vanilla] Ice, who topped the charts in the early '90s with the hit *Ice Ice Baby*, was shunned by many hip-hop fans and the media, after it emerged that the gangster background he claimed to have was concocted to give him street credibility" (Vanilla Ice 2003).

The Real Eminem

So who is the "real" Eminem or the "real" Marshall Mathers who is capable of producing a "real" song? Ironically, of course, we have to move away from the individual person/persona and back to the performance to attempt to answer that question. For even as Dyer asserts that we evaluate the performance based on its correspondence to the person's persona, it is still the performance we begin with. A review of *The Slim Shady LP* by Sloppy Joe (n.d.) on a web page titled "10 Rap Commandments" serves as a reasonable beginning. Here the author makes comments about Eminem's first major-label album and on its signature style and its realness:

> You cannot walk away from this album without being affected by the graphic and gory imagery that Eminem spits more frequently than any rap artist in history. At first it is kind of funny, but his obsession with his demented imagination gets a little old as he raps about nothing other than drugs, and his own inner turmoil. Still I applaud Eminem for his bold surreal approach and for simply keeping it real.

So there it is. Eminem is "keeping it real." But what exactly is being kept? What is real? There is no comment here about the truthfulness of his lyrics, but rather the graphic nature of his imagination. So, in part, the author may be assuming that the lyrics are "real" for the "demented imagination" of the person Marshall Mathers as displayed in the persona of Eminem. But how, exactly, is that "real"?

None of the standard meanings of *real* seems to adequately cover the sense of the word as it is being used in the musical community in relationship to Eminem. Chris Matthew Sciabarra (n.d.) provides a workable definition of the standard meaning of *real* in the context of rap music when he writes that "rap artists have always prided themselves on 'keeping it real,' telling stories that reflect the truth about people's lives." But the commentary around Eminem indicates the flexibility or evolution of "real" into something a little different. (This change is most clearly highlighted by rap artist Will Smith's comment in Maria Montoya's article (2001) that he was "trying to keep it real for real" while writing a children's story.) Again, as Dyer contended, the shift seems to be away from a sort of communal "real" to an intensely personal one. It is not required that the artist represent the truth about "people's lives" (in the broad sense of *people*) but rather that they represent the truth about their own individual (in the narrow sense) personal lives.

Oddly, however, the world of rap music seems to condense the personas of its performers into a specific set of types—meaning that only a few personas are acceptable as "real." Nick Hasted (2003) notes that a variety of different people end up with roughly the same public image—one involving crime and posturing: "There seems to be something in the demands of hip-hop and its followers, for 'keeping it real,' ostentation and machismo, that makes so many of its stars pass through a courtroom. Mild, music-loving Dre and bohemian, Shakespeare reading Tupac are among those who have forced their personalities into tough guy masks" (p. 114). Ironically, then, while being "real" is supposed to be about matching your own personality, in the end it doubles back on itself. To be "real" is more about fitting a specific idea or ideal held by the audience. It is not *really* tied to the individual in any way other than how that individual conforms to the expectations for "realness" in a given arena.

When dealing with a person/persona like Eminem, this kind of flattening is even more of a concern. Many of his critics have dubbed Eminem a caricature. Joe S. Harrington (2000) laments that music critics would even have to listen to his music. "It should shame any critic to even have to waste his time listening to such a prefabricated creation as Eminem." O'Hagan (2003) goes so far as to compare Eminem to "a cartoon character, like Bart Simpson or Dick Tracy: not so much self-invention as someone drawn into life by the power of the surrounding culture."

Such comments lead Anthony Lamar Rucker (n.d.) to comment on the shift in meaning of "real" when he writes, "It is the suggestion that Eminem doesn't mean what he's saying that I find very perplexing.... To believe that Eminem isn't keeping it real by presenting a true persona contradicts the very heart of an audience's attraction to an artist: credibility."

The Real Real

So what, then, allows one to keep it real, if being real is not enough? Dyer (1991) begins, I think, to suggest an answer when he considered the difficulties of finding a "real" representation of an artist whose work must, of necessity, be somewhat "unreal"—in that it is recorded, scripted, edited, and so on: "We must know that her star quality has nothing to do with recording techniques, with mechanical reproduction (even though what we are watching is perforce a recording), but is grounded in her own immediate (= not controlled), spontaneous (= unpremeditated) and essential (= private) self" (p. 139). Ah, but in our current age, everything is potentially premeditated. Even in the real of the immediate and spontaneous, there are doubts about the lack of control and lack of premeditation. Reality TV, for example, purports to present real people doing real things in an unscripted way, but it is still frequently accused of having a script (from *Survivor* to *Last Man Standing*, there have been accusations and, in some cases, admissions of editorial control). And it is in this framework that I think *real* is elevated to a god word. It is obviously enough a positive word. No one wants non-real food, and the advance of "reality" television certainly indicates a desire for "realness," but how are we to get it? How can we know that someone or something is real—uncontrolled, unpremeditated, and private? What, in other words, has Eminem got that Levy and company do not?

In short, he has (or rather his persona has) projected a willingness to upset people. Boehlert (2000) provides a snapshot of these ideas while critiquing music critics:

> *Time Out New York* thought this incestuous, quasi-rape fantasy about Jennifer Lopez was "sidesplitting." *The Times of London* agreed it was "extremely funny." *CDNow* insisted, "The man is fearless." Why? Because he has the courage to insult, among others, pop stars Puff Daddy, Will Smith, Britney Spears and 'N Sync. Eminem also has things to say about quadriplegic Christopher Reeve. Talk about picking fights you can't possibly lose.

Neuberg (2000) contends that, indeed, the appeal of Eminem originally stemmed from his willingness to say anything: "He's still Eminem, but the 'Just Don't Give a Fuck' days are gone (they had to go, I guess, and don't tell me about how it was all just a posture—never *real*—to begin with)." Here, the author specifically equates realness with a disregard for the evaluations of others.

Neuberg (2000) continues, "but if he is not real, why bother? What was so compelling about Eminem when he first blew up was his mix of recognizably authentic fucked-upness and razor-sharp commercial smarts." Another potential meaning of "realness," then, is a sort of craziness (I suppose most clearly akin to the sense of craziness that Robert M. Pirsig [1974, pp. 316–17]) describes in *Zen and the Art of Motorcycle Maintenance* as falling outside the normal understanding of the rest of society)—operating in ways not acceptable or understandable to the "normal" or "sane."

None of these examples assumes that "realness" has any direct connection to "truthfulness" or accuracy in the reproduction of the day-to-day issues faced by today's youth. Indeed, many authors have directly refuted the connection of Eminem's "realness" to his truthfulness.

Real Ethics?

I want to stop for a moment and return to the question at hand. It seems clear to me that "real" is about credibility. This is a central issue for those of us who study communication, and it is well worth noting that people are actively discussing in the nonacademic world what it would take to have source credibility.

Now, again I need to be careful. There is nothing in particular about credibility that requires a connection to ethics. As Johannesen (1990) warns, "*Ethos* [the audience's perception of the character of the communicator] *and ethics should not be viewed as synonymous concepts* [emphasis added]. Of course, a communicator judged by an audience as being unethical probably will have low ethos with it. And an audience judgment of high ethicality often contributes to its positive perception of a communicator's trustworthiness" (p. 116). Unfortunately, the standards set down for credibility here tend to foster a strange sort of ethic. The rule is, ostensibly, "To thine own self be true" (to borrow from both high and low culture, you can sing Shakespeare's lines for Polonius to Bizet's "March of the Toreadors" and end up with *Gilligan's Island*). This ethic would seem relatively useful and liberating for the speaker—all one must do is really believe what you say and you are ethical.

In practice, however, the ethic of "real" would seem to be something quite different and much more constricting for the speaker. Speakers, after all, do not get to determine their own credibility. They cannot demonstrate their belief and commitment to their rhetoric directly to the audience, so the audience is left to intuit any speaker's ethical standing.

The result here is that, according to contemporary popular culture, one *cannot* be credible without being rude, hateful, mean-spirited, or any number of impolite things. Or, to quote the lead-in to MTV's reality television show *The Real World*, "This is the true story of seven strangers, picked to live in a house to find out what happens when people stop being polite and start getting real. *The Real World!*" Why is politeness seen as the antithesis of "real"? Perhaps because of a sense in Eminem's audiences that humans are essentially cruel and nasty—developing niceties like ethics only when they separate from their natural state. Neuberg (2000) provides a good example of this view:

> The song ["Stan"] *should* end with the splash of the car as Stan drives into the water. Instead Eminem comes back in—as "himself"—and proceeds to rap about how he's sorry he's so late writing back and "you got some issues Stan / I think you need some counseling." *Weak!* Even weaker is what Eminem said to the *L.A. Times* about the song: "[Stan]'s crazy for real and he thinks I'm crazy, but I try to help him at the end of the song. It kinda shows the real side of me." That's the spin. Unfortunately, the spin made it into the song.
>
> Eminem got a lot of fans because he was crazy for real. Crazy enough, anyway.

Notice here that Neuberg put scare quotes around "himself" and labels the last section of the song as "spin." She expresses these doubts despite the claims by Eminem himself that this final portion of the song reveals at least part of the "real" Eminem—or perhaps of the "real" Marshall Mathers.

How can she be so sure? I think the answer is revealed in part by her contrasting of "real" with "weak." Eminem espouses what might be considered a pro-social position at the end of "Stan" and, as a result, expresses some ideas that might be socially acceptable. He does not say things that challenge the status quo and, therefore, does not engage in risk taking (although the actual risks involved in saying anything on a commercial recording are certainly debatable, Eminem at least engages in the perception of risk taking). More likely, this move is a result of an "us" versus "them," in the minds of the audience. Adults, parents, politicians, and teachers will be shocked by what he has to say, so he has been "real" by defying their authority. Boehlert (2000), in his commentary on other music critics, recalls the story of how Christina Aguilera came to be attacked by Eminem in a song and the critics' reaction to that song:

> "Don't let your guy disrespect you," Aguilera urged her young viewers. And for that common-sense message she has been slandered in a Top 40 song that MTV can't stop playing.

> Did anybody come to her aid? Hardly. In fact, the *Washington Post* cheered on Eminem's attack: "We're all tired of pop moppets like Spears and Aguilera, and he obliges us by slurring them both."

So here we come down to it. The simplest meaning of being "real" might roughly be described as being "in your face." Well, more accurately, in someone else's face. Eminem is "real" because he attacks other pop stars. He is real because politicians disapprove of him (though they might, to a different audience, be seen as "real" because of their willingness to get in his face).

In this context, the refusal to constantly challenge the system is taken by Neuberg as a sign of weakness in Eminem, a sign that he is no longer being true to himself, no longer ignoring the opinions of other people (and I mean other people in the general sense, for I think Neuberg *does* want Eminem to pay attention to her opinion).

As we can see, in Eminem and the idea of the "real," we have a strange ethic. One must not show any signs of compassion or humanity, for those are signs of weakness. Interestingly, the true self may be savage, but must not desire money. Weakness, it would seem, is also displayed by "selling out"—that is, altering rhetoric in an attempt to make money by appealing to the wrong audience (of course, Eminem continues to make a good deal of money by being perceived as *not* selling out). While "keeping it real" seems to offer the kind of credibility that could be used as a platform to speak out about social conditions in the United States, this "realness" places extreme limits on what Eminem and other "real" communicators can do and say.

Real Consequences

From the perspective of popular culture, concerns about "ethics" and "values" are quite dangerous—something to be avoided. That is to say that analyzing a pop culture artifact drains it of its enjoyment. If one were to draw an ethical principle from popular culture as a whole, it might be that entertainment should not be considered a valid subject for ethical and academic considerations: one should not confuse entertainment and intellectual pursuits. bell hooks (1994), for example, recalls "the day a student came to class and told me: 'We take your class. We learn to look at the world from a critical standpoint, one that considers race, sex, and class. And we can't enjoy life anymore.' Looking out over the class, across race, sexual preference and ethnicity, I saw students nodding their heads" (pp. 42–43).

Eminem (2000) himself, in the introduction to his book *Angry Blonde*, argues that people should not take him seriously and analyze his lyrics. In responding to concerns about a line in one of his songs, he writes, "to me, there was nothing homophobic about that line. IT WAS JUST A LINE! It was just something funny, but like most of my lyrics, it got analyzed too much" (p. 4).

"Real," then continues to prove elusive. "Real" people don't stand for analysis. And at any rate they would seem to have no interest in what those who are not "real" think about them. "Real" rather fits what Kevin Murphy (2003) writes about "cool" in his attempt to review the movie *Kill Bill: Vol. 1*: "You can't define it, but you know it when you see it. Moreover, Cool is impossible to criticize. Those who get it are Cool, and those who don't are not. It is an immeasurable, unassailable aesthetic." Any attempt to analyze "real" will likely result in the complaint that we are thinking too much about the issue.

This argument is clearly disingenuous, however. Eminem (as quoted in Weiner 2002) himself has said that "damn near every song that I do has a message" (p. 110). If his songs have a message, how then are we to avoid analyzing them? How much analysis is enough to understand and react to the message, and how much analysis is too much?

As an ethic for communicators, I find "realness" quite lacking, but the conversation surrounding "keeping it real" and Eminem provides all of us an opportunity to connect academic discussions of ethics to our lived experiences. If we do not attempt to find connections between what we study and what we do, if we do not get ourselves dirty in the popular culture artifacts that do matter to the greater society, and if we let our society (or popular culture specifically) divorce the things that matter to them from the concepts and ideas we study, then ethics truly are irrelevant.

In any case, this sense of "realness" seems to be pervasive—existing in all facets of our lives, not merely in our music. Of course, I am sensitive to the views expressed by Tom Patrick in the epigraph to this chapter. In the end, perhaps, this is just paper. Even Eminem is just a musician whose words and music are also preserved on paper, and "real" is just four letters on the page. However, "real" people do influence the *real* world. Words and paper and even pop stars can influence how we see and think about our world. These ideas do also extend beyond the world of ethics and beyond the world of music. Micah L. Sifry (1999), for example, was reporting on a person who was rising to national prominence in politics at almost the same time Eminem was rising to national prominence in music, a person who would eventually become a governor: Jesse Ventura. He includes in his descriptions of Ventura's supporters a "middle-aged car dealer in a sweat shirt who voted for Ventura because 'he's real people.'"

What made Ventura "real"? What made this former UDT (Underwater Demolitions Team) member, former professional wrestler, former football color commentator, and radio personality "real"? Or, at least, was he more "real" than the other candidates for governor? Well, it was in part the belief that he was uncontrollable and unpremeditated. Sifry (1999) also remembers "the middle-aged shuttle who picked me up at the airport was a typical and enthusiastic Ventura voter. 'I don't know what he'll do. But he's going to tell all those Bible-thumpers on the right and the tree-huggers on the left to vote for their own, and he'll unite all the disaffected voters in the middle in a new party.'"

Dennis Cass (1999) was also recording the story of the Minnesota gubernatorial election that year. He recalls attending a rally for Ventura, meeting some of his supporters, and soliciting their justifications for supporting the soon-to-be governor:

> The stage diving prompts me to go back downstairs and enter the fray. I push my way toward the podium and end up next to a group of frat boys who are punching one another's stomachs and pinching one another's nipples. One of them has plastered a Jesse Ventura bumper sticker over his team-logo baseball cap. I ask them if they'd like to comment on Ventura's campaign, and the alpha male jostles past his buddies to get closer to my tape recorder. His voice is hoarse as he yells about how this country needs a "real man" and how Ventura is a "real man," and he says "real man" so many times I almost beg him to stop.

And so it is almost time to stop. Still, it is interesting to note that the public discussion of Ventura mirrored in many ways that about Eminem. He was unpredictable, would get in the face of someone, and above all was "real" in a way that defied specific description.

"Real," as considered here, poses several challenges to communicators and to ethics. To what extent can a communicator be "real" and use that credibility in any meaningful sense? To what extent does being "real" require the communicator to find a third party to attack in order to be or keep it "real"? Does being "real" require the speaker to subordinate his or her individual personality to a socially constructed one? How can we connect ethics to a concept that resists analysis and discussion? Can "real" make ethics more *real* to communicators? Regardless of the answers to these questions, it seems clear that "real" is a defining concept, a god term, in popular culture.

References

Boehlert, E. (2000). Invisible man. Salon.com, June 7. Retrieved December 15, 2003, from http://dir.salon.com/ent/music/feature/2000/06/07/eminem/index. html.

Cass, D. (1999). An action figure for all seasons. *Harper's Magazine*, February. Retrieved February 7, 2004, from http://findarticles.com/cf_dls/m1111/1785_298/54029661/p3/article.jhtml?term=.

Dyer, R. (1991). A star is born and the construction of authenticity. In C. Gledhill (ed.), *Stardom: Industry of desire* (pp. 132–40). New York: Routledge.

Eminem. (2000). *Angry blonde*. New York: HarperCollins.

Gunderson, E. (2004). Academy making progress. *USA Today*, February 9, p. D2.

Harrington, J. S. (2000). The last word on Lester. Elis Eil's Zine. Retrieved December 12, 2003, from www.eliseil.com/zarchive1/read1.htm.

Hasted, N. (2003). *The dark story of Eminem*. London: Omnibus.

Hooks, B. (1994). *Teaching to transgress: Education as the practice of freedom*. New York: Routledge.

Johannesen, R. (1990). *Ethics in human communication*, 3rd ed. Prospect Heights, IL: Waveland.

Montoya, M. (2001). Will Smith writes life lessons for kids. *USA Today*, May 4. Retrieved December 8, 2003, from www.usatoday.com/life/books/2001-05-04-will-smith-pens-kids-book.htm.

MTV.com—Real World. Retrieved March 8, 2004, from www.mtv.com/onair/realworld/.

Murphy, K. (2003). The cinema of the cool. [Review of the motion picture *Kill Bill: Vol. 1*]. *A Year at the Movies*, October 10. Retrieved April 7, 2004, from www.ayearatthemovies.com/reviews_10_07_03.htm.

Neuberg, E. (2000). Music reviews: *The Marshall Mathers LP*. New York Press, June 7. Retrieved December 12, 2003, from www.nypress.com/13/23/music/musicreviews.cfm.

O'Hagan, A. (2003). Imitation of life. *New York Review of Books*, November 6. Retrieved December 12, 2003, from www.nybooks.com/articles/16735.

Pirsig, R. M. (1974). *Zen and the art of motorcycle maintenance: An inquiry into values*. New York: Bantam.

Rock on the net: Eminem. (n.d.). Rock on the Net. Retrieved April 7, 2004, from www.rockonthenet.com/artists-e/eminem_main.htm.

Rucker, A. L. (n.d.). Elton John and Eminem: A perfect combination? All Things Deep. Retrieved June 25, 2001, from www.allthingsdeep.com/articles/emandeltonduet.htm.

Sciabarra, C. M. (n.d.). The paradox of Eminem: Will the real Slim Shady please stand up. *Sense of Life Objectivists*. Retrieved December 15, 2003, from http://freeradical.co.nz/solo/sciabarra_eminem.html.

Sifry, M. L. (1999). Working class hero? *Salon Newsreal*. Retrieved February 7, 2004, from www.salon.com/news/1999/01/11news.html.

Sloppy Joe (n.d.). 10 Rap Commandments. www.msu.edu/user/dalrymp6/slimshady.html

Terkel, S. (1972). Tom Patrick, fireman. In *Working* (pp. 578–89). New York: The New Press.

Vanilla Ice: I'm Eminem's guideline. (2003). *Contactmusic News*, December 17. Retrieved March 8, 2004, from www.contactmusic.com/new/xmlfeed.nsf/0/BCCE8F27F77E0FF580256DFF003209BE?opendocument on.

Weaver, R. (1953). *The ethics of rhetoric*. Chicago: Henry Regency.

Weiner, C. (2002). *Eminem "talking."* London: Omnibus.

Williams, R. (1976). *Keywords: A vocabulary of culture and society*. Oxford: Oxford University Press.

CHAPTER TEN

(Re)Constructing the Vietnam Veterans Memorial Wall: Ethical Choicemaking and the Construction of Self in Online Popular Culture

Scott Titsworth and Jeffrey St. John

> The tangled connection between past and present—or, in the idiom that has become so common in our postmodern era, between history and memory—seems particularly apt when considering the place of the Vietnam War in American culture and society.
>
> —Robert J. McMahon

During the early-morning hours of April 30, 1975, eleven U.S. Marines were evacuated by helicopter from the U.S. Embassy in Saigon, Vietnam, thus officially ending U.S. presence in the country and signaling an end of the Vietnam conflict. Yet, nearly thirty years after the official end to hostilities, America continues to wage ideological war over meanings associated with collective national identity generally, and moral and ethical dimensions connected to the Vietnam War specifically. Though not fought with conventional weapons of war, the ideological battles for (re)shaping collective memories of Vietnam are nonetheless emotionally charged, visceral, and ongoing.

Discourses shaping collective memories of the Vietnam War are complex and multidimensional in the ways in which they cut across traditionally distinct discursive forms. As R. J. McMahon (2002) observes, the conceptual battleground over Vietnam

> is a struggle that was joined first in the mid- and late 1960's, when raging debates about the morality and efficacy of U.S. involvement triggered

the most profound societal division since the Civil War. It has continued without surcease ever since the war's end as various claims-makers,
operating from a wide diversity of motives—political leaders, military
officers, veterans, intellectuals, filmmakers, television producers, writers,
artists, monument-builders, and more—have tried to fit this turbulent
chapter of America's recent past into the wider compass of the nation's
history and purpose. (p. 160)

Thus, modern battles over Vietnam are particularly fruitful for understanding interrelationships among ethics, morality, and identity
as they shape and are shaped by the discursive nature of public
memory.

Our intent in this chapter, in part, is to develop an informed
reading of ethical dimensions surrounding the Vietnam Veterans
Memorial website. As a "virtual companion" to the Vietnam Veterans Memorial in Washington, D.C., the Vietnam Veterans Memorial
website was launched in 1996 to honor those who died in Vietnam
(Vietnam Veterans Memorial Page [VVMP] 2003). Our initial intent
was to limit our analysis to the Memorial Wall website in particular;
however, after embarking on this task it became clear that the wall
website (hereafter referred to as the Virtual Wall) could not be understood in isolation from the Vietnam Veterans Memorial in Washington (hereafter called the Memorial Wall). In fact, the relationship
between the Virtual Wall and the Memorial Wall highlighted ethical
forces at play in contemporary discourses, particularly those discourses spanning tangible and virtual worlds.

In framing our analysis we draw from potentially competing
perspectives on the ethical nature of discourse and identity. In articulating his views on ethics and identity construction in our digital culture, Kenneth Gergen argues broadly that securing or finding
a stable sense of self in a fragmentary cultural landscape is a close
to impossible task. In contrast, Charles Taylor suggests that it is
only through the securing of a coherent, stable self that a citizen can
then meaningfully negotiate the complications of contemporary
life. These two viewpoints sharply diverge on key assumptions and
outcomes, and yet we find much that is useful in these divergences
and in commonalities we detect in them at the same time. After
discussing both overlapping and exclusive elements of these perspectives, we unpack ethical discourses surrounding the Memorial

and Virtual walls. Specifically, we argue that those who visit the Memorial and Virtual walls enact ethical selves through a particular form of subjective patriotism that politicizes what are intended as memorial spaces. Through subjective stances, participants communicate subtle political messages about the nature of war, trust in government, the meaning of service, and patriotic obligation. In the final section of the chapter we conclude that the subjective patriotism enacted by visitors to the walls illustrates a potentially interesting permutation between Taylor's ethical self and Gergen's fragmented self.

The rationale for focusing on the Memorial and Virtual walls stems from our observation that these sites of discourse are rhetorically unique when compared with other popular culture discourses about the war. As explained by McMahon (2002), "Popular culture … has been instrumental in reflecting and reinforcing societal misgivings about the Vietnam War, thereby helping fix essential elements of the antiwar paradigm in the nation's collective consciousness" (p. 177). Unlike films (for example, *Apocalypse Now*), literature (*The Things They Carried*), or even Broadway productions (*Miss Saigon*), discourses found at the wall (in "real" or virtual form) are not limited by any particular perspective or "fixed meaning" about the war. Both sites, because of their public nature, represent open spaces for multiple voices and opinions to be heard. In this sense, the Memorial and Virtual walls are sites where multiple discourses about one of the most troubling topics in American history are enacted—sites that, in our opinion, offer valuable insight on how members of a discourse community grapple with complex questions of ethics, identity, and memory.

A second reason for selecting the Virtual Wall as a focus of study concerns the singular moral and ethical dilemmas faced by members of virtual communities. Online discourse proves troubling for some observers at the level of sheer conceptualization: the very idea of it can be difficult to swallow. After all, an online chat room is a physically nonexistent "place" in which immaterial voices "gather" to "talk" (soundlessly) in hopes of forming a "community," one consisting of nonpresent persons who may or may not be who they claim to be, and who may or may not be the true authors of the views they have "gathered" to espouse. Merely thinking about what it means to be a person in such a context is troublesome in itself, because in an online environment options for forming or refining new identities—and new modes for expressing those identities—are ostensibly inexhaustible.

Unlike other communication technologies, which emphasize one-to-one interaction (for example, the telephone) or one-to-many interaction (mass communication), the Internet is unique in the way that it allows for many-to-many interactions. As Gary Burnett (2002) explains, the Internet promotes the formation of virtual communities that function in strikingly similar ways as face-to-face communities. Placed in this context, the Virtual Wall is similar to other online communities where members negotiate codes of conduct and rules for interaction (Baym 1998), while at the same time providing participants with an outlet for cathartic venting and therapeutic affiliation (Song 2002). What makes the Virtual Wall unique from other online communities is the morally and ethically charged nature of the common interest drawing community participants together—the Vietnam War. Unlike chat rooms focusing on television shows or multiuser domains allowing participants to engage in virtual combat, the Memorial Wall website has tangible connections to life-and-death struggles in the "real world." In particular, the visceral nature of Vietnam prompts community participants to enact self in ways likely not found in virtual communities addressing more trivial and mundane matters.

Contemporary Ethical Perspectives

Constructing and enacting an ethically responsive self is inarguably one of the central challenges of contemporary life. Constructing the self is necessary, difficult, and generally thankless. There are few if any cultural rewards offered for the sheer *sustaining* of one's self-coherence; *enacting* the self, as a reflexive process, is just as unrewarding and is fraught with all manner of social and cultural peril. What causes us more grief or strain or trouble on a daily basis than those small miscalculations of speech and action that we would dearly love to take back or reenact, but cannot? *To be* is, in many respects, no less contingent and arduous an effort for computer programmers, assistant professors, and soccer players than it was for Hamlet. The main difference is that the stakes are now far higher in one crucial sense: our words and deeds are more likely than ever before to be recorded, surveilled, reviewed, assessed, and criticized.

Defining and deploying the self is a process rendered even more complex by the fragmented, anonymous, and multivariate personas available to participants in online communities. To elaborate on these tensions, we explore Taylor's and Gergen's respective claims about the relationship(s) between contemporary selves and online ethical behavior, for two reasons. First, we seek to provide a clear context for our ensuing analysis of discourse in and around the memorial. Second, we seek to frame a pair of themes that thread their way through our discussions of both theorists' ideas. These two themes are (1) the ongoing construction and presentation of online selves, and (2) the application of those selves in a discourse community, in this case the online memorial community. We identify and apply these themes for several reasons. First, we need to distinguish meaningfully between the ongoingness of a person's constructing and refining of self, and that self's real-world application in a particular discursive venue. Second, we want to demonstrate similarities, not just differences, between Taylor's and Gergen's ideas. Finally, we use these themes to draw conclusions about the differing applicability of Taylor and Gergen to various ethical conundrums, contexts, and choices. We focus, then, not on the relative strengths and weaknesses of these two ethical systems, but rather on how elements of each may best be applied, rhetorically and pragmatically, in the service of our evaluation of memorial discourse.

Taylor's Ethically Charged Self

Alasdair MacIntyre (1981) begins *After Virtue*, his influential account of modern moral argumentation, with what he terms a "disquieting suggestion" (p. 1). MacIntyre claims that a distinctive feature of contemporary argument is its disputants' tendency to be generally unreflective about the language they use to denounce each other's positions. If, as MacIntyre observes, part of a person's central claim is (for example) founded on the rejection of another's claims to moral absolutism, may the first person justifiably use absolutist language to advance that claim against the second person? The claim "I'm right," for instance, is predicated on far more than the mere belief that "You're wrong." "I'm right" is semantically *and ethically* rooted in at least two assumptions: (1) that there is a right and a wrong that can serve as a valid framework for argumentation, and (2) that this right and wrong can be discovered and applied through linguistic means. But verbal disputants, MacIntyre observes, often fall into a self-contradiction like the one described above without realizing that they are doing so, and this happens in part because they fail to acknowledge the implications of those two assumptions. We almost always argue ethically—that is, we make "ought to" or "ought not" claims—on the footing of an unstated but deeply consequential presumption that we know what right and wrong are and that this knowledge can serve in some sense as self-justification for the ethical prescriptions we advance in response to public disputes.

The same kind of problem plagues disputants who *are* more or less conscious of argumentation's debt to language. MacIntyre (1981) notes that "if those who claim to be able to formulate principles on which rational moral agents ought to agree cannot secure agreement on the formulation of those principles ... [then] there is once again *prima facie* evidence that their project has failed" (p. 21). In other words, our taken-for-granted assumptions about rightness or wrongness (in discourse) too often undermine attempts to resolve moral disagreements before the substance of the competing arguments is ever deliberated in any appreciable sense. More to the point, again, those assumptions about right and wrong are themselves the ground of ethical disagreement: they provide a coherent field in which we evaluate what is said, establish a range of possible responses, and then take action.

MacIntyre argues that both unself-conscious and self-conscious disputants regularly and unwisely attempt to extricate their notions of the self from the language that informs that self. "It is wrong to separate the history of the self and its roles," MacIntyre (1981) asserts, "from the history of the language which the self specifies and through which the roles are given expression" (p. 35). Why? Because "what we discover is a single history and not two parallel ones" (p. 35). The self is best understood, then, in the context of the linguistic choices it makes. Those choices are what hold selves, and arguments about right and wrong, together.

Taylor's (1989) major work on moral identity, *Sources of the Self*, anchors its understanding of the ethical self on a premise very similar to MacIntyre's. Taylor puts his position bluntly: "It is a form of self-delusion to think that we do not speak from a moral orientation which we take to be right. [To speak from such an orientation] is a condition of being a functioning self" (p. 99). For Taylor, the self is intrinsically ethical; there is no getting around the fact that we are inclined to speak on any given topic as if we were right. How else, he implies, would the conditions for argument ever arise?

Taylor (1989) asserts that the chief problem of contemporary ethical argument (within what he terms the broader "modern moral culture") is that people cannot agree with any regularity about what counts as good (p. 498). This absence of consensus has enormous implications for the very idea of communal action (for reasons obvious to anyone who has ever tried, for example, to launch a concrete campaign for social change in an atmosphere of abiding political divisiveness). It also reduces a once-majestic conception of "morality" to the status of an artificial situational ethics; that is, what can I (or must I) do at this place and at this moment? Taylor concludes, "Morality is [today] conceived purely as a guide to action. It is thought to be concerned purely with what it is right to do rather than with what it is good to be" (p. 79). This argument is important to the development of our understanding of ethical behavior in online discourse in at least two respects.

First, Taylor notes that treating "ethics" separately from grand philosophical questions about right and wrong is misguided, because people do not tend to argue with any such distinction in mind. Rather, they argue—even about small, local, finite problems—with the goals of (1) *establishing* rightness or wrongness on that grander scale, or of (2) *confirming* their existing beliefs about rightness or wrongness (on that same scale). Taylor here recapitulates Aristotle's characterization of *eudaimonia*, the good life. Writing in another vein, the classicist philosopher Martha Nussbaum (1986) confirms Taylor's invoking of Aristotelian goodness: "To find out about our nature seems to be one and the same with finding out what we believe to be the most important and indispensable elements of our lives" (p. 350). Recall MacIntyre's claim above that we argue in part to remind ourselves who we think we are. In some crucial sense, defining the self is complementary to defining right and wrong as extensions or confirmations of one's self-identity in the public world.

The second argument deriving from the passage quoted above focuses on the relationship between what we take to be good and what we think our obligations are with respect to that good. Taylor insists that these two considerations are opposite sides of the same ethical coin. In his view, to speak exclusively of what is owed or incurred at this moment or in that interaction is to elide the ethical landscape in which such questions are asked. Taylor's position is echoed in Mikhail Bakhtin's (1993) rejection of systematized ethical systems divorced from morality. "Formal ethics," he warns, "provides no approach to a living act performed in the real world" (p. 27). This claim is consonant with Taylor's call for a holistic understanding of the good and our obligations thereto.

In sum, Taylor seeks to persuade us that the ethical self must be vigilantly reflective about its standing in relation to the good, and about its obligations to that good. What defines and gives meaning to an "ethical self" is its continuous enactment of its own subjectivity in the context of those two concerns. In turn, those concerns, working through the "ought to" and "ought not" of language, give shape to what we believe ourselves to be; they mold us within the frame of what we think is right and wrong. Arguments about right and wrong reveal, then, not only something about where we stand, but about who it is that is standing there.

Gergen's Saturated Self

Gergen's (1991) view of the contemporary self proceeds largely from one key insight: that what a person thinks about his or her self cannot be separated from that conception's consequences in the social world. Gergen is not simply arguing that we are and do what we think we are and do. Rather, he claims that an overabundance of potential human contact (for example, a bewildering array of media) has made it difficult to achieve and maintain a firm sense of self. He terms this assault and its psychic consequences "social saturation" (p. 16). Within his description of social saturation, Gergen stresses the effects of external stimuli on the self's internal functioning, and in so doing distinguishes his version of selfhood from Taylor's.

"Social saturation," Gergen (1991) contends, "brings with it a general loss in our assumption of true and knowable selves" (p. 16). The necessity of displaying multiple selves in multiple contexts in our lives strains us psychically to the point of breaking. The first thing to crumble is our intrinsic sense of self-coherence. We fail to see the negative repercussions of this saturation, however, in part because we are enamored of the false promise of multiple selves. In the fragmented context of saturation, argues Gergen, "each of us comes to harbor a vast population of hidden potentials—to be a blues singer, a gypsy, an aristocrat, a criminal. All the selves lie latent, and under the right conditions may spring to life" (p. 71). The problem here is that those "right conditions" presume a nearly endless wellspring of social and psychological energy that most persons do not possess. Gergen's argument here is a more technical version of the maxim that one "can't be all things to all people"— and that the effort to achieve that ideal will end in exhaustion and in the disintegration of the self.

For this reason, a self's initial foray into a fast-paced, multivocal environment (such as an online discursive community) may prove especially burdensome. The pressures placed on the self's sense of itself in such a context may lead to a kind of alienation, one in which the self is distanced both from its own bearings and from healthy contact with others. Gergen (1971) cautions that "not know-ing precisely how to act, running the risk of failure in not knowing, feeling as if [one's] actions are out of joint with standard modes of being—all contribute to feelings of estrangement" (p. 89). This sense of social and psychological estrangement has been discussed in a number of contexts, particularly within contemporary critical theory. The silencing of minority voices, the institutionalization of oppressive forms of power, the hidden violence of language—all have been examined closely for their effects on selves and communities. Arjun Appadurai (1996), for example, has studied globalization and its relationship to selfhood and modernity, and has concluded that the pressures placed on the modern self have given rise to artful but confusing amalgams of the real and the unreal. "Lives today," he writes, "are as much acts of projection and imagination as they are of known scripts or predictable outcomes" (p. 61). Absent a manageable milieu for social and cultural interaction, people adapt in whatever ways they can. Some jettison older rules for what the self is, or should be, in public contexts. Other lose a grip on selfhood altogether.

The interplay of estrangement and adaptation is closely addressed in Erving Goffman's (1959) work on the public performance of self. Goffman reveals that the social forces that would eventually produce Gergen's "saturation" were fully at work in the public culture of 1950s America. Consider a representative passage from Goffman's major work, *The Presentation of Self in Everyday Life*:

> Socialization may not so much involve a learning of the many specific details of a single concrete [public role]—often there could not be enough time or energy for this. What does seem to be required of the [self] is that he learn enough pieces of expression to be able to "fill in" and manage, more or less, any [role] that he is likely to be given. The legitimate performances of everyday life are not "acted" or "put on" in the sense that the performer knows in advance just what he is going to do, and does this solely because of the effect it is likely to have. (1959, p. 73)

Goffman's words illuminate a crucial difference between Gergen's and Taylor's positions. Note that Goffman acknowledges the pressure on persons to handle or manage a variety of roles, and suggests that this pressure is applied from external sources. This view presages Gergen's like-minded belief: that pressures felt by modern selves are (largely) externally produced or constructed. Unlike Taylor, who accords significant power to the self to decide for itself what it is, and *to actuate* that version of self as an ethical agent in public contexts (see Taylor 1989, pp. 510–12, 516), Gergen's account follows Goffman's in concluding that the self is in many respects a passive recipient of its own identity.[1]

Gergen (1991) devotes the fourth and fifth chapters of *The Saturated Self* to the painstaking development of his claim that the self is substantially the product of external forces (pp. 84–138). This claim embodies his most serious disagreement with Taylor. In Gergen's estimate, radical perspectivalism and social fragmentation have effected an "undermining of being" that has become "a self-sustaining way of life" (p. 138). "Belief in clear and separable things-in-themselves deteriorates across a broad spectrum," Gergen concludes, and as they do, the "boundaries of the self become blurred" (p. 138). Contra Taylor, whose account of identity retains possibilities for fixed, deeply held meaning(s) as derived through ethical enactment, Gergen declares that relativity has won out: "No transcendent [cultural] voice remains to fix the reality of selves. As rational coherence is increasingly questioned, so does the traditional view of identity as fixed by [longitudinal] continuity lose its appeal. When anything goes, so does personality as a discriminant category. In the end consciousness of construction turns reflexive" (p. 138).

In light of our focus on online popular discourse, this conclusion begs several questions. First, how can a self act *ethically* in a world drained of authoritative meaning? What is the standard of evaluation or judgment that would inform recognizably "ethical" (as opposed to "unethical") speech and action in that world? Gergen's answer—that selves derive meanings about the good from the particular communities they inhabit (1991, p. 170)—diverges sharply from Taylor's more stabilized formulation. If "no transcendent voice remains," how can communities serve as legitimate resources for localized ethical meaning? Doesn't the voice of a community "transcend," by definition, the voices of its individual members? Are the meaning-making efforts of the many somehow intrinsically more valid than those of the one? And: If *all* meanings are constructed, why then should meanings constructed by a community take precedence over meanings constructed by an individual self? Let us stress that we do not pose these questions for purposes of judgment, but for juxtaposition: clearly, Gergen and Taylor see the ethics of discourse very differently. For Taylor, a person crafts, refines, and deploys an ethically accountable self, whereas Gergen argues that the world in which Taylor's selves live and act is not quite so stable as the latter would have it. For Gergen, the self is far more mutable, manifold, and relativized. The contrast between the two positions is striking, and given our present focus, usefully so.

With these differences in mind, we return to the field of our inquiry: the online discourse community surrounding the Vietnam Veterans Memorial. The relationships between that community as a whole, its electronic gatekeepers, and its individual members, is delicate and complicated, and evaluating those relationships for their ethical content is far from easy. This is the case in part because claims about right and wrong necessarily imply a need for responses, whether favorable or unfavorable, from those selves whose participation in communities makes them ethically accountable for what is said and done there. The form and content of those responses are the focus of the remainder of this chapter.

The (Virtual) Vietnam Veterans Memorial Wall

In April 1979, Jan Scruggs and a group of fellow veterans campaigned to create a memorial recognizing the service and sacrifice of Americans who served in Vietnam (Hass 1998). The culminating effects of their efforts resulted in a nearly $9 million fund and P. L. 96-297, a joint resolution to establish a Vietnam Veterans Memorial in the Constitution Garden, near the Lincoln Memorial, in Washington, D.C. President Jimmy Carter signed the joint resolution on July 1, 1980.

The Memorial Wall is shrouded in conflicting discourses. For some the Memorial Wall provides discursive space for expressing guilt and seeking redemption (Carlson & Hocking 1988), for others the wall provides space for remembrance (Ehrenhaus 1988), and for others the wall has become "a cultural phenomena as an agent of healing" (Theriault 2003, p. 421). Although initial reactions from Vietnam vets were perhaps typified in the statement "I think it sucks ... some kind of hole or something like that ... some fucking gash in the ground" (Braithwaite 1997, p. 435), for many Vietnam vets the wall "made mourning in this country a more public and acceptable experience. Now you can cry out if you need to" (Updike 2000, p. 24). The wall is in this sense simultaneously participatory and redemptive.

Visitors to the Memorial Wall in Washington are active participants in the textual representation of the wall. Kristen Ann Hass (1998) observes that objects brought to the wall serve a variety of functions for those who bring them; as she explains, "The great majority of objects mark specific individual memories, some speak to the problems of patriotism or community, some are negotiations between the living and the dead, some work to establish a community of veterans, and some make explicit political speeches" (p. 95). Indeed, A. Cheree Carlson and John E. Hocking (1988) note that such active participation allows viewers to redefine the war "in such a way as to allow them to live with the reality of Vietnam" (p. 213). Textually, the Memorial Wall is more than the names carved in granite; the Memorial Wall requires audience members to "read" the entire experience, including other persons visiting the site, the commentary of veterans who volunteer to "guide" people in their visit to the site, and artifacts left by other visitors.[2] As Sonja K. Foss (1986) explains, the Memorial Wall lacks explicit cues and allows for "a wide variety of referents to be attributed to its various visual elements" (p. 336). Thus, the text of the Memorial Wall is constantly in flux for the reader. Kim Servart Theriault (2003) notes, "the minimalism of Lin's architecture advocates its contemplative qualities. These essential forms both allow and preempt attempts to attach programmed meanings to them" (p. 424).

Sixteen years after President Carter authorized space on the National Mall for the Vietnam Memorial, former members of the 4th Battalion 9th Infantry Regiment created a virtual memorial of sorts, the Vietnam Veterans Memorial website (we encourage readers to view this website at www.thewall-usa.com). In addition to providing a searchable database of names on the Memorial Wall, the Virtual Wall provides viewers with the opportunity to view "Today's Birthdays" of those on the wall, a casualty listing for the day, photos, literature, a listing of Medal of Honor recipients, a guestbook, and a message center. As of December 10, 2003, over thirty thousand persons had added entries to the guestbook.

Like the Memorial Wall, visitors to the Virtual Wall are active participants in the rhetoric of the site. "Since it first went on line in 1996 [the Virtual Wall] has evolved into something more," proclaims the website. "It is now a place of healing for those affected by one of the most divisive wars in our nation's history" (VVMP 2003, n.p.). Such therapeutic narratives are most apparent in the guestbook, where visitors are able to upload photographs, literature, messages about individual soldiers listed in the database, and messages for other visitors. Through such therapeutic narratives participants are able to (re)mold their own sense of identity and self.

We analyze discourses enveloping both the Virtual Wall and the Memorial Wall.[3] In particular, we suggest that a synecdochic relationship (see Burke 1969) exists between the Memorial Wall and the Virtual Wall.[4] Visitors to the Virtual Wall have carved out space where they can actively create meaning and interact with the memorial. In that sense, a visit to the Virtual Wall *represents* re-demptive hope much like the redemption found through visits to the Memorial Wall (see Carlson & Hocking 1988). Our reading of the visitors' messages to the Virtual Wall suggests that contributors enact self and establish ethical identities by (re)constructing narra-tives of subjective patriotism. As we observe, participants rely on two general rhetorical strategies, remembrance and community, to display the political, ethical, and moral dimensions of patriotism while at the same time denouncing specific aspects of the war and those who propelled it. We call this subjective patriotism because it falls somewhere in between strict views of nationalistic patriotism on the one hand and cosmopolitan individualism on the other (see Gordon 2000).

The Subjective Patriotism of Remembrance

Although traditional memorials serve to legitimize sacrifice and sanctify "the virtues of accepting as legitimate future calls for sac-rifice" (Ehrenhaus 1988, p. 57), visitors to the Virtual Wall enact subjective patriotism by remembering those who died while at the same time opposing unjust and unnecessary war. Virtual Wall visitors emphatically vow to "never forget" those who died in Vietnam. For example, civilians write to keep the memory of their loved ones alive: "My husband was 101st Airborne, 1968 to 1970. In memory of those who did not return home, you are ALWAYS with us. In our home, our hearts, our minds. YOU WILL NEVER BE FORGOTTEN! (Wendy, November 2, 2003). Veterans also write to help remember fallen comrades. As expressed by Bill, "So many years have passed but the sadness remains.... You are missed, Duane, and the heroic sacrifice you made will always be remembered" (September 23, 2003).

In addition to "never forgetting" those who served in Vietnam, a number of visitors to the Virtual Wall express gratitude for the sacrifices of those who served. Shirley writes, "The men and women whose names appear on the Wall gave the ultimate sacrifice.... I say thank you from the bottom of my heart. Without men and women like you, we would be no better than the rest" (October 13, 2003). By recognizing the sacrifice of those who served, some visitors use remembrance to ease their dissonance over the war. "I spent the last 35 years heart broken over this country's decision to send a whole generation of young men to their deaths," writes Brenda. "It breaks my heart to think of all the young men, my age who have given their lives. They are greatly missed and so deeply appreciated" (September 29, 2003).

Messages of remembrance left at the Virtual Wall are not unlike similar messages left at the Memorial Wall. Laura Palmer (1987) notes that "the memorial, unexpectedly, became a place not only to honor but to communicate with the dead. The Messages that have been left speak eloquently of loss and remembrance" (p. xi). Similarly, messages left at the Virtual Wall call upon us to not forget those who served and also provide assurances to fallen loved ones that their memory will remain. In some ways, both the Memorial and Virtual walls are portals to another time and place, where connections are kept between the living and the dead; that one wall is "real" and the other "virtual" seems to mean little to visitors. Such discourses force participants to take moral and ethical stands in the

larger battle over public memory about the war. In focusing on the
people who fought in the war, these participants are able to avoid
supporting the act of war while at the same time embracing those
who carried out the battles.

The Subjective Patriotism of Community

Vietnam veterans also use the Memorial and Virtual walls as places
to maintain communal bonds. Many veterans enact subjective patriotism by discussing the notion of "brotherhood" as endemic to
the veteran community. Van writes, "Brothers you will not be forgotten. Ashaw and all the other places. REMEMBER BROTHERS. I
thank GOD that he let return from there. I have my memories, but
GOD let me live. THANK YOU" (October 2, 2003). By defining their
connection as a brotherhood, veterans are able to form community,
mold identity, and engage in value-centered discourses about characteristics of the community.

    One example of value-centered discourse about the veteran
community is the expression of what "service" means. Veterans
expressly define service in terms of an obligation to the values of
the country. As Alen writes, "Just a time to ponder on this day of
celebration of our country's founding of how many have lost their
lives protecting our freedom. From even before the Revolutionary
War, people have been dying for our country. Dying for a belief in
what they were doing was right and just. Our fallen comrades from
Vietnam are no different.... God Bless all those fallen soldiers listed
on The Wall" (July 4, 2003). Many of the veterans describe service
from a moral perspective by expressing pride. Even though many
Vietnam veterans were ridiculed, and in fact tormented, because of
their service, many veterans use the Virtual Wall as an opportunity
to morally redefine their experience: "It took me a long time to even
tell anyone that I was a Viet-Nam vet.... When I first came back
people would shame you and make fun. After a while that really
affects you. I will hold my head up and be proud of what I was sent
to do" (Don, August 15, 2003).

    In addition to expressing pride, veterans also express guilt—
another form of value-centered discourse. Most indications of
guilt stem not from participation in the war, but from "surviving"

when others did not. On particularly poignant story is from Calvin, who writes,

> Well buddy another one has slip by. I just didn't have the ball's to enter this on the 26. The day was another tuff one to get through. That day is still embeded in my pea brain, I can close my eyes and see everything that happen and I still see the bottom's of your boot's you were laying so still and I knew that you didn't see the bunker. I let you down that day and it cost you your life. There's not a day goes by that I don't think about you. I always wonder what kind of life you might have had. Roger Guest, KIA 8/26/69. (September 4, 2003)

Such expressions of guilt are important, for they represent "the goal of achieving individual peace and release from pain" (Carlson & Hocking 1988, p. 210). Yet the apparent grief and guilt expressed by some veterans leaves open the question of whether true redemption can be found. Indeed, one is left to wonder whether some veterans feel that true redemption can only be found when they join their fallen brethren. As expressed by Darreld, "I feel so guilty I made it home. So many of my brothers did not…. When I die I sure hope to meet everyone of those 59,300 men and women [whose] names that is on the Wall" (October 25, 2003).

A final example of value-centered discourse defining the Vietnam veteran community, as indicated by Virtual Wall postings, is the creation of "us versus them" dimensions. Many veterans point out, "When I returned from Vietnam I kept quiet—has seen too many hippies spit on our heroes. I told everybody I was in college, traveling, anything but the dreadful truth" (August 28, 2003). Another veteran, Jim, explains,

> Many took the easy way out and let the rest of us carry a very heavy load. They even took pride in that fact, flaunting it in our faces. Meanwhile we fought, sacrificed and endured under the worst possible conditions…. What had they learned in their safe little college classrooms except how wonderful socialist revolutions were. Bottom line is, not one of them will ever measure up to you, my fellow vets, my comrades, my buddies. (August 21, 2003)

In using such "us versus them" representations, veterans make explicit moral arguments about politicians, reporters, "hippies," and those who avoided the war for whatever reason.

From our reading of participants' contributions to the Virtual Wall, we conclude that a synecdochic relationship exists between the two memorials. In particular, both memorial sites serve as places of remembrance and redemption (Carlson & Hocking 1988) and provide discursive space where visitors can contribute to discussions of public memory about the war (Hass 1998). Through such discourses, participants enact self through subjectively patriotic stances that allow them to take sides, establish moral boundaries for right and wrong, create hero figures and villain figures, and form communal bonds.

Ethics and the (Virtual) Wall

When read in combination, the Memorial Wall and the Virtual Wall provide a unique vantage point for exploring similarities and differences in discourses taking place in "real" and "virtual" public spaces. In this final section we discuss our analysis of the memorials in relation to ethical dimensions of the self as described by Taylor and Gergen. First, we argue that ethical identity is intertwined, constructed and reconstructed within narratives of subjective patriotism enacted by people at the two sites. Second, we consider how discourse communities are faced with ethical dilemmas that influence the agency of actors in those communities. In developing these arguments we intend to support the overall conclusion that Taylor's view of the self remains both productive and insightful when considering discourses spanning both "real" and "virtual" spaces.

Political controversy has attended the Memorial Wall since its inception, with the majority of public criticism targeting the unusual design of the memorial. West Point graduate, Pentagon lawyer, and Vietnam vet Tom Carhart called the Memorial Wall "a black gash of shame and sorrow" and asked, "Can America truly mean we should feel honored by that black pit? In a city filled with white monuments, this is our reward for faithful service" (quoted in McCombs 1982, p. A1). The fact that Maya Lin (the designer of the wall) was not a veteran, was a woman, and was of Asian descent further embroiled the memorial in controversy (Theriault 2003). The *Chicago Tribune* claimed that the design was a "monumental insult to veterans," and over two dozen congressmen asked that the design be reconsidered prior to the groundbreaking in 1981 (McCombs 1982, p. A1).

Controversy surrounding the Memorial Wall underscores its place as a focal point for ethical discourses about the meaning of memorializing, personal and public memories of the Vietnam War, and the larger question of public trust in governmental entities (Foss 1986). Following the initial controversy surrounding its design, the physical "place" of the Memorial Wall has been actively (re)constructed by participants as a site for value-centered discourses spanning both geographic localities (that is, the physical location of the wall) and time.[5] It should not be surprising, then, that discourses aimed at making sense of political issues surrounding the war have spilled into other venues, such as the Virtual Wall.

According to its developers, the Virtual Wall was created as "the first internet site dedicated to honoring those who died in the Vietnam war" (VVMP 2003, n.p.). After its launch in 1996, visitors to the Virtual Wall began interacting with it in much the same way that visitors interact with the actual wall in Washington. Visitors are able to upload photographs, stories, poetry, and ask questions; more than twenty thousand such remembrances and entries have been uploaded to the Virtual Wall. These active texts left by visitors to the Virtual Wall are iterations of similar texts left by visitors to the Memorial Wall, which, as Foss (1986) argues, "encourages us to look at the personal consequences of war—death of individuals— and to oppose such a method of the destruction of life" (p. 337). Although our analysis suggests that opposition to war is only one possible reading of these texts, we agree with Foss that narratives cocreated by visitors to both the Memorial and the Virtual walls are laced with social and political meanings.

Ethical discourses at the Virtual Wall enact what we refer to as subjective patriotism, or what Igor Primoratz (2002) calls "moderate patriotism" (p. 457). According to Primoratz, moderate patriotism allows one to "show special concern for his country" while at the same time allowing for the possibility that under some circumstances "the concern for human beings in general will override the concern for one's country" (p. 457). Discourses found at the Virtual

Wall show concern for those who died in the war, yet at the same time (re)present views that the war was unnecessary and harmful.

Such politically charged discourses offer concrete foundations from which to assess Gergen's and Taylor's notions of ethical behavior. From Taylor's perspective, intrinsic ethical stands are discernible in the discourse. Whether participants seek redemption through remembrance or community through brotherhood, or call the wall a "black gash of shame and sorrow," each brings to his or her discourse a decidedly moral lens. These same discourses embody elements of Gergen's "saturated" self, at least in the sense of offering subjective meanings associated with the war. Of course, the discourse analyzed was not interactive per se, and it is probable that web-based discussions of other, perhaps more "popular" topics would provide examples more resonant of Gergen's contingent ethical selves.

In addition to forging political meaning, discourses surrounding the Virtual and Memorial walls are also faced with unique challenges. Though we view the relationship between the two memorial sites as synecdochic in nature, we realize that the relationship is not perfectly identical. In fact, striking differences exist between the two spaces. First, the Virtual Wall decontextualizes visitors' reading of the memorial, and second, the Virtual Wall imposes certain limitations on the discourse that potentially limit the multiplicity of meanings derived from the memorial.

The decontextualized nature of the Virtual Wall stands in stark contrast to the Memorial Wall. In comparison, the Virtual Wall is visually, physically, and psychologically decontextualized. Visitors to the Virtual Wall must explore a series of layers in the website to find information; each layer of the website becomes more and more decontextualized. When visitors initially access the site they encounter a page with a slate-gray background reminiscent of the Memorial Wall. Of course, the two-dimensional nature of a web page decontextualizes it from the serene beauty of the National Mall. Perhaps as an artifact of hypertext programming, visitors to the Virtual Wall must read a progressively fragmented text that fails to emulate the "power [of the Memorial Wall] to evoke an emotional response" (p. 217). Although the creator of the Virtual

Wall, Alan Oskvarek, attempts to "bring The Wall to your living room" (quoted in Gilje 1999, p. E1), such placement of the reading also decontextualizes the reader from the experience of seeing all 58,325 names, other visitors, the distinctive (and meaningful) polished granite surface, and other distinguishing features of the Memorial Wall experience. As such, the Virtual Wall limits visitors' ability to fully immerse themselves in the broad range of emotions felt by those who visit the Memorial Wall.

Although details found in the database and in other sections of the website provide information about individuals and events, the text-based presentation also limits visitors' agency in extracting meaning. Through its text-based discourse, the Virtual Wall has "greater constraints such as grammar and denotative meanings that limit, to some degree, the referents and meaning options available to the audience" (Foss 1986, p. 336). In addition, the Virtual Wall is more explicit in terms of its intended purpose. As stated on the front page of the site, "The Vietnam Veterans Memorial Wall Page is dedicated to honoring those who died in the Vietnam War.... Every effort is made to continually update this site with the most accurate information regarding the Names on The Wall in Washington, DC as possible. We remain dedicated to displaying the information in the dignified manner that it deserves" (VVMP 2003, n.p.). Thus, the "reading" of the Virtual Wall proffered for readers is somewhat fixed. Although readers are able to add stories, pictures, and even literary work to the site, the prominent features of the site, namely the database of names provided on the front page, remain unchanging.

Finally, visitors' ability to engage in multiple discourses at the Virtual Wall is also hampered by active censoring, or "mindguarding," which takes place at the memorial. Key actors in the discourse of the Virtual Wall actively discourage messages that are contrary to the stated purpose of the memorial. In an interview, Oskvarek notes, "I don't want stuff in there about [President] Clinton being a draft dodger. That doesn't stay. And I don't want to hear about L.B.J.'s ... policies; 58,193 people died in Vietnam. They have family, friends, comrades. This is for them" (quoted in Gilje 1999, p. E1). Such censoring of alternative messages is also evident in the interactive pages (for example, the guestbook). As noted by one participant, "This website is about the men and women who I had the privilege of serving with and had their lives taken from them.... If you have nothing to say about them then stay the hell away" (Big John, August 4, 2003).

Decontextualized and fragmented texts, fixed meanings, and active mindguarding all potentially contribute to a loss of agency for participants. Such loss of agency, on its face, appears to transcend any possibility of a fixed and continuous ethical identity. After all, the Virtual Wall actively discourages certain political statements and explicitly condones certain functions for the website; those who fail to communicate within those rules risk ejection from the community. Here, Gergen's warning of the relativistic ethical self seems to garner support. Or does it? The discourse community spanning "spaces" of the Virtual and Memorial walls does not require others to join. Those wishing to remember lost loved ones or form community with fellow veterans could (theoretically) find ample opportunities to do so without visiting either wall. Yet the act of participating in particular discourse communities (for example, visiting the Memorial or Virtual wall) explicitly indicates a willingness to contribute (though not necessarily conform) to that community. Such an action is, itself, evidence of an individual's perspective on *eudaimonia*—in the case of the Virtual and Memorial walls a life characterized by reverence for fallen "heroes," a community of brothers, and a solemn remembrance of sacrifice.

The interpretation of virtual and embodied participants in the cultures of the wall is necessarily as active and complex as the words and deeds enacted in those cultures. We offer two guarded conclusions, and at the same time encourage future analyses of these and other online cultures. First: the fears of earlier cultural commentators, those writing at the dawn of the multimedia age, that an imagistic orientation toward public culture would necessarily produce mass conformity are refuted (in the present case) by the textual data. The calculus of Daniel Boorstin's famous warning—"The passivity of conformity is the passivity of fitting into images. The prevalence of images makes possible the prevalence of conformity" (Boorstin 1961, p. 192)—is countered here by the variety and vigor of the responses that the wall's online community has engendered.

Every visitor to the Virtual Wall confronts images, not the physical memorial itself. Yet every visitor is moved to write something distinctive, something original. Even the most consonant expressions of patriotism, remembrance, solidarity, or regret are worded uniquely. To underscore the point: each visitor responds in his or her own voice, not someone else's. Conformity of structure is undeniable; the nature of the (online) venue requires that written comments take a certain form. But conformity of *response* is simply nowhere to be found.

Our second tentative conclusion, one that builds from the first, is that Taylor's account of the self is generally more useful as an analytic frame than is Gergen's "saturated" self. The reason, in hindsight, is clear: participants (that is, discussants) at the Virtual Wall site make ethically infused claims. Even expressions of emotional conflict or indecision are housed in the language of "ought" or "ought not." Taylor's claim that our most intrinsic sense of self is indelibly stamped by our beliefs about right and wrong—particularly as articulated in public contexts—resonates much more strongly with the textual record of discussants' comments than does Gergen's claim that we are now fully relativized to the point of incoherence. The persons who have left their written testimonies at the Virtual Wall do not believe that they are relativized. They do not write as if they somehow do not exist as coherent, identifiable selves. Quite the opposite: they write as if what is at stake is no less than their most fundamental understanding of what it means to pursue the good in a conflicted societal milieu in conflicted times. Finally, they write to persuade. Whether to convince themselves alone, or a few others, or every person who visits the site, these discussants seek to persuade someone of the rightness or wrongness of particular beliefs—beliefs that are laced throughout the subjective patriotic stances we observed.

In *The Ethics of Authenticity*, Taylor (1991) argues that contemporary public efforts to achieve common ground are fueled by an almost visceral rejection of a growing cultural fragmentation. Detecting the presence of an atomized assortment of "people increasingly less capable of forming a common purpose and carrying it out" (p. 112), Taylor claims that the origin of the problem is the erosion of shared identity, particularly political identity. That kind of identity is fostered through public discussion of how it is that what people think ethically informs who they believe themselves to be personally. At the end of such discussion, Taylor argues, are renewed possibilities for "successful common action" of a type that "can bring a sense of empowerment and also strengthen identification with a political community" (p. 118). Consciously or otherwise, it is the search for these possibilities that we see online discussants making in their discourse about the memorial and its meanings in and for contemporary public culture. Thus, computer-mediated discourse offers some possibility for individuals to enact ethical selves and join together within the confines of a virtual *eudaimonia* and community.

Authors' note: We would like to thank our colleagues Drs. Roger Aden, Lynn Harter, and Arvind Singhal for their helpful suggestions for this chapter.

Notes

1. We are emphatically not arguing that Gergen believes that the self has *no* role in its own formation. Gergen makes no such claim. We are asserting, however, that Gergen far more freely ascribes agency to external cultural and social forces than Taylor does, and that Gergen's emphasis on constructed selves greatly exceeds the degree of agency Taylor is willing to assign to the social world.
2. As estimated by the National Parks Service (2001), the Memorial Wall is second only to the Washington Monument in terms of attendance at National Mall tribute sites, with nearly 4.5 million annual visitors. Additionally, the National Parks Service estimates that over sixty thousand items ranging from handwritten letters and teddy bears to bottles of liquor have been left as remembrances at the Memorial Wall (Updike 2000).
3. Our analysis of "discourses" included analyses of the Memorial Wall by academicians, popular press articles about the Memorial Wall and the Virtual Wall, content on the Virtual Wall website, and entries to the Virtual Wall guestbook by visitors. We read all guestbook entries dating back to September 1, 2001, for our analysis. When quoting material from the guestbook, we identify the visitor's first name and the date their entry was posted to the website.

We have opted not to use "[sic]" to comment on the spelling and grammar of visitors' entries. In our view such notations would disrupt the narratives and would contribute to a perception of "intellectual elitism."

4. Synecdoche, according to Burke (1969), is a rhetorical representation in which a "relationship of convertibility" is established between two things (p. 508). A representative sample used by social scientists, substituting "9/11" in reference to terrorism, and various nonverbal emblems are all examples of synecdochic relationships commonly found in our culture. In the case of the Virtual and Memorial walls, visitors have created uses and functions for the memorials that have caused the two "sites" to have a clear synecdochic relationship.

5. The argument that the Memorial Wall "space" should be read to extend beyond the physical/geographic location of the memorial is consistent with postmodern interpretations of rhetorical space. For an excellent analysis of meanings associated with space, see Massey (1994).

References

Appadurai, A. (1996). *Modernity at large: Cultural dimensions of globalization.* Minneapolis: University of Minnesota Press.

Bakhtin, M. (1993). *Toward a philosophy of the act* (V. Liapunov, trans.). Austin: University of Texas Press.

Baym, N. (1998). The emergence of on-line community. In S. Jones (ed.), *Cybersociety 2.0: Revisiting computer-mediated communication and community* (pp. 35–68). Thousand Oaks, CA: Sage.

Boorstin, D. (1961). *The image: A guide to pseudo-events in America.* New York: Harper & Row.

Braithwaite, C. A. (1997). "Were YOU there?": A ritual of legitimacy among Vietnam veterans. *Western Journal of Communication* 61: 423–47.

Burke, K. A. (1969). *A grammar of motives.* Berkeley: University of California Press.

Burnett, G. (2002). The scattered members of an invisible republic: Virtual communities and Paul Ricoeur's hermeneutics. *Library Quarterly* 72: 155–78.

Carlson, A. C., & J. E. Hocking. (1988). Strategies of redemption at the Vietnam Veterans Memorial. *Western Journal of Speech Communication* 52: 203–15.

Ehrenhaus, P. (1988). The Vietnam Veterans Memorial: An invitation to argument. *Journal of the American Forensic Association* 25: 54–64.

Foss, S. K. (1986). Ambiguity as persuasion: The Vietnam Veterans Memorial. *Communication Quarterly* 34: 326–40.

Gergen, K. J. (1971). *The concept of self.* New York: Holt.

———. (1991). *The saturated self: Dilemmas of identity in contemporary life.* New York: Basic Books.

Gilje, S. (1999). Web site brings Vietnam Wall to your home. *Seattle Times*, June 2, p. E1.

Goffman, E. (1959). *The presentation of self in everyday life*. New York: Anchor Books.

Gordon, R. H. (2000). Modernity, freedom, and the state: Hagel's concept of patriotism. *Review of Politics* 62: 295–325.

Hass, K. A. (1998). *Carried to the wall*. Berkeley: University of California Press.

MacIntyre, A. (1981). *After virtue: A study in moral theory*. Notre Dame, IN: University of Notre Dame Press.

Massey, D. (1994). *Space, place, and gender*. Minneapolis: University of Minnesota Press.

McCombs, P. (1982). Reconciliation: Ground broken for shrine to Vietnam War veterans. *Washington Post*, March 27, p. A1.

McMahon, R. J. (2002). Contested memory: The Vietnam War and American society, 1975–2001. *Diplomatic History* 26: 159–84.

National Parks Service. (2001). 20 most-visited sites in the National Park System, 1999. *World Almanac and Book of Facts*. New York: Newspaper Enterprise Association.

Nussbaum, M. C. (1986). *The fragility of goodness: Luck and ethics in Greek tragedy*. Cambridge: Cambridge University Press.

Palmer, L. (1987). *Shrapnel in the heart: Letters and remembrances from the Vietnam Veterans Memorial*. New York: Random House.

Primoratz, I. (2002). Patriotism: A deflationary view. *Philosophical Forum* 33: 443–58.

Song, F. W. (2002). Virtual communities in a therapeutic age. *Society* (January/February): 39–45.

Taylor, C. (1989). *Sources of the self: The making of the modern identity*. Cambridge, MA: Harvard University Press.

———. (1991). *The ethics of authenticity*. Cambridge, MA. Harvard University Press.

Theriault, K. S. (2003). Re-membering Vietnam: War, trauma, and "scarring over" after "The Wall." *Journal of American Culture* 26: 421–31.

Updike, W. A. (2000). War and remembrance. *National Parks* 74 (September/October): 20–26.

Vietnam Veterans Memorial Page. (2003). Wall information. Accessed October 2, 2003. Available at: www.thewall-usa.com.

When You Lie with *Friends*

Diana L. Rehling

> Ethical conduct is important in interpersonal interactions. While the interpersonal setting is often our place of greatest trust, it is also our place of greatest vulnerability.
>
> —Stanley Deetz

Interpersonal relationships, such as friendships, provide us with some of our most basic needs, from a sense of belonging and stability to provisions of assistance and reassurance of our worth (Hobfoll and Stokes 1988; Weiss 1974). Friendships are, as Deetz (1990) notes above, also places of great trust and great vulnerability. Friendships provide contexts in which to learn about relationships, places to practice "relationshipping" (Duck 1991). Friends become "benchmarks that tell us how we should react appropriately, and they correct or guide our attitudes and beliefs in both obvious and subtle ways" (p. 12). In a culture without codified ethical guidelines for interpersonal relationships (Hardwig 2002), friendships are a place in which we work out what it means to communicate ethically with friends.

Popular culture may, however, provide insight into how friendships in the culture are generally enacted. In seeming contrast to the personal world of private friendships, mass culture provides us with a window into the common culture. Paul Cantor (2001) argues that in viewing current popular culture as a way to understand our times we are following in the footsteps of Plato, who interrogated the popular poets of ancient Greece to "reveal the horizon of common opinion" (p. 37). Cantor goes on to suggest that "the American people have increasingly come to understand their world in terms of what they see on television, which often provides them with both the raw data and the categories with which to analyze them" (p. 37).

Betwixt and between the more private world of personal friendships and the public world of mass culture appears *Friends*, NBC's hit situation comedy. Rob Walker (2002) of *Slate* describes the show as "basically about three guys and three gals who live in suspiciously large New York apartments, humorously cope with the problems that come along with being incredibly good-looking white people, and occasionally sleep with each other." The relationships among the six are complicated, including Monica (a chef) and Ross (who studies dinosaurs) as brother and sister; a friendship between Monica and Rachel (who works in the fashion industry) that extends back to high school; and former college roommates Ross and Chandler (who works in an undefined area of business). Phoebe, a woman who once lived on the streets and Joey, a struggling actor, joined the circle later, through living in close proximity to the others. An ongoing romantic entanglement between Ross and Rachel, including the birth of their daughter, and the romance and eventual marriage of Chandler and Monica provide a complex relational history among the group. For ten seasons the show has made common to America the relational ups and downs, the everyday joys and woes of Monica, Rachel, Phoebe, Chandler, Joey, and Ross. In the hoopla that built around the show's final season in 2004, NBC ran ads that described *Friends* as the "best comedy ever" (Bauder 2004).

Whether measured by the conventional means of Nielsen ratings (on average 13.4 million viewers in the 2001–2002 season) and Emmy awards (best comedy in 2002) or the less conventional means of magazine covers and fan-based websites, *Friends* has clearly been embraced by America (Ryan 2002). The show's high ratings among the demographic category of 18–49ers has caused advertisers to pay prices among the highest ever, rivaling the prices paid for Super Bowl slots (Bauder 2004). And with ten years of shows in syndication worldwide, the friendships among the characters are for many people more known, developed, and discussed than many real-life relationships.

Typical of its genre, *Friends* tends to focus upon relational issues in which actual or imagined problems are introduced into the relationships, conflict erupts, and, before the half-hour is over, order is restored. As with other popular situation comedies, the continuing relationships among the principal characters provide the show's continuity. *Friends* is in many ways characteristic of situation comedies. Exploring the dynamics of communication and ethics within *Friends* can, therefore, provide insight into understanding this popular genre, as well as raising questions for real-life relationships.

Friends provides a popular culture artifact in which we can examine communication among some of the best-known friends in America—a place to watch "relationshipping" happen and ethical dilemmas being played out—a window into a shared understanding of friendship. Various aspects of ethics in interpersonal communication could be considered by examining *Friends*, such as forgiveness (see McBride 2003), sexual behavior within friendships, or even notions of family loyalty. I am focusing on the fundamental ethical concern of truthfulness and deceit, as represented by lying. Keith E. Davis and Michael Todd (1985) find that among our most basic expectations of friends is that they will be honest and open and that they will trust us and also be trustworthy. Lying, as ethicist Sissela Bok (1978) suggests, threatens to undermine that fundamental trust:

> The function of the principle of veracity is evident when we think of trust. I can have different kinds of trust: that you will treat me fairly, that you will have my interest at heart, that you will do me no harm. But if I do not trust your word, can I have genuine trust in the first three? If there is no confidence in the truthfulness of others, is there any way to assess their fairness, their intentions to help or do no harm? How then can they be trusted? (p. 31)

In examining acts of lying among the Friends (the group of characters in *Friends*), we are able to consider the entwined ethical and relational dimensions of a communication behavior that has implications for the very foundations of friendship. We can consider if all untruths undermine friendship and trust or if some level of deception is necessary, even among those closest to us, to living together in harmony.

In deciding what communication acts should be considered lies, communication scholars and ethicists alike generally agree that we should be concerned about the intentionality of the speaker rather than about the accuracy of their representation (Bok 1978; McCornack and Levin 1990; Miller and Stiff 1993). While we may tell someone something that is not true because we lack information or because of a misunderstanding, a lie is a deliberate act intended to mislead the relational partner, to cause the partner to believe something the liar does not believe to be true.

Lies the Friends Tell

Deceptions or lies occur with regularity on *Friends*. The lies they tell generally fall into three sometimes overlapping categories distinguishable by what appears to be the primary motivation of the liar: white lies or lies that are viewed as insignificant deceptions, primarily done to help another save face or to avoid confrontation over what is deemed as an insignificant issue; lies to protect the lied-to person or another person; and lies to protect the liar or advance his or her own self-interest.

White Lies

White lies are probably the most common type of lies on *Friends*, just as they appear to be in the lives of most people (DePaulo 1985). Many of these are the boring little lies told to keep social interactions pleasant and to make us generally more agreeable to others, lies of the "no, those pants don't make you look fat" variety. And, as is common on situation comedies, these are often played for a quick laugh, as in the following scene:

> Rachel: Hey Pheebs, can I talk to you over here for a second?
>
> Phoebe: Yeah!
>
> Monica: Subtle, guys!

Phoebe: What?!

Monica: I know you're planning my surprise bridal shower.

Rachel: (Laughs.) Well, okay—Well, don't ruin it! Just play along at least!

Monica: Okay. Sorry. (She goes into the guest bedroom.)

Rachel: (To Phoebe.) Oh my God! We have to throw her a shower?!

("The One with Ross and Monica's Cousin," 719)[1]

More elaborate white lies are also common on *Friends*, such as the verbal and nonverbal efforts made by the others throughout an entire episode to conceal from Rachel that the layered dessert she has made (one of her first cooking efforts) tasted truly awful because she had mistakenly combined two recipes ("The One Where Ross Got High," 609). The rationale behind the lie appears to be that nothing would have been gained by telling Rachel how terrible her dessert actually tasted. Such lies often provide a basis for humor throughout an entire episode.

The group not only tells white lies on a regular basis, but is aware that they are a common feature of their interactions with others. The following dialogue, which takes place among the Friends after Phoebe has returned from an unsuccessful date, reflects this understanding:

Phoebe: He walked me to the subway and said, "We should do this again!"

All: Ohh. Ouch.

Rachel: What? He said, "We should do it again," that's good, right?

Monica: Uh, no. Loosely translated "We should do this again" means "You will never see me naked."

Rachel: Since when?

Joey: Since always. It's like dating language. Y'know, like "It's not you" means "It is you."

Chandler: Or "You're such a nice guy" means "I'm gonna be dating leather-wearing alcoholics and complaining about them to you."

Phoebe: Or, or, y'know, um, "I think we should see other people" means "Ha, ha, I already am."

Rachel: And everybody knows this?

Joey: Yeah. Cushions the blow.

Chandler: Yeah, it's like when you're a kid and your parents put your dog to sleep, and they tell you it went off to live on some farm.

("The One with the Thumb," 103)

The above exchange not only suggests that the Friends are familiar with and have participated in such white lies, but that they see them as performing a necessary social function ("cushioning the blow"), even when the lied-to party is likely to realize or later discover the truth.

Two widespread and long-running white lies have been told by the Friends throughout the ten-year run of the show. The Friends lie regularly to spare Phoebe the ugly truth that she doesn't sing well, that her songs are sometimes amusing but memorable only for their strangeness (can anyone who has heard it forget "Smelly Cat"?), and that her guitar playing is mediocre at best. The Friends also lie to Joey about the quality of his acting projects, rolling their eyes or grimacing to each other, only to tell him some face-saving lie. While it can be argued such long-running lies spare Phoebe and Joey a hurtful truth, when the issues are central to the person's sense of self, as Phoebe's musical ability and Joey's acting seem to be, such excuses seem to beg a larger question. How would Phoebe or Joey react if they were made aware of the group's conspiratorial lie? Would they feel betrayed? Or humiliated? They have in a sense been made the butt of a joke of which they are not aware. The group, however, seems to accept and agree upon the need for these lies and at times even treats them as evidence of caring for each other. While Phoebe lies about Joey's acting, Joey takes part in the deception about Phoebe's music.

Lies to Protect the Lied-to Person or Another Friend

Some lies told by the characters of *Friends* appear to be motivated by a sense of loyalty to the person lied to or to protect another one of the Friends. Season 5 included a storyline that mandated lies by most of the characters. A series of lies was told among the Friends to conceal the fact that Monica and Chandler had begun a romantic relationship. While Monica and Chandler cover up their relationship from the beginning with multiple lies to the others (lies more appropriately considered as lies to protect oneself), the lying to protect others begins when Joey finds out about the relationship and is then convinced by Monica and Chandler to lie to the others. In spite of his reluctance and his unease about the deception, Joey does his best to keep the relationship between his two friends secret from the others ("The One with All the Kips," 505).

Slowly, each of the others finds out the truth and each is enlisted in the cover-up until only Ross is unaware of the growing romance between the two. Despite the multiple and lengthy series of lies told among the Friends, when the romance is finally known, other than a few playful jabs at one another, all is forgiven in the celebration of their happiness for Monica and Chandler or, as is the case when Ross discovers the truth, the deception is viewed as an act of concern for the person lied to:

> Ross: (Upset, to Chandler.) I thought you were my best friend, this is my sister! My best friend and my sister! I—I cannot believe this!
>
> Chandler: Look, we're not just messing around! I love her. Okay, I'm in love with her.
>
> Monica: I'm so sorry that you had to find out this way. I'm sorry, but it's true, I love him too.
>
> (There's a brief pause.)
>
> Ross: (Happily.) My best friend and my sister! I cannot believe this. (He hugs them both.) (To Joey and Rachel.) You guys probably wanna get some hugs in too, huh? Big news!
>
> Rachel: Awww, no, it's okay, we've actually known for a while.
>
> (There's another pause as Ross gets angry again.)
>
> Ross: What? What? What?! You guys knew? (Joey and Rachel back up against the door.) You all knew and you didn't tell me?!!

Rachel: Well, Ross, we were worried about you. We didn't know how you were going to react.

(Pause.)

Ross: (Happily again.) You were worried about me? You didn't know how I was going to react? (He hugs them both.)

("The One Where Everyone Finds Out," 514)

Similarly, when Phoebe deceives Joey by pretending to be her identical twin sister Ursula in order to tell him bad news Ursula is unwilling to tell him and the ruse is discovered, Joey is touched by Phoebe's show of concern for him ("The One with Two Parts," part 2, 117).

The Friends lie not only out of concern for each other, but also to protect their own dignity. When Ross tries unsuccessfully to convince Rachel and Joey that he is "fine" with them seeing each other, he defends his pretense by saying that he wants to be fine with their dating and will be eventually ("The One Where Ross Is Fine," 1002).

Lies about serious matters among the Friends are, however, relatively infrequent—and dialogue in the show at times even seems to openly discourage deception, although the basis for disapproval seems somewhat unclear. In one instance what begins for Chandler as a deception to protect Joey turns into a lie to protect himself when Chandler finds that he is very attracted to Kathy, a girl Joey is dating. Chandler deceives Joey into believing that he dislikes Kathy and would rather not be around her. As the storyline progresses and Chandler finds out that Kathy is also attracted to him, they kiss several times. When Chandler tells the other Friends what has transpired, they urge him to tell Joey the truth, while also warning him that Joey will be angry:

Chandler: No. Is there any way, any way you think he'll understand this?

Ross: No the—the sad thing is, if you had told him how you felt before you kissed her, knowing Joey, he probably just would've just stepped aside.

Chandler: Oh, don't say that! Don't say that. That's not true. Is it?

Phoebe: I think maybe, yeah.

Monica: He loves you.

Chandler: Then why didn't you tell me to do that?!!

Ross: Well, I said—I said something to Phoebe.

Phoebe: Yeah! No, that's right. And I thought it was a really good idea.

Rachel: I know, I remember that!

Monica: I remember you did.

Chandler: God!! (Sits down in disgust.) What am I gonna do?!

Rachel: Well, Chandler, you're gonna have to tell him.

Chandler: Why?! Why do I have to tell him?!

Rachel: Because you do.

Chandler: Yeah, I know.

("The One Where Chandler Crosses the Line," 407)

The prediction by the Friends that Joey would have understood earlier, but following the deception will be very angry, is proved accurate when Chandler finally owns up to his feelings for and actions with Kathy to Joey. The basis for Joey's feelings of betrayal are unclear, however. The principles involved are simply treated as a metaphorical line:

Chandler: You're right, I have no excuses! I was totally over the line.

Joey: Over the line?! You—you're—you're so far past the line that you—you can't even see the line! The line is a dot to you!

The storyline is pursued into the next episode, in which Joey threatens to move out of their apartment because of Chandler's betrayal, which is characterized as not knowing "what it is to be a friend." The friendship is redeemed, however, when Chandler agrees to do penance by living in a box. Interestingly, Joey does not feel betrayed by Kathy, and when she arrives to talk with Chandler, to tell him she doesn't want to destroy his friendship with Joey, Joey relents, the friendship is saved, and everyone is happy again.

The "line" that Chandler crossed in pursuing the relationship with Kathy seems to be less that of deceiving a friend than not receiving Joey's permission to pursue the relationship with Kathy. When viewing the show across the span of its existence, an involved set of ethical guidelines about beginning romantic or sexual relationships with the past or present romantic partners or family members of other friends emerges. When Ross kisses Chandler's mother, or Chandler becomes involved with one of Joey's sisters, or Ross is attracted to Joey's girlfriend Charlie, or Rachel and Joey want to begin seeing each other, while the initial reaction is to lie in order to stay out of trouble, ultimately the ethical guidelines that involve seeking permission are enacted. It is likely that this code of ethics, rather than one about deception, is the basis for Joey and the other Friends judging Chandler's behavior with Kathy as terribly wrong.

Lies to Protect Themselves or Advance Their Own Self-Interest

Occasionally, the characters lie to their friends in order to protect themselves. When they do, however, the lies tend to be very short-lived and without apparent relational consequences. Some such lies are deemed so transparent and of so little consequence that they aren't even addressed. When Joey lies about his pet duck being sick all over the apartment that he and Rachel share and insists it was *not* because the duck ate her face cream, no one even bothers to dispute his claims ("The One with Rachel's Book," 702).

More typical of the lies told for self-protection is an instance in which Chandler and Joey babysit Ross's son Ben and inadvertently leave Ben alone on a bus. Their attempts to deceive Ross about the afternoon's events are quickly discovered and, despite the potential seriousness of the situation, not brought up in subsequent episodes ("The One with the Baby on the Bus," 206). In a similar vein, when Chandler lies to Joey about having viewed an audition videotape Joey has prepared, Joey discovers the lie when Chandler never says anything about the Japanese "Ichiban: Lipstick for Men" that is the topic of the tape. Before the end of the show, as penance, Joey requires Chandler to declare before the others while wearing the lipstick that "Lying is wrong" and that "I'm a pretty little girl" ("The One with Ross's Grant," 1006). With that bit of humiliation and humor, all is forgiven and forgotten.

The majority of examples of Friends lying to Friends involve lying to protect themselves, although there are also several examples of lies to gain small advantages. Some of these might more appropriately be considered white lies about insignificant matters. For example, Rachel lies to Phoebe about where she bought the apothecary table ("The One with the Apothecary Table," 611) in order to be able to keep it. Like most lies on the show (other than some of the long-running white lies), these lies tend to be found out very quickly and seem to be understood by the person to whom the lie is told. In the instance of the apothecary table, Rachel actually becomes complicit with Phoebe so that each can get what she wants:

> Rachel: Okay! Okay-okay, look—no I did, I just wanted this stuff and I know how you feel about Pottery Barn. Just ... Come on, don't be mad.
>
> Phoebe: No-no-no, but I am mad! I am mad! Because this stuff is everything that is wrong with the world! And it's all sitting up in my living room and all I can think about is how I don't have that lamp!
>
> Rachel: Well, then, honey, buy the lamp! Hey, we have that sixty bucks from Ross.
>
> Phoebe: I can't! I can't! Unless ... Well, are you saying that—that you would move out if—if I didn't buy that lamp?
>
> Rachel: What?! No! I'm not gonna move out!
>
> Phoebe: But are you saying that you would move out if I didn't buy that lamp?
>
> Rachel: (Gets it.) Oh. Yes! I would so move out!
>
> Phoebe: Okay, then I don't have a choice! I have to buy that lamp.
>
> ("The One with the Apothecary Table," 611)

Lies that don't appear to seriously harm anyone and yet gain an advantage for a Friend are acceptable among the group.

But even lies that harm the others seem to be quickly forgotten and seem to have no relational consequences. For instance, when

Ross's lie to an attractive young woman that he is a masseur results in Phoebe losing a client and eighty dollars a week of income,
after a failed attempt to shift the blame to Phoebe for not canceling
the appointment, a quick "Oh, you're right, you're right. I'm sorry"
fixes the situation. The confusing situation is made comprehensible
and acceptable to Joey, who has been witnessing the exchange,
with the quick explanation that an attractive woman was involved,
to which Joey replies simply "Gotcha" ("The One with Monica's
Book," 702).

In contrast, the Friends seem to see little wrong with lying to
others outside their tight-knit circle of friends, whatever their motivations. Lies to others are far more frequent than among the six
main characters, and the liar is not generally discouraged from or
disparaged for that kind of lying by the others. When Chandler
lies and says that he is moving to Yemen rather than trying once
again to break off his on-again, off-again romance with Janice, the
Friends do not openly participate in the lie, but neither are they
much bothered by it, since although all of them know Janice, none
of them really likes her ("The One with All the Rugby," 415). In just
one episode, Rachel tells a number of lies at her workplace ("The
One with the Engagement Picture," 704). She lies to her new assistant when she takes his picture and then tells him that the human
resources department requires it. She lies to a coworker by saying
that her assistant is gay in order to discourage the coworker's romantic interest in him, and when her assistant asks her about her
comments about him being gay, she lies to protect her earlier lie. All
of this without regard for how it may impact her relationships with
her coworkers.

Lies to strangers occur with great regularity. Joey and Chandler
lie about their being Ben's father to the autotransit guy to regain
custody of the baby ("The One with the Baby on the Bus," 206).
And the two men regularly lie to try and pick up women (for example, "The One with Joey's Porsche," 605). Monica lies about her
age to her younger lover ("The One with the Ick Factor," 122), and
everyone seems to lie to their parents and has been doing so for
years (for example, "The One Where Ross Got High," 609). All of
these lies seem quite easily accepted, although not always deemed
wise, by the other Friends.

For example, after Rachel, who has no medical insurance, sprains her ankle, she convinces a reluctant Monica to lie to the hospital so that she might use Monica's insurance program ("The One with Two Parts," part 2, 117). Although the two women do eventually correct the lie by filling out a new hospital form with accurate information, it is the complications that arise and the fear of getting in trouble that motivate them to abandon the lie.

The exception to the Friends' seemingly wanton disregard for the truth when dealing with strangers, and perhaps an indication that the characters are maturing, occurs in the final season, when Chandler and Monica are looking to adopt a baby ("The One with the Birth Mother," 1009). The adoption agency has mixed up Chandler and Monica's file with another couple's, and the birth mother, who is interviewing them as prospective parents for her child, mistakenly believes that Chandler is a doctor and Monica a reverend. When during the interview Chandler and Monica realize the mix-up, Monica, desperate to be chosen by the young woman, pretends that she is indeed the reverend the young woman believes her to be and nonverbally persuades Chandler to go along with the pretense. Later, when they are alone, Chandler argues that the lie "is wrong" because the decision the young woman faces, to choose parents for her baby, is a momentous one. Although Monica asserts that they would make great parents and therefore the child wouldn't be harmed by the lie, she eventually succumbs to Chandler's pressure. When Chandler reveals the truth to the young woman, she is furious that they have lied to her, but is eventually persuaded to give them her child.

The Patterns and Underlying Principles
about Lying in *Friends*

Lying is a fairly regular and recurring pattern of communication with the six main characters in *Friends*. White lies and lies to protect one of the group or to make relationships easier are not only deemed reasonable and acceptable within the group, but are sometimes viewed as evidence of their shared friendship and commitment to each other. Because such lies are attributed to a desire to make social interaction more pleasant or to spare someone's feelings, the lies do not appear to be seen as character deficits or to predict the Friends' behavior or honesty in other more critical situations. When such lies backfire, the fault is assigned to lying poorly or misjudging the chances the lie will be discovered.

The attitude toward lies to protect oneself or to advance one's own interests is more ambiguous. In the instances in which Friends lie to each other to protect themselves, it is typically in an instance in which the lie is covering up an earlier mistake or instance of bad judgment by the liar. When other Friends become upset with the liar, it is difficult to determine if it is the lie or the earlier mistake or act of bad judgment that is giving offense. Is Joey upset with Chandler because he kissed Kathy or because he had earlier deceived Joey about his feelings for her? Is Ross upset with Chandler and Joey because they tried to deceive him about what had happened with Ben or because they left Ben on the bus in the first place? Since both of the earlier acts (kissing a friend's girlfriend and leaving someone's baby alone on a public bus) could reasonably be considered grievous acts in their own right, it is not clear that the attempts to obscure the truth about them is a significant source of anger for the aggrieved or a part of their feeling wronged. The desire to protect oneself from the consequences of an earlier mistake appears to be understandable to the Friends and isn't necessarily seen as a character flaw or moral weakness.

When the lies among the Friends are about gaining an advantage, the lies are typically about relatively inconsequential matters (such as a table), and when the situation is understood by the lied-to person, the lies are not problematic in terms of the relationship. The rationale for such lies generally comes in some form of "I didn't think it would hurt anyone." As a result, since the liar did not intend to harm, there is not only a kind of understanding but a kind of acceptance. There is even a sense of "I'll agree to accept your petty, self-serving lies, if you'll support mine. After all, we all want what we want."

In the instances in which the Friends lie to people outside their circle, whether strangers, acquaintances, or parents, lying is accepted as a fact of life, if not condoned as always wise. Moral considerations are not part of deciding the issue. Instead, the decision of whether or not to lie is based on strictly pragmatic grounds. Is a lie the easiest way to get what we want? Is the lie believable? Will we be in serious trouble if we are discovered in the lie? The storylines that hinge on such lies appear to assume that no one will be seriously harmed by the lie. Monica is reluctant to lie to the hospital, because she fears the legal consequences if they are found out, not because she finds the lie morally wrong. She and Rachel eventually abandon the lie because of the complications it creates. Similarly, Chandler's inability to fire one of his staff and the subsequent lies to her and to his supervisor are a source of amusement among the Friends because of the complications that arise ("The One with Two Parts," part 1, 116). And when in season 6 Ross begins dating a student of his, which could cause him to be fired, while none of the Friends thinks the relationship is a wise one, no one condemns his attempts to deceive others at the university. Monica's lie about her age to a younger boyfriend is derided not because the others think it is wrong, but because they think it is an unbelievable lie. When Chandler and Phoebe lie and say that Phoebe is Chandler's dying fiancée in order to retrieve from another couple the engagement ring Chandler has chosen for Monica, neither is bothered by the deception; they are simply thrilled that they have regained the ring ("The One with the Ring," 623). Sometimes it is even agreed upon among the Friends that a lie is the only solution to a problem, as when Chandler and Joey lie to Chandler's new roommate, Eddie, who they are trying to oust from the apartment so Joey can move back in ("The One Where Eddie Won't Go," 219). Moral considerations or a sense of ethical responsibility to those outside the circle of Friends do not generally appear to be concerns.

The exception to this general pattern of lying to those outside their small circle remains the instance in which Monica and Chandler decide not to continue their lie to the woman looking to place her child in an adoptive home, although Monica's first instinct was to lie to get the child she wanted. When talking with Monica later, Chandler clearly calls upon their ethical responsibility to the young woman. He argues to Monica that lying would be wrong because of the serious nature of the decision the young woman is facing and rejects Monica's counterargument that the child would still have a good home, even if not exactly the kind of parents the young woman imagines. Have the characters, by the middle of season 10, matured ethically? Or are there situations serious enough to cause the characters to rethink their general position of lying as acceptable if no obvious harm is done? Or did the writers believe that the characters of Monica and Chandler might be seen as unsympathetic if they had maintained their lie to a young woman in such a situation simply to get what they desired? Perhaps because during the interview scene they talked at length with the woman and were able to see her dreams and aspirations for the child, Monica and Chandler were able to see her as a person, and hence to imagine an ethical responsibility to her.

When the Friends are lied to by others outside the group, however, they are often offended by the lack of truthfulness. Monica is upset when she finds out that the younger boyfriend she has lied to about her age has deceived her and is actually a senior in high school, not college. She is also teased at great length by the others for being so gullible as to not see through his lies. Chandler is offended when, despite their friendly behavior toward him, he finds out that the staff members he supervises do not like him and make fun of him behind his back ("The One with the Ick Factor," 122). Monica and Chandler are offended when they find out that Janine, one of Joey's girlfriends, has lied about liking them and enjoying their company, while seeming to understand that Joey lied to them about it to spare their feelings:

Chandler: So she was just pretending to have a good time last night? She was lying to our faces?!

Monica: Ugh, I cannot believe this! I mean, who is she to judge us? We could not have been nicer to her!

Chandler: And I am not blah, I am a hoot!

Joey: I know! I know! Come on, please—please, you guys, don't—don't be mad. I'm sure she just—she just said that stuff because she was nervous and you guys are like my best friends! Y'know? And it was our first date! Plus, she's really sick!

Chandler: No, you sh—No you said you made that up!!

Joey: I know, but don't you think the sick thing is way better than the play thing?

Chandler: Eh, they're both good. I generally just go with, Monica's drunk again.

("The One with the Apothecary Table," 611)

The above dialogue not only illustrates Monica and Chandler's anger at being lied to by Janine, but, with the final comments between Joey and Chandler, makes it apparent that both men regularly and consciously employ the same covering lies that have so upset Monica and Chandler when told to them. In Joey's attempts to persuade Monica and Chandler to give Janine one more chance, Joey not only tries to excuse her behavior by explaining that she was nervous about meeting them, but even reminds the pair that they "owe him" for the lies he told when he initially covered their budding romance—a kind of "lie tolerance exchange." His appeal to them, however, is not based upon the moral compromises required of him to support the deception but that he "looked like an idiot!" and was "humiliated."

When You Lie with *Friends*

There are few negative consequences for the six main characters of *Friends* when they lie, regardless of the person to whom they lie or their motivation in doing so. The lies among the Friends, like those on other situation comedies, are often played for laughs and often appear more amusing than hurtful. Additionally, when the lies are typically disclosed or discovered within the same half-hour episode, the lied-to person is almost never, unlike in real life, put in a position of acting or making decisions based upon the deception. Similarly, when we consider the lies the Friends tell to those outside their circle, we never see negative consequences for the people to whom they have lied. In many instances the people to whom they have lied are strangers with whom the Friends will have no future contact, and so the harm done by the lie would not be knowable to the liar. In contexts in which the Friend is likely to have an ongoing relationship with the lied-to person, as at Rachel's place of work,

the impact of multiple deceptions on the reputation and relationships of the Friend are simply not revealed on the show.

The harms that ethicists like Sissela Bok suggest always come
from telling lies, even the most innocuous ones, are not typically
evidenced in the show. Bok (1978) argues that lies always harm
the liar, diminish the level of trust in relationships, and harm
"the general level of trust and social cooperation" in a society (p.
24). We might easily imagine a friend, acquaintance, or coworker
who lied with the regularity of the characters on *Friends* gaining
a reputation for untruthfulness, resulting in our reduced trust in
or respect for the individual. With *Friends*, however, there is no
evidence that the main characters lose credibility with each other
or respect each other less, even though they know of the lies each
has told.

In one instance, notable for its distinctiveness, Joey seems to
briefly recognize his friends' lack of veracity. After Chandler and
Monica have agreed to allow Phoebe to play guitar and sing at their
wedding, he comments, "Yeah! Well, I think we'll see if they actually let you play. Huh? I mean they tell you anything you want to
hear like—like, 'You look nineteen,' and then they just take it away
like—like, 'No you don't'" ("The One with Monica's Thunder," 701).
The price to be paid for regularly lying to the Friends is, however,
fairly low, since Phoebe is reassured when Chandler gives her a
one-dollar deposit to symbolize his and Monica's serious intention
to have her as their wedding singer and Joey never again shows a
lack of faith in his friends' honesty. In actual lived relationships,
regaining our reputation for honesty or the trust of our relationship
partners is seldom accomplished with so little effort.

Not only do the Friends seem to trust in each other despite their
regularly lying to each other, they also seem to maintain their individual sense of themselves as honest and truthful people and good
friends. In an early episode, in which Phoebe is about to tell Rachel
that Paolo has made a pass at her, Phoebe attempts to establish her
credibility by saying, "Ok, um, [clears throat] we haven't known
each other for that long a time, and, um, there are three things that
you should know about me. One, my friends are the most important
thing in my life, two, I never lie, and three, I make the best oatmeal

raisin cookies in the world" ("The One with the Dozen Lasagnas," 112). Phoebe then opens a tin and offers Rachel a cookie. Phoebe's truthfulness is confirmed for Rachel when after tasting the cookies she decides Phoebe's oatmeal raisin cookies are indeed the best in the world (and hence Phoebe has not lied) and Rachel, therefore, must accept Phoebe's version of the encounter with Paolo.

Because the episode occurs so early in the history of the show, one might argue that Phoebe's lying ways as a character have not been fully developed or even decided upon by the writers. More likely, however, is that the character, as with many people, does not see herself as being a liar, despite the untruths she tells. Phoebe, like many people, may not see her lies as "real lies" that hurt or harm others, especially since her lies are generally intended to protect others and she is allowed to ignore or avoid the harms caused by her more self-serving lies. The other Friends similarly seem to see themselves as good friends and honest people. Liars, however, are seldom the best judges of the harm done by their lies.

There is throughout the show no sense that the Friends recognize that they may be contributing to a general social breakdown by lying to others outside their circle. The Friends see their lies as expedient or convenient, without considering that the lied-to stranger or acquaintance may be more suspicious, less cooperative, and even less honest with others as a result of their experiences with the Friends. Only with the young woman screening prospective adoptive parents do the characters reflect upon the impact of their lies on others. Furthermore, the characters accept—if perhaps at times resent—that others may not always be honest with them.

There seems to reign within the world of *Friends* an ethic that tolerates lies, especially when they are seen as justified or deemed excusable. Among the Friends themselves, good intentions are an acceptable reason for a lie, but, barring these, an understandable need to protect oneself or a desire to gain an insignificant advantage also justifies deception. The Friends must explain to Ross that they were trying to protect him by not telling him about Chandler and Monica's romance, but once this is known, Ross is appreciative of their good intentions. Chandler and Joey are not held morally responsible for their deception about leaving Ben on the bus, because

Ross would be angry with them and lying to avoid his anger appears to be excusable. And although Rachel begins to apologize to Phoebe about lying to her about the apothecary table coming from Pottery Barn, her explanation makes the lie acceptable, particularly if she will participate in the lie necessary to allow Phoebe to buy the lamp she wants.

Even when the Friends are lied to by others outside their group, while initially upset by the deceptions, the offended Friend is calmed when excuses or justifications are provided. Chandler comes to see that subordinates are bound to deceive their boss about their feelings about him or her. Monica and Chandler begin to understand that someone who is nervous or ill might lie about her feelings. Monica comes to realize that a man wanting to sleep with her would deceive her and that perhaps she even bears a responsibility to expect and be on guard for such deception.

This general tolerance on *Friends* for lying is difficult to understand, however, when we consider what Bok (1978) argues are typically different perspectives taken by the liar and the lied to. She suggests that what will often serve as "good reasons" for the liar or for those unaffected by the lie are seldom deemed so by the one deceived:

> Liars find the moral claims that their lies will be beneficial, perhaps prevent harm, or support fairness or prior obligation, much more persuasive than do those lied to or those not directly affected. Liars are quicker to argue that honesty will hurt them in practices where "everybody cheats"; they are more easily convinced that a lie which benefits them will harm no one else; and their concern for the effect of deceit on their own character and practices is minimal. (p. 87)

In contrast to the reasonableness of lies when looked at from a liar's perspective, if we are the lied to we may not feel so sanguine.

The depiction within *Friends* of the characters' tolerance for lies, as well as the lack of significant harms resulting from deceptions, can in part be explained by the context in which they occur. *Friends* is after all a situation comedy. As in all situation comedies, lies, their detection, or the complications flowing from them can provide humorous moments and entertaining storylines. Showing characters struggling with moral dilemmas, portraying the damage done to friendships, or focusing on other injurious consequences resulting from lying would not generally be amusing. Similarly, in that the primary characters need to continue to be likable enough for viewers to care about or identify with them and that the premise of the show requires ongoing relationships among the characters, the writers are not likely to develop storylines that hold the characters responsible for their lies in ways that show them in a bad light or that create irreparable breaches in the relationships. Additionally, as fictional characters, the betrayal, disappointment, or injury actual humans might feel when lied to can simply go unrepresented as the writers create the scripts if such developments are not humorous or do not further the desired storyline.

An additional and not necessarily mutually exclusive explanation for the pattern of lies observed in *Friends* also presents itself. Does the general tolerance of deception shown on *Friends* represent an ethic of acceptable lies within the culture? Does the popularity of its characters and the long-running nature of the show suggest that an ethic has become widely accepted that tolerates lies when we are not the one lied to or when there are good excuses or justifications offered, explicitly or implicitly, or when there is not demonstrable harm caused by the deception? Has the segment of the population represented by the fans of *Friends*, or perhaps have we as a culture generally, become more comfortable with the perspective of the liar than that of the lied to? Certainly such a perspective is easier in many ways; it is less moralizing and more convenient. Such a perspective allows us to avoid judging others, and, we can hope, allows others to similarly avoid judging us. It also provides a position from which we can pursue our own interests more easily than one that holds us responsible for the societal harms of our actions. In circumstances in which we do not know the other or in which we believe we have justification or do not believe there will be significant harm, we can lie, even to our friends, with less fear of the consequences.

Adopting a tolerance for lies within real-life friendships is not likely, however, to be without long-term consequences for the relationships and the individuals involved. Unlike the friendships of the situation comedy, actual lived relationships are likely to be battered by regular patterns of lies. Without script writers to forget, minimize, and overlook the deceptions, the foundation of trust on which friendships are built and maintained is bound to be eroded by regular convenient or protective lies among friends. As Bok (1978) suggests, if we cannot have confidence in the veracity of our friends, how can we trust in their fairness or their intentions?

An examination of the patterns of deception and a consideration of the underlying belief system in one popular culture artifact, such as *Friends*, can raise intriguing questions but provides few clear or definitive answers. Examining other related texts, such as HBO's *Sex in the City* or ABC's *Home Improvement*, and considering similar texts from another era, such as *I Love Lucy*, might reveal if *Friends* is an anomaly in its representation of deception or whether it represents a shift in popular culture's depiction of deception. Certainly deceptions are a staple in situation comedies. Lucy lied regularly and often drew Ethel into her lies in *I Love Lucy*, and Tim in *Home Improvement* frequently tried to escape trouble through lying. I suspect, however, that in these shows the characters who habitually turned to deception were the exception among the cast of characters in their shows. In addition, I believe the veracity of the characters who lied with regularity was often called into question as a result of their lying ways. What strikes me as new in *Friends* is the general acceptance and pervasiveness of deception among the characters and the lack of harms incurred from lying. Additional research would help confirm or disconfirm my suspicions.

If the patterns of deception I've outlined within *Friends* represents a change within situation comedies, as I suspect, is the tolerance of lies detected within *Friends* related to a growing tolerance of "bad behavior" within popular culture generally—for example, within music videos, among sports stars, or in the public behavior of celebrities? Or does the pattern of lies observed in *Friends* suggest an even larger cultural shift? Have we as a society come to tolerate and even expect deceptions from friends, acquaintances, and strangers within our everyday lives? If such a tolerance of lies characterizes our personal lives, how can our reputations and relationships survive if we have as little regard for truthfulness as do Monica, Phoebe, Rachel, Joey, Ross, and Chandler? Bok's contention that all lies harm the liar, the level of a trust within a relationship, and the trust within the society generally suggests that the topic of the representation of deception in popular culture is worthy of further exploration. Such exploration may offer insight into the popular culture that surrounds us every day and may provide provocative discussions about truth and deception in our everyday relationships.

Note

1. In identifying particular episodes of *Friends*, I am following a format begun by others. The official title of each episode, as named by NBC, begins with the phrase "The One." The three- or four-digit number following the title identifies the season in which the episode appeared as well as the number of the episode in that season. For example, "The One with Monica's Thunder," 701, appeared during the seventh season and was the first episode of that season. While I have watched all of the episodes noted in this paper and have taken notes and transcribed dialogue from them, I have also relied on the following websites to determine episode names and for episode guides and transcripts of the shows: www.thecfsi.com/home.htm, www.angelfire.com/tv/chocgal/, www.nbc.com/Friends/index.html, and www. tvtome.com/Friends/.

References

Bauder, D. (2004). NBC tones down *Friends* praise in ads. Cincinnati.com— Cincinnati Enquirer/Post, January 24. Accessed February 11 from http://customwire.ap.org/dyanc/stories/T/TV_FRIENDS_PRAISE?SITE.

Bok, S. (1978). *Lying: Moral choice in public and private lives*. New York: Quartet Books.

Cantor, P. A. (2001). The art in the popular. *Wilson Quarterly* (summer): 26–39.

Davis, K. E., & M. Todd. (1985). Assessing friendship: Prototypes, paradigm cases and relationship description. In S. W. Duck & D. Perlman (eds.), *Understanding personal relationships*. London: Sage.

Deetz, S. (1990). Reclaiming the subject matter as a guide to mutual understanding: Effectiveness and ethics in interpersonal interaction. *Communication Quarterly* 38: 226–43.

DePaulo, B. (1985). On a study in which participants kept a daily diary of lies. *New York Times*, February 12, A8.

Duck, S. (1991). *Understanding relationships*. New York: Guilford.

Hardwig, J. (2002). In search of an ethic of personal relationships. In J. Steward (ed.), *Bridges not walls: A book about interpersonal communication*, 8th ed. (pp. 338–47). Madison, WI: McGraw-Hill.

Hobfoll, S. E., & J. P. Stokes. (1988). The process and mechanics of social support. In S. W. Duck (ed.), with D. F. Hay, S. E. Hobfoll, W. Ickes, & B. Montgomery, *Handbook of personal relationships*. Chichester: Wiley.

McBride, M. C. (2003). More than just "I'm sorry": The ethic of forgiveness between *Friends*. Paper presented at the National Communication Association Convention, Miami, FL.

McCornack, S. A., & T. R. Levin. (1990). When lies are uncovered: Emotional and relational outcomes of discovered deception. *Communication Monographs* 57: 117–38.

Miller, G. R., & J. B. Stiff. (1993). *Deceptive communication*. London: Sage.

Ryan, J. (2002). NBC's *Friends* can't beat CBS. *E Online*, October 1. Accessed February 9 from www.eonline.com.

Walker, R. (2002). How *Friends* wins advertising friends. *Slate*, October 9. Accessed February 9 from http://slate.msn.com.

Weiss, R. S. (1974). The provisions of social relationships. In Z. Rubin (ed.), *Doing unto others*. Englewood Cliffs, NJ: Prentice-Hall.

CHAPTER TWELVE

You Are Forgiven: Interpersonal and Familial Ethics in the Films of Wes Anderson

Greg Carlson

In the grade school, high school, and college classroom, cinema and other forms of popular culture often provide teachers with a dynamic and commanding context in which meaningful discussion of communication ethics can be situated. E. O. Marshall (2003) argues effectively that popular films can be appropriately and valuably integrated into the classroom as a resource for teaching about ethics and morals. Morals, ethics, and a focus on both virtuous and malevolent characters form the heart of storytelling thematics, and debates about the effects of too much violence on young television viewers, for example, continue to capture headlines in the mainstream press. Joseph H. Kupfer (1999) explains:

> Interest in the virtues has never really been far from the thoughts of mass audiences whenever they read novels, watched plays, or viewed movies. Narrative arts have always emphasized the character of their characters, whether the protagonist be a Scrooge, or a Ulysses, an Othello, or a Huck Finn. Audiences, elite and popular, are drawn to questions of virtue and vice perhaps because so much of our own welfare depends on our own character and because we prosper and suffer at the hands of other people on account of their moral traits. (p. 25)

Because the nature of all dramatic arts requires some kind of conflict, whether it be internal or external, cinema provides a wealth of examples that readily demonstrate ethical issues, including archetypal struggles such as good versus evil and the construction of character.

Good versus evil is a mainstay motif of several genres of film, including the western, the crime/gangster film, the war or combat film, and the science fiction and fantasy film. Wildly popular film franchises such as *Star Wars*, *The Lord of the Rings*, *The Matrix*, and *Harry Potter* construct detailed and elaborate universes with dozens of major characters and even specially designed "sciences" that govern the physics and metaphysics of the worlds co-constructed by the authors, moviemakers, and fans and consumers who participate in the spin-off cultures that include fiction and fan-written fiction, video games, customizable card games, and toys.

Movie director and critic Peter Bogdanovich makes an argument that Hollywood filmmaking has historically enshrined the outlaw and the criminal by fetishizing the brutal gun violence that attends the western and gangster genres (Valenti, 2000, p. x). While it is certainly not a new idea to make the claim that cinema is a sensationalist medium, or that it contributes to the moral decay of society, the vast majority of immoral characters "pay for their crimes" with their lives, reinforcing the notion that wicked behavior will ultimately be punished. Bogdanovich writes that

> glorification of gangsters and outlaws is virtually a Hollywood tradition, from James Cagney as *The Public Enemy* or Edward G. Robinson as *Little Caesar* to Humphrey Bogart in *High Sierra* to Warren Beatty and Faye Dunaway as *Bonnie & Clyde*. Indeed, the brutal slow-motion massacre of Bonnie and Clyde was the ultimate (and much imitated) antiauthoritarian deification. (Valenti, 2000, p. x)

What Bogdanovich does not include, however, is an acknowledgment that the characters he references all pay the ultimate penalty for their moral and ethical transgressions: Cagney's Tom Powers, after he has apparently decided to reform, is kidnapped and murdered by a rival gang; Robinson's Enrico Bandello dies in a hail of police gunfire; Bogart's Roy Earle is picked off by a sharpshooter. Bonnie and Clyde, as well as the other gangster characters, might all be depicted as heroes (or anti-heroes), but the underlying moral implication remains clear and well-standardized: crime does not pay.

Film can be a tremendously effective setting for the consideration of morals and ethics. Keith Tester (1994) argues, "It is through the media that individuals become aware of some of their moral duties towards others" (p. 83). Tester even goes on to suggest that the media actually create moral concerns and issues. Arguably, because narrative, feature-length cinema relies on the literary conventions of conflict and resolution, the stories and characters depicted in popular cinema tend to reflect the concerns of the social communities they describe. For millions of people who consume television and film, the fictional plot arcs offer strong indications of right and wrong, and model scenarios in which good is rewarded and evil is punished. Truly subversive or antisocial features are rare; even movies that depict "bad" characters getting away with murder, theft, or other crimes tend to emphasize isolation, ostracism, madness, or other negative results of having to live with what has been done. Overwhelmingly, however, characters who participate in immoral behavior, whether it be a white lie or a capital offense, reveal their transgression in a public manner, and moral order and balance is restored to the universe.

Filmmaker Wes Anderson's Artistic Orientation

Filmmaker Wes Anderson dramatizes the interpersonal and familial relationships of unique and unorthodox characters for a sophisticated audience. Among Anderson's creations are individuals who manage and negotiate deceitfulness and deception while ironically maintaining sets of deeply moral behaviors. In all three of his feature films, *Bottle Rocket*, *Rushmore*, and *The Royal Tenenbaums*, Anderson focuses his attention on central characters who lie, cheat, steal, and in some cases intend to become criminals as a "career choice." These characters, however, are also possessed of highly regulated, self-monitored codes of ethics, and are typically kind-hearted, well-meaning, and motivated by desires to achieve and maintain positive recognition for certain responsibilities like fatherhood, friendship, and romantic love. Anderson's characters are also articulate and communicative, and hopeful and needful of acceptance and forgiveness when they have been caught in duplicity. An exploration of honesty and dishonesty in Anderson's characters will illuminate some of the ways in which filmmakers create nuanced portraits of ethical choicemaking and behavior.

Wes Anderson belongs to the tradition of filmmaking that places importance on directors as singular visionaries creatively and artistically responsible for their movies. With only three feature films to his credit, Anderson has already achieved noteworthy critical acclaim, and, as indicated by the entry devoted to him in *Current Biography*, has won accolades such as "Debut of the Year" from the Lone Star Film and Television Awards, the "New Generation" award from the Los Angeles Film Critics Association, "Best New Filmmaker" from the MTV Movie Awards, and "Best Director" from the Independent Spirit Awards. Along with his cowriter Owen Wilson, Anderson has also been nominated for "Best Screenplay" from the Writers Guild of America, the British Academy of Film and Television Arts, the Online Film Critics Society, and the Chicago Film Critics Association. A native of Houston, Texas, Anderson attended the University of Texas at Austin, where he earned a bachelor's degree in philosophy (Thomas 2002).

Anderson's movies intensely examine families and friendships, and the director has described his interest in organizing his stories around these basic, familiar themes in terms of several of his major cinematic influences. Speaking with Gavin Smith and Kent Jones for *Film Comment*, Anderson said of *The Royal Tenenbaums*, "Another thing was that I wanted to do this family history thing, inspired by *The Magnificent Ambersons*," (p. 28) and goes on to specify "And a certain kind of movie that I really like is the romantic-feeling house movie, you know, family intrigues in a house, like *Rules of the Game*" (p. 28). Anderson goes on to identify himself with the Margot and Eli characters in *The Royal Tenenbaums*, suggesting that he always maintains an extremely personal, and at least marginally autobiographical, connection to his movies: "And Margot does these plays, too. I'm a middle child and the middle-child dynamic is something I've always felt was significant. I also feel a connection with Eli, Owen's character, because there's this family that he wants to get himself adopted into. And I've experienced that with a number of families over the years. Not that I didn't want to be with my own family, but there were just certain families that would have so much going on that I would just want to be over there" (p. 28). Anderson's identification with his characters is a crucial building block in gaining the sympathies of viewers, particularly because underneath the archetypal interpersonal conflicts familiar to virtually all viewers, the accoutrements of the personalities Anderson creates bear the outward trappings of eccentricity and aloofness. Commentary relating to family relationships continues as a thread throughout the remainder of the *Film Comment* piece, and in other interviews, Anderson cites specific literary works (dominated by themes relating to the family) as influences on his filmmaking. In an interview with Tod Lippy, Anderson spoke about his orientation toward creating drama that focused on familial relationships by acknowledging the frequent comparisons between the characters in *The Royal Tenenbaums* and J. D. Salinger's Glass family. When asked by Lippy if the Glass family is an inspiration for his characters, Anderson replies: "Yeah, I guess so. Really more than being an inspiration, it was an easy way to communicate to people something more or less similar to what we're doing" (p. 110).

Since the theatrical release of his debut feature film *Bottle Rocket* in 1996, writer and director Wes Anderson has gradually been embraced by both the critical establishment and mainstream audiences as a talented creative artist worthy of identification as an auteur filmmaker. Anderson's trio of movies encompasses a myriad of emotional signposts, freely ranging from gentle comedy to moving drama even within individual scenes. The director's ability to attract major Hollywood stars, including Gene Hackman, Danny Glover, Gwyneth Paltrow, and Bill Murray, to appear in his relatively low-budget films additionally attests to his inspired and stimulating inventiveness. With the appearance of *The Royal Tenenbaums* in 2001, Anderson was hailed as a visionary in a *Film Comment* cover story written by Kent Jones—despite the fact that the movie itself was released to mixed reviews in the popular press. Jones's article, however, solidified Anderson's reputation as a director of "art" films, and Anderson's current project, *The Life Aquatic*, is the subject of much anticipation and speculation. Critic David Thomson, in the 2002 reissue of his influential collection of film-world biographies, raised eyebrows in the cinema community by including the following as the entire entry for Anderson: "Watch this space. What does that mean? That he might be something one day" (p. 18).

Anderson's Communication of Ethics

Several ethical issues are consistently embodied in the films of Wes Anderson. Relevant to people who wish to discuss morality are the dialectical tensions of truthfulness and deceitfulness in work relationships, family relationships, and public and private interactions. Defying the typical criticism that popular culture fails to understand the complex nuances of real human interaction, Anderson designs and develops characters who demonstrate the subtle internalization of self-doubt and who employ strategies that encompass the utilization of truth-telling and lying as means to achieve personal goals. Even while the director employs a highly stylized aesthetic in the rendering of his fantasy constructions of people and places that do not exist in concrete reality (for example, the inclusion in *The Royal Tenenbaums* of the "375th Street YMCA"—a made-up New York City location meant to evoke a certain type of wistful nostalgia), the emotional core of identifiable human emotions like longing and regret are palpable in the depictions of the protagonists. In this manner, Anderson's work becomes an ideal vehicle through which we can discuss ethical communication issues within popular texts.

This essay focuses on Anderson's perspective on the communication ethics of his characters and discusses the director's status as a sensitive, humanistic portrayer of familial structures and relationships. In order to arrive at a conclusion regarding Anderson's apparently ironic treatment of "good people who do bad things," however, Kenneth Burke's (1984) discussion of "perspective by incongruity" in *Permanence and Change* provides the basis of a critical approach by which scholars of popular culture can usefully examine both the ethical and unethical actions of the director's creations. The value of applying Burkean concepts to popular culture will be illuminated through an analysis of Anderson's movies as examples of narratives that reveal nuanced depictions of detailed and complicated interpersonal relationships that on occasion transcend the usual limitations of popular culture to mimic the complications of everyday interactions we have with our own family members.

The Burkean Conception of Piety and the Function of Comedy

In the preface to Ross Wolin's *The Rhetorical Imagination of Kenneth Burke* (2001), editor Thomas Benson notes:

> Burke was a monumental figure in twentieth-century rhetorical studies, a critic and theorist of vast erudition, wide curiosity, cranky individuality, comic genius, and grand vision. His major writings, most of them decades old, are still in print. A society formed in his name holds conferences about his work, the great themes of which are part of the vocabulary of every rhetorical critic and theorist. (p. vii)

Kenneth Burke said very little about modern mediated communication, but in *Permanence and Change* (1935, 1984), Burke does not ignore technology altogether. By the early 1980s, Burke had established a viewpoint that essentially set up technology as the dialectical agon of humankind. This certainly has not stopped rhetorical critics from applying Burkean concepts to movies, television, and the media, and Robert Cathcart (1993), James Chesebro and Dale Bertelsen (1996), and Barry Brummett (1984, 1994) have all successfully used Burkean frames as the basis of rhetorical criticism.

While the concept of piety has been traditionally situated within religious contexts, Kenneth Burke expanded the representation of the term to include a non-sacred philosophical definition appropriate to rhetorical discussion. Using a metaphor to explain his broader application of the word, Burke (1984) suggests that "It [piety] would as well be present when the potter moulds the clay to exactly that form which completely gratifies his sense of how it ought to be" (p. 71). Burke argues that society inherently assumes customs, protocols, and a sense of decorum that steers and guides—as well as limits—our behaviors based upon the idea of what is appropriate in any and every social interaction. Thomas Rosteck and Michael Leff (1989) understand Burke's approach to piety as an orientation as well as a process of organizing and categorizing, writing that the notion of piety operates as "stable frames of reference which direct human perception and determine our judgments about what is proper in a given circumstance" (p. 329).

Burke's interest in social structures led him to contextualize his notion of piety within the dialectic of the social order and the challenges to that order. Burke recognizes a social fusion of how the debates over what is "proper" and "improper" can symbolically morph into pairs that are always linked precisely because they are opposites (i.e., black and white, war and peace, life and death). As two seemingly opposite things are inextricably linked together by their polarization, Burke sees a nexus for linking refinement with vulgarity because they seemingly oppose one another.

According to Burke (1984), it follows that society's insistence on defining terms partially in the negative (in other words, by what the thing "is not"), notions of what is deemed appropriate and correct will gain status in large part by a stance opposite that which is seen as inappropriate and incorrect. Therefore, Burke is able to make the seemingly odd and contradictory conclusion that "vulgarity is pious" (1984, p. 77) because piety requires an antithesis such as vulgarity in order to reveal what Rosteck and Leff refer to as "the difference between standards of decorum defined in opposition to one another" (1989, p. 328). This line of thinking argues that it is possible to be, for example, a "perfect" liar or an "ideal" thief. The practitioners of vulgar behaviors sanctify, justify, and execute their anti-societal orientation with self-determined attitudes of decorum and orthodoxy.

Sissela Bok (1978) describes the familiarity of familial deception by stating, "We may never have to worry about whether to lie in court or as experimenters or journalists; but in our families, with our friends, with those whose well-being matters most to us, lies can sometimes seem the only way not to injure or disappoint" (p. 205–6). Bok argues that adults often elect to purposefully ignore realism and accuracy when sharing stories and myths with young children, because the sense of invention, imagination, and play is highly valued in our culture. Additionally, lies are told within families in order to offer comfort, protection, and respite from trauma and fear. Bok's assumption that deceitfulness is a regularized part of family life can easily be connected to the rhetorical orientation of Burke on the matter, which is discussed in the following paragraph.

Richard L. Johannesen (1975) writes of Richard M. Weaver and Kenneth Burke that the two rhetorical theorists "believe that the idea that language can be used in a completely neutral and objective manner is untenable" (p. 13). It is central to an understanding of Burke's philosophical orientation that language usage is innately fraught with the subjective colorations of our personal morals, beliefs, and agendas. Johannesen continues, "They [Weaver and Burke] argue that language use (our selection of words) inherently expresses the communicator's choices, attitudes, tendencies, dispositions, and evaluations—and thus channels the perceptions both of sender and receiver" (p. 13). This "sermonic" orientation of language insists that all communication is persuasive, regardless of whether that communication is intended to reflect truth or harbor deceit.

Johannesen describes two additional dimensions of communication ethics that illuminate human interaction, and particularly, the intimate yet complex manner in which families reveal and conceal information from one another. Reiterating one of the basic premises of Joseph Fletcher's 1966 discussion of situational ethics, Johannesen writes, "There is *one* absolute ethical criterion to guide situational evaluations—namely, *love* for fellow humans in the form of genuine affection for them and concern for their welfare" (1975, p. 61). Because love is at the very least a concept often identified in the relationships of family members (to the extent that sometimes it is taken for granted that mothers love their children, sisters love their brothers, etc.), the absolutism of love as a justification for situational ethics carries substantive weight in the discussion of family in popular culture.

The other notable precept in Johannesen's consideration of communication ethics has to do with ethos: "The degree to which an audience has a positive or negative perception of a communicator's personal qualities plays an influential role in determining whether the audience will accept the communicator's information, arguments, or proposal" (1975, p. 69). As children, it is commonplace to accept the word of parents without ethical scrutiny; because we are taught to trust our mothers, fathers, and adult guardians even before we learn how to speak, it is not until several years later that we begin to realize that we might have been lied to "for our own good" during formative growth years. Burke would certainly argue that it is impossible to raise children without lying to them, just as children sooner or later learn how to lie to their parents and other adults. Anderson manages to capture many of the nuances of how family members withhold and distort the truth in their interpersonal communication with each other, so commentary on his orientation toward family provides a helpful frame for understanding some of the thematic underpinnings of his filmmaking.

While they also display elements of psychological disappointment, sadness, and melancholy, Anderson's movies are typically referred to as comedies. Burke (1959) suggests that "comedy requires the maximum of forensic complexity" (p. 42). Burke also distinguishes comedy and tragedy by articulating what he sees as their primary literary and philosophical functioning: "Comedy deals with *man in society*, tragedy with the *cosmic man*" (p. 42). In other words, Burke insists that comedy is "essentially humane," as it allows for a kind of audience identification that permits people to recognize their own shortcomings and limitations. In the tragic frame, a kind of deep character flaw that engenders evil distances us from fully recognizing ourselves in the bad actions of fictional characters (this same distancing also suggests to us that we can be rid of evil by ostracizing those who do evil). Identification within the comic frame aids us by suggesting that we all make errors, but we can learn from them. Because families tend to operate from within the comic frame—and because Anderson's depictions of family rely on forgiveness—the value of Burke's discussion on the comic reveals itself as worthwhile in this discussion.

Anderson's Construction of Family

It is important to note that any discussion of moral and ethical behavior intersecting with the concept of the family is likely to call to mind the misunderstood term "family values." Stephanie Coontz (1997) questions the core notion itself, suggesting that "today's interpretation of what constitutes a 'values' question, for example, is even more narrow than the truncated definition of what counts as an economic issue" (p. 6). While Coontz goes on to suggest that conservative groups have taken ownership of the term as a code that privileges parental responsibility, she makes the point that "the reduction of morality to questions of sexuality, marriage, and parenthood leads to some serious instances of moral blindness" (p. 7). Coontz (1992) also debunks the concept of the moral life cycle of families as unsustainable (p. 265), and argues that the world in which we live is complicated, and especially complicated for families. Anderson, whether deliberately or subconsciously, transcends some of the basic limitations of popular culture with his more complex depictions of families. Included in his trio of films are portrayals of adoption, economic factors (including debt and financial security), sibling rivalry, incest, divorce, and death.

Family structures and family units, from nuclear to extended and from blood relations to socially connected groups (like gangs or roommates, for example), are among the most popular types of relationships to depict in the dramatic narratives of feature films. Whether one identifies traditional families consisting of blood and marital relations, or extends their view to incorporate groups that function as families, popular culture focuses on family and family-style relationships consistently. While Lawrence Mintz (1985) was specifically referring to half-hour format television comedy when he wrote that "all sitcom is 'domestic' or family-oriented if we extend the definition to non-blood-related groups that function as families" (p. 116), his comments can readily be extended to include feature narrative films. In a discussion of ideal norms, David Altheide and Robert Snow (1979) also support the idea that mediated popular culture is arguably dependent on a structure that includes the depictions of traditional and nontraditional families:

> Typically, the television ideal-norms format works best through a family setting. Although the contemporary family may be a parent without a partner, it still is the primary socialization and problem-solving institution in American society. This is reflected in the number of successful TV sitcoms and dramas, from the days of *Donna Reed, Father Knows Best,* through *Bonanza* to *Happy Days,* and *One Day at a Time,* where we have witnessed the family as the problem-solver. Even programs without a traditional family structure develop a quasi-family appearance. (p. 41-42)

Families immediately connote aspects of "what goes with what" in terms of archetypal identifiers that govern the special pieties of kinship. In Anderson's work, the major elements of family ties that audiences expect are firmly established: (traditional, and perhaps outmoded) patriarchal governance of the unit, deep and lasting bonds that transcend petty squabbles, and unspoken but symbolically demonstrated commitments to the family unit itself. While the Tenenbaums, despite their unusual status as a "family of geniuses" and the eccentric behavior that attends that moniker, are the most outwardly traditional of Anderson's family groups, similar family groups are on display in both *Bottle Rocket* and *Rushmore*.

Anderson is keenly interested in exploring both blood relations and the kinds of connected groups that emerge from formal and informal organizations that operate as families. He is also inclined to devote a great deal of time to fathers, surrogate fathers, and father figures. Examining both the expected pieties acted out by fathers, and the impieties engendered in failures and shortcomings related to fatherhood, Anderson's films appear more comfortable addressing paternal connections than they do mothers and motherhood. This is not to suggest that mothers are ignored completely; while absent in *Bottle Rocket*, *Rushmore* ruminates on Max's deceased mother Eloise as a consistent motif, and in *The Royal Tenenbaums*, audiences have their clearest view of motherhood in Anderson's films to date, with Etheline Tenenbaum (Anjelica Huston) taking an important role in the narrative. Smith and Jones (2001) suggested to Anderson that Royal seems to be the only character "who seems to have an emotional understanding of the people around him" (p. 28), and Anderson responded, "Like the mother: she has a good nature towards everyone, she's encouraging, she wants them to succeed, but she's sort of got a glaze over everything, she's not seeing it sharply" (p. 28).

In *Bottle Rocket*, Anthony (Luke Wilson) and Dignan (Owen Wilson) join forces with their friend Bob (Robert Musgrave) to embark on a series of criminal misadventures that Dignan believes will gain the respect and attention of Mr. Henry (James Caan). Both Dignan and Mr. Henry represent father figures, with widely divergent levels of effectiveness. Dignan behaves paternally toward Anthony and Bob, expecting them to submit to his authority despite his own glaring naïvete and ineptitude. Much of the humor in *Bottle Rocket* is derived from Dignan's zealous overplanning and impetuous demand to be treated as the leader of the burglary team he has organized. Dignan is often not taken seriously by Anthony and Bob, and as a result responds by behaving like an angry child. In this way, Dignan emerges as an ironic father figure—an inversion of the wise protector and moral guide.

Dignan is enamored of the authority wielded by local under-world figure Mr. Henry, who possesses the circumspection and skill Dignan lacks. Even so, Anderson parallels Dignan and Mr. Henry, playing with the symbolically rich theme of children imitating their parents. Dignan exerts tremendous effort in his bid to impress Mr. Henry, all the while being unwittingly duped by the older man. Mr. Henry ultimately demonstrates his patriarchal superiority when he uses Dignan as a decoy on a phony break-in job at Hinckley Cold Storage in order to steal the valuable possessions contained in Bob's family's house.

A similar paralleling device is used effectively in *Rushmore*, which contains a number of unique family units. Max Fischer (Jason Schwartzmann) can be read as a son on many levels, including (most obviously) the blood relationship he has with his father, barber Bert Fischer (Seymour Cassel). Initially, Max is ashamed of his humble home life, and eagerly seeks acceptance as the symbolic "son" of both Rushmore Academy and of millionaire industrialist Herman Bloom (Bill Murray). Interestingly, Max is also periodically cast into the father role, directly expressing his approval and dispensing his advice to chapel partner Dirk Calloway (Mason Gamble), as well as to the many participants in the clubs Max heads on campus. Like Dignan, Max demonstrates social vulgarity without the ability to correctly identify it as such. Just as Dignan is convinced that he can implement a "seventy year plan," complete with retirement, based on the idea of burglarizing private homes, Max thinks nothing of destroying Rushmore's baseball diamond in order to begin unlicensed, illegal construction on a lavish, but only partially funded, aquarium.

As nearly the diametric opposite of what he will become by the end of the film, Royal Tenenbaum (Gene Hackman) is introduced in *The Royal Tenenbaums* as an absentee father unworthy of love and admiration from any of his three children. As in his other films, Anderson toys with expectations of what is proper, expected, and appropriate by emphasizing the ways in which Royal fails to meet the criteria for socially respectable fatherhood through his blunt, coarse, and (initially) unsympathetic demeanor. Royal is more often than not insulting and belligerent, and his self-centered attitude usually obscures the possibility that underneath it all, he might in fact be capable of positive change. Royal constantly reminds his daughter Margot (Gwyneth Paltrow) that she is adopted, and Anderson never specifically indicates any motive for Royal's callousness aside from playing with stereotype by identifying Royal's occupation as a once-prominent litigator. It is interesting to note that son Chas (Ben Stiller) sued Royal twice, and was responsible for having him disbarred, presumably because Chas was upset that Royal stole bonds from Chas's safety deposit box when Chas was fourteen.

The Truthful Liar

In his discussion of piety, Burke (1984) understands the ironic nexus of linking opposing social norms through a definition that allows seemingly irreconcilable behaviors to enjoy the same level of symbolic respect. As discussed earlier, Burke's application of piety takes into account the work of people who would not normally be considered valuable to the functioning of a law-abiding society. Yet examples of this kind of piety can be found any place one chooses to look: members of the Special Forces are artists when it comes to learning the best ways to kill with bare hands, and drug dealers hone unique skills that allow them to evade detection by law enforcement agents. Burke's own examples discuss poet Matthew Arnold trying to fit in with the "gashouse gang" of street toughs—and failing miserably, for Arnold lacks the necessary skills to be one of them—and the ability of a drug fiend to "take his morphine in a hospital without the slightest disaster to his character" (p. 77).

Burke's deceptively effortless ability to bring opposites into proximity with each other defines the "truthful liar," or the person who must practice dishonesty in order to get at the larger truth. In Anderson's films, the truthful liar operates in much the same fashion. While these characters lie frequently to others and often to themselves, the ultimate repercussions of their falsehoods unlock profound truths and stunning self-realizations that ironically inter-twine reliability and fraudulence. Lying allows Anderson's char-acters to discover deeper meanings not possible without the initial self-delusion. This unique characteristic represents another way that Anderson's work manages to escape some of the traditional limitations of popular culture.

In each of Anderson's movies, lying and deceitfulness is central to both plot and character. While the most direct, and arguably sim-ple, manifestation of a conscious choice to commit fraud appears in Dignan's misguided efforts to start up a theft ring, Max Fischer and Royal Tenenbaum craft extensive mistruths in order to try to get what they desire. In one colorful set-piece in *Rushmore*, framed by Anderson's flair for adolescent theatricality, Max arranges his battered bicycle under a streetlamp outside the window of Miss Cross (Olivia Williams) in order to curry her sympathy. Gaining en-try through a window, Max explains to Miss Cross that he has been hit by a car, and pretends to need medical attention for a phony cut on his forehead. While Miss Cross is in the bathroom preparing bandages and hydrogen peroxide, Max takes the opportunity to set the mood with a cassette tape of Yves Montand's sweet, romantic crooning. While attending to Max's abrasion, Miss Cross discovers that Max has instead smeared his head with fake blood, and she orders him to leave.

What makes the scene interesting is Anderson's ability to reveal deeply submerged truths as conversational counterpoint to Max's fantasy of a romantic encounter with Miss Cross. While reclining on the bed in a room that is filled with the only physical remind-ers of Miss Cross's dead husband, Edward Appleby, Max and Miss Cross are able to engage in an open and honest discussion of their feelings. While the encounter is predicated on one of Max's many falsehoods, the scene includes dialogue in which Miss Cross reveals to Max that Edward drowned, and Max tells Miss Cross that his mother died of cancer. This thematic coupling of lying and honesty illustrates a unique contradiction that exists as a theme throughout Anderson's work.

Royal Tenenbaum, apparently jealous that his estranged wife Etheline intends to marry Henry Sherman (Danny Glover), the family's longtime accountant, tells his family that he has "a pretty bad case of cancer" in order to be allowed to move back to the family home on Archer Avenue. While some members of the Tenenbaum clan, notably bitter son Chas, are dubious of Royal's bombshell, Royal sets up shop with some borrowed medical equipment, including heart monitors and IV stands, that allows him to complete the illusion of his illness. Interestingly, Royal claims that his cancer diagnosis is the reason that he wants to "make things right" with his family, and Anderson reveals later that Royal is indeed capable of positive change. In other words, Royal lies in order to get close to his family following years of absenteeism and neglect, but his motivation to be a better person turns out to be genuine by the conclusion of the story. By the time Royal does actually die (heart attack, not cancer), he has demonstrated compassion and selflessness—two traits that had been missing in his character for decades.

Royal has an epiphany that occurs strategically when he has been outed by Henry Sherman as a phony cancer patient and Chas insists on kicking him out of the house. Royal says, "I know I'm the bad guy on this one, but I just want to say that the last six days have been the best six days of, probably, my whole life." Immediately following this line of dialogue, the film's narrator is heard in voice-over, saying, "Immediately after making this statement, Royal realized that it was true." The juxtaposition of those two statements in the film implies that Royal had become so accustomed to lying that he could not distinguish between genuine sentiment and spurious distraction. Anderson compresses Royal's shift to the good by dramatizing Royal's rescue of his grandsons Uzi (Jonah Meyerson) and Ari (Grant Rosenmeyer) on Etheline's wedding day, when Royal pushes them out of the path of Eli Cash's (Owen Wilson) careening, out-of-control convertible.

Other characters within the ensembles also exhibit traits of deceptiveness that can surprisingly, and quickly, intersect with frank, candid, and blunt honesty. Margot Tenenbaum is arguably the most effective case study for the purpose of illustrating Anderson's handling of the truthful liar, for she combines brutal, even hurtful insights about others while protecting her own fortress of insulation and seclusion. The film's introduction to Margot visually reinforces the character's desire for privacy: she is locked in the bathroom and requires specific information from her husband before she opens the door. Additionally, the narrator fills in some of the traits that define Margot: "She was known for her extreme secrecy. For example, none of the Tenenbaums knew she was a smoker, which she had been since the age of twelve. Nor were they aware of her first marriage and divorce to a recording artist in Jamaica. She kept a private studio in Mockingbird Heights under the name Helen Scott."

While Margot has hidden so much from her family, any time one of her previously unseen characteristics is revealed, she responds with such clarity that the result can be startling. The most poignant example of this takes place when she and Richie converse in his tent following his return from the hospital. Not only does Margot offer details about her brief marriage to the Jamaican musician Desmond, she admits her love for Richie. Exiting the tent, she says, "I think we're just going to have to be secretly in love with each other and leave it at that, Richie." Margot exemplifies the truthful liar because she so flexibly navigates between honesty and secrecy, and because her lies provide the thematic framework necessary to discovering truth's close relationship to falsehood.

The Lovable Rascal

Because Anderson's films are primarily identified as comedies, one expects that the behavior of the characters—even when depicting transgressions ranging from mild half-truths all the way to illegal activity—is intended to function within the definition of humor that rewards lighthearted and relatively harmless "pranks" and "indiscretions." Anderson's protagonists, as well as many of the peripheral ensemble, function as lovable rascals: wily tricksters and smart smooth-talkers who take advantage of situations through the application of considerable charisma and intellectual guile. The lovable rascal is a person who can get away with a great deal, and this supports the comic device that identifies the "naughty" violations and trespasses against the social order as merely excessive righteousness or an overexuberant orientation toward things of value. There is little doubt that Anderson's protagonists easily fit this category, for their ethical miscalculations inevitably stem from the motivation to win the love of peers and relatives.

Royal teaches Ari and Uzi to shoplift, throw water balloons at passing cabs, bet on dice games in the street, run out in front of on-coming traffic, and hitch rides on the back of garbage trucks. Max cuts the brake line to Herman's car, releases a swarm of bees in Herman's hotel room, and takes photos of Herman and Miss Cross in the hopes that she will be fired from her job for consorting with a married man. Dignan steals a car, holds up a bookstore, and stages a heist (which results in incarceration). These are all vulgar behaviors, but in the end, Dignan, Max, and Royal are clearly seen in a posi-tive light by Anderson, who consistently concludes his films with a wistful sense of melancholy that things did not quite turn out the way in which the characters fantasized that they would. Instead, the summarizing scenes (or codas)—Dignan romanticizing his life of crime as he is visited in jail by Anthony and Bob, Max hosting the "Heaven and Hell Cotillion" as he comes to terms with the need for Miss Cross and Herman to be together, and Royal making peace with his family—return everything to a morally righteous balance of the world. Anderson introduces enough closure to suggest the appearance that the characters have been made somewhat account-able for their vulgar impieties, but using the Burkean frame, one could claim that the vulgar displays of lying, cheating, and stealing were merely a reinforcement of pious behavior all along.

Bottle Rocket includes a montage in which Anthony and Dignan are seen breaking and entering a house and stealing the valuable contents of jewelry boxes, as well as coin collections and other items. Anderson does not preface the sequence with the traditional identi-fication of setting or context. As a result, the audience is delighted and surprised to discover the "truth" about Anthony and Dignan's domestic caper: the pair has robbed Anthony's own house. Not only does this revelation reinforce the idea that Anthony and Dignan are unlikely to develop into successful thieves, it also provides Ander-son with an opportunity to display the cleverness and imagination of his likable characters. Anthony and Dignan can simultaneously be interpreted by the audience as sweet and kind-hearted as well as rambunctious and subversive—even if the sense of "subversive" is limited to transgressing against one's own family.

Certainly Anderson portrays his characters as worthy of the love of friends and family—the lies told by the protagonists do not require the kinds of consequences associated with tragedy, such as lasting isolation from society or punitive banishment from the family group. While it is apparent that the deceitfulness of Anderson's central characters does indeed render legitimate social consequences (that is, Dignan going to jail, Max being expelled from Rushmore, Royal being thrown out of the house by Chas), the comic framing insists that Anderson's clowns are embraced and forgiven by their friends and families no matter the transgressions. Tragedies depend upon wickedness inherent in the characters who transgress. The unethical actor in a tragedy is beyond redemption and deserves a harsh consequence for violating the ethics of honesty and trust. Dignan robs more than one small business, Max's actions directly cause both Miss Cross to leave her job at Rushmore and Herman to get a divorce, and for more than two decades, Royal treats his children with cavalier disdain, yet all of these people—subject to their corrective humility—take comfort in the forgiveness of their loved ones.

Family Values and the Subverting/Supporting
of Institutional Norms

Liars, cheats, and thieves threaten and challenge the cherished values of interconnected society. On first consideration, therefore, Anderson's films would seem to operate as subversive, antiestablishment celebrations of vulgarity through their depictions of delinquency. By subtextually addressing liars (through their prominent roles as the protagonists of his movies), Anderson seeks to target the illusion of piety in contemporary society. Ironically, however, each of Anderson's "wrongdoers" concludes his story arc by recognizing the limitations of deception—particularly when it comes to the lies that are told to one's loved ones. Rather than genuinely subverting the values of the institutions of family and society, then, Anderson merely reinforces the traditional viewpoint that the pleasures of misbehavior are no substitute for the love and acceptance afforded by traditional family values.

In this sense, Anderson actuates the popular literary tradition of "comeuppance," or the idea that one's sins must be cleansed, one's crimes paid for in full. In *Bottle Rocket*, Dignan arguably presents the most subtle illustration of this idea because his incarceration operates punitively on one level (the idea that serving jail time for the perpetration of crimes is part and parcel of repaying a "debt" to society), but also serves as the previously missing link to criminality that validates Dignan's dubious career choice as the leader of a theft ring. Dignan's romanticizing of life behind bars—visually represented by the nonchalant, over-the-shoulder look he gives to Anthony and Bob when they are leaving the prison on visitor's day, delivered in the stylistically charged, in-camera slow-motion effect that Anderson employs in each of his movies—can easily be read as naïve and juvenile (few people view serving prison time as enjoyable). Yet Dignan seems to understand that he was destined to be arrested. During the Hinckley Cold Storage break-in, Anthony and Dignan argue briefly over who will stay behind to help Applejack, and Dignan convinces Anthony that he really "needs" to show his leadership by inviting certain arrest ("Give me this one," says Dignan).

At the "Heaven and Hell Cotillion" that concludes *Rushmore*, peripheral and supporting characters trade stories about Max's now-legendary transgressions. Like Dignan, who despite his fanciful ideas about being a heroic crime boss must face up to the reality of incarceration, Max has been chastened by his realization that he is indeed too young to pursue a romantic relationship with Miss Cross. Max's elaborate staging of his play "Heaven and Hell," complete with pyrotechnics courtesy of illegally purchased dynamite, affords Anderson another opportunity to play with the notions of subversiveness by showing us that Max is unafraid to continue pushing the limits of acceptability, but the conversation Max shares with Miss Cross reveals that a lesson has been learned. When it is suggested by Max that nobody was hurt (referring to the explosive staging of "Heaven and Hell"), Miss Cross says, "Except you." Once again, Anderson returns his characters from the edges of their vulgar misbehaviors to a state of traditionally sanctioned piety. The dialogue that remains in *Rushmore*'s final scene neatly ties up loose ends by clearing up several of Max's previous lies (for example, Miss Cross's date, the surgeon John Coats, played by Luke Wilson, discovers that Max's father is not a brain surgeon but a barber). Max also claims Margaret Yang as his girlfriend, reassuring the audience that his age-inappropriate pursuit of Miss Cross has come to an end.

The Royal Tenenbaums also features a coda in which Anderson reveals that Royal managed to return to a position of respect within his family only after he accepted the marriage of Etheline and Henry. Royal, whose own vulgar behaviors supply much of the plot and the comic circumstances that have come before, is revealed as a doting, supportive father and grandfather who makes peace with estranged son Chas and bonds with grandsons Ari and Uzi. Just as he had done in *Bottle Rocket* and *Rushmore*, Anderson presents an ironic juxtaposition of his previously vulgar main characters chastened by the somewhat formal acceptance of piety. Royal's final appearance is attended by narration that explains how Chas was the only witness to his father's death, which serves to reinforce the repaired bond between father and son. An epilogue shows Royal's funeral, which allows Anderson a final opportunity to depict Royal as a trickster. In one shot, the presiding priest reads Royal's headstone epitaph, which suggests that Royal died while rescuing his family from a sinking ship. Of course, the audience—and the priest—know that this is patently false, but the sentiment contains another of Anderson's wistful half-truths: Royal did, in fact, save his family by bringing them all together following years of bitterness and separation.

Anderson simultaneously manages to take aim at society's conventions and expectations, and reinforce them. His movies, then, all manage to illustrate Burke's concepts of piety and vulgarity through their ironic connection of truth and falsehood. Dignan, Max, and Royal—as well as many of the colorful gallery of supporting players—serve as mouthpieces for Anderson's belief in the sanctity of moral tradition. The central characters masquerade as duplicitous, selfish narcissists, but they also seek and receive forgiveness from their loved ones once caught up in their lies. Their personal ethics end up reflecting the ethics and regulations of society, which allows audiences to enjoy the displayed misbehavior and vulgarity that precede the epiphanous summarizations that conclude each film. The vulgarity of Anderson's protagonists can be consumed safely because there exists an expectation that Anderson will return his imaginatively constructed world to the familiar one in which boundaries of decorum and protocol are expected and implemented in everyday behavior. In real life, we might hold ourselves in check even if a desire to behave like Dignan, Max, or Royal exists within the imagination. The cinema offers an opportunity to dramatize make-believe fantasies in which people do and say things that are consistently repressed in daily activity. More often than not, however, customary and sanctioned moral norms are reinforced rather than subverted.

The application of ethical communication to motion pictures provides an opportunity for reflection and consideration, not just in the classroom, but also in everyday conversation. Directors like Anderson might be more attuned than many other mainstream and independent filmmakers to an ethic of love and personal consideration, and this is due in part to the nature of acceptance and forgiveness embodied in the comic corrective. Arguably, an understanding of Burke's constructs provides an opportunity to identify the appropriate narrative responses to characters whose actions are rooted in the art of lying. Rather than functioning as scapegoats who must suffer tragic ostracism (or perhaps, even death) in retribution for their transgressions, Anderson's characters teach the benefits of humility and compassion that result from functioning as comic clowns worthy of pardon and grace. It is in this fashion that Anderson's characters resemble our own friends and families, and by recognizing the parallels, we come to a deeper understanding of how popular culture can positively impact the way we see the world and ourselves.

Appendix: Film Plot Summaries/Primary Cast

Bottle Rocket (1996)

Directed by Wes Anderson. Written by Wes Anderson and Owen Wilson.

Primary Cast:
    Anthony Adams: Luke Wilson
    Dignan: Owen Wilson
    Bob Mapplethorpe: Robert Musgrave
    Abe Henry: James Caan
    Inez: Lumi Cavazos
    John Mapplethorpe/Future Man: Andrew Wilson
    Rocky: Donny Caicedo
    Applejack: Jim Ponds
    Kumar: Kumar Pallana
    Rowboat: Tak Kubota
    Grace: Shea Fowler
    H. Clay Murchison: Brian Tenenbaum
    Bookstore employee: Deepak Pallana

Anthony Adams leaves the health facility where he had voluntarily committed himself following some kind of nervous breakdown. Anthony's friend Dignan doesn't realize that Anthony elected to stay at the hospital of his own free will, and has devised an elaborate escape. Not wanting to disappoint his friend, Anthony plays along, and Dignan is delighted that their plan went off without a hitch. Dignan, who has been working for Abe Henry, a local figure involved with criminal activity who also own a legitimate landscaping business called the Lawn Wranglers, dreams of becoming a career thief, and suggests a "seventy year plan" to Anthony in which they will rob homes and businesses.

Enlisting the help of their friend Bob (because he has a car), Anthony and Dignan hold up a bookstore and then head out of town in order to keep a low profile until "thinks blow over." At a roadside motel, Anthony falls in love with Inez, a beautiful housekeeper who speaks very little English. As Anthony's priorities shift from crime to romance, Dignan quickly comes to resent Anthony's relationship with Inez. Dignan and Anthony eventually reconcile, however, as an opportunity to pull a job for Mr. Henry emerges. While Dignan, Anthony, and Bob rob Hinckley Cold Storage, however, it is revealed that the naïve young men have been duped: Mr. Henry has robbed Bob's house while the phony cold storage job was under way. Dignan takes the fall for the break-in, and winds up in jail, where he romanticizes elaborate escape plans along with his newfound pride at being a "real" criminal.

Rushmore (1998)

Directed by Wes Anderson. Written by Wes Anderson and Owen Wilson.

Primary Cast:
    Max Fischer: Jason Schwartzman
    Herman Blume: Bill Murray
    Miss Cross: Olivia Williams
    Dr. Guggenheim: Brian Cox
    Bert Fischer: Seymour Cassel
    Dirk Calloway: Mason Gamble
    Margaret Yang: Sarah Tanaka
    Magnus Buchan: Stephen McCole
    Dr. Peter Flynn: Luke Wilson
    Mr. Adams: Deepak Pallana
    Mr. Littlejeans: Kumar Pallana
    Coach Beck: Andrew Wilson
    Mrs. Guggenheim: Marietta Marich

Max Fischer, despite his participation in numerous extracurricular activities, is academically one of the worst students at Rushmore Academy, a private prep school. The threat of expulsion seems to hang like a cloud over Max's head, but he ignores his studies in favor of serving as the creative director of the Max Fischer Players, a theater troupe that stages popular but reckless theatrical productions (often featuring dazzling pyrotechnics). Max hears millionaire industrialist Herman Blume speak in chapel. Deeply impressed by Blume's unorthodox style, Max seeks out the older man (whose twin sons attend Rushmore), and the pair forms an unlikely friendship.

Max and Herman forge a close bond, but their relationship is jeopardized when both fall for Miss Cross, a new teacher at Rushmore. Max is naturally far too young to be taken seriously as a suitor by Miss Cross, and the teacher is further surprised to find herself attracted to Blume. Humiliated and defeated, Max makes life miserable for Herman and Miss Cross, cutting the brake line on Herman's car, setting bees on him, and revealing the couple's affair to Herman's wife and the administration of Rushmore. As a result, Max is expelled, and is forced to enroll at a public school. Max begins to come to terms with the things he has done, and he reunites Blume and Miss Cross at the premiere of his latest play, a Vietnam epic he wrote to honor Blume.

The Royal Tenenbaums (2001)

Directed by Wes Anderson. Written by Wes Anderson and Owen Wilson.

Primary Cast:
  Royal Tenenbaum: Gene Hackman
  Etheline Tenenbaum: Anjelica Huston
  Chas Tenenbaum: Ben Stiller
  Margot Tenenbaum: Gwyneth Paltrow
  Richie Tenenbaum: Luke Wilson
  Eli Cash: Owen Wilson
  Henry Sherman: Danny Glover
  Raleigh St. Clair: Bill Murray
  Dusty: Seymour Cassel
  Pagoda: Kumar Pallana
  Narrator: Alec Baldwin
  Ari Tenenbaum: Grant Rosenmeyer
  Uzi Tenenbaum: Jonah Meyerson

Royal Tenenbaum, a once-prominent litigator, has separated from his wife Etheline and left his three children. Considered at one time a family of geniuses, the Tenenbaum children, with the support and encouragement of their mother, distinguished themselves while still minors. Chas was an entrepeneur, buying real estate and managing large sums of money. Margot, who was adopted, won a fifty-thousand-dollar grant while in the ninth grade for her playwriting talents. Richie, a failed painter, excelled on the tennis court, turning pro at the age of seventeen and winning the U.S. Nationals three years in a row. Now adults, the Tenenbaum children have not spoken to their father in a long time. Royal discovers that Etheline intends to marry the family's accountant, Henry Sherman.

Hatching an elaborate scheme to ingratiate himself with his estranged family, Royal claims to have cancer in order to be allowed to move back to the family mansion. His ruse works for some time, but when it is discovered he has been lying, Chas insists that he be evicted. Surviving a suicide attempt, Richie reveals to Margot that he has loved her since they were children. Margot responds that she loves Richie as well, and because she was adopted, the pair see no reason why they cannot be together. On Etheline's wedding day, Royal saves Ari and Uzi from the out-of-control car driven by family friend Eli Cash. Chas is moved by Royal's selflessness, and the two begin to repair their badly damaged relationship. Royal dies of a heart attack, and the film concludes with his funeral, attended by all the members of the Tenenbaum family.

References

Altheide, D., & R. Snow. (1979). *Media Logic*. Beverly Hills, CA: Sage.

Anderson, W., & O. Wilson. (1999). *Rushmore*. New York: Faber & Faber.

———. (2001). *The Royal Tenenbaums*. New York: Faber & Faber.

Bok, S. (1978). *Lying: Moral choice in public and private life*. New York: Pantheon Books.

Brummett, B. (1984). Burke's representative anecdote as a method in media criticism. *Critical Studies in Mass Communication* 1, 161–76.

———. (1994). *Rhetoric in popular culture*. New York: Bedford/St. Martin's.

Burke, K. (1959). *Attitudes toward history*. 2nd ed. Los Altos, CA: Hermes Publications.

———. (1984). *Permanence and change: An anatomy of purpose*. 3rd ed. Berkeley: University of California Press.

Cathcart, R. (1993). Instruments of his own making: Burke and the media. In J. Chesebro (ed.), *Extensions of the Burkeian system* (pp. 297–308). Tuscaloosa: University of Alabama Press.

Chesebro, J. & Bertelsen, D. (1996). *Analyzing media: Communication technologies as symbolic and cognitive systems*. New York: The Guilford Press.

Coontz, S. (1992). *The way we never were: American families and the nostalgia trap*. New York: BasicBooks.

————. (1997). *The way we really are: Coming to terms with America's changing families.* New York: BasicBooks.

Fletcher, J. (1966). *Situation ethics: The new morality.* Philadelphia: Westminster Press.

Johannesen, R. (1975). *Ethics in human communication.* Columbus, OH: Charles E. Merrill Publishing Company.

Jones, K. (2001). Family romance. *Film Comment 37,* 24–7.

Kupfer, J. (1999). *Visions of virtue in popular film.* Boulder, CO: Westview Press.

Lippy, T. (ed.) (2000). *Projections 11: New York film-makers on New York film making.* New York: Faber & Faber.

Marshall, E. O. (2003). Making the most of a good story: Effective use of film as a teaching resource for ethics. *Teaching Theology and Religion 6,* 93–9.

Mintz, L. (1985). Situation comedy. In B. Rose (ed.), *TV genres: A handbook and reference guide* (pp. 107–29). Westport, CT: Greenwood Press.

Rosteck, T., & Leff, M. (1989). Piety, propriety, and perspective: An interpretation and application of key terms in Kenneth Burke's *Permanence and Change. Western Journal of Speech Communication 53,* 327–41.

Smith, G. & Jones, K. (2001). At home with the royal family: Wes Anderson interviewed by Gavin Smith & Kent Jones. *Film Comment 37,* 28–9.

Tester, K. (1994). *Media, culture and morality.* New York: Routledge.

Thomas, C. F. (2002). Wes Anderson: Screenwriter and film director. *Current Biography 63,* 3–6.

Thomson, D. (2002). *The new biographical dictionary of film.* New York: Alfred A. Knopf.

Valenti, F. M. (2000). *More than a movie: Ethics in entertainment.* Boulder, CO: Westview Press.

Wolin, R. (2001). *The rhetorical imagination of Kenneth Burke.* Columbia, SC: University of South Carolina Press.

CHAPTER THIRTEEN ———————————

Judge Judy and Dr. Phil:
Advice with an Attitude

Debra K. Japp

"Dear Ann, Abby, Martha, Carolyn, Randy, Click and Clack ..."
Few are the daily newspapers that do not carry an advice column—
experts responding to inquirers—on a variety of topics. Add
magazines of all sorts—for example, women's, teen, fitness, home,
garden—and the shelves of volumes available at local bookstores,
the wide selection of tapes and videos, radio and television programs, Internet sites, support groups, and other venues, and one
realizes that dispensing advice on everything from relationships
to carpet cleaning is both an American avocation and a major economic industry.

On a daily basis, Americans seem willing, if not compelled, to
ask for and dispense advice on matters from the serious ("He hit
me; should I leave him?") to the mundane ("I didn't receive a birthday card from her!"). Of course to the inquirer, the latter may well
be considered a serious relational problem. If not actually giving or
receiving advice, Americans apparently love to watch, listen, and
read about advice given to others; we are a nation of advice voyeurs, if you will. Kenneth Burke (1974), writing over half a century
ago and before the advent of televised advice programming, noted
that Americans love to read literature that provides strategies of
"easy consolation" for the difficult situations of life. Such literature
tends to "play down the realistic naming of our situation and play

up such strategies as make solace cheap." Moreover, by reading we vicariously address our difficulties and attain resolution without actually undertaking the hard work of changing habits or reshaping difficult relationships (pp. 298–99).

Sixty years later, Burke's observations are even more pertinent, as Americans tune in to television's myriad of talk shows in addition to perusing the shelves of self-help literature available in bookstores. There are two compelling reasons for venturing into this vast, varied, and fascinating domain of popular media: first, as documented above, advice-giving and receiving are firmly lodged in and shaped by popular cultural values and practices; second, the practices are inescapably in the realm of communication ethics. Advice seekers inquire, implicitly or explicitly, "What *should* I do?" Advice givers invoke the *shoulds* and *oughts* that comprise our social values: "Do you think you *should* have done that?" Advice voyeurs comment on others' judgments: "I don't think he *should* be allowed to get away with such behavior!" The realm of the *should*, stated or implied, suggests standards or norms, whether of relationships or rug cleaning, that seekers, givers of advice, and observers invoke as the way things *ought* to be. Being a nation of rule makers and prescribers as well as advice givers and receivers ("Ten simple steps to a better relationship" or "Eight rules for winning at work"), inquirers, the experts they query, and observers seem sure there exists a simple and effective answer to every human dilemma.

I've selected two extremely popular television advice givers, Dr. Phil McGraw and Judge Judy Sheindlin, to engage the ethical issues involved in seeking and dispensing advice for the edification and entertainment of viewers.[1] While these two programs might seem quite different—as do their hosts—they are excellent examples of the complex communication and ethical issues involved in advice situations. Dr. Phil is a relaxed and folksy psychologist from Texas with a major focus on personal, relational, and family problems. From losing weight to disciplining children to revitalizing a marriage, he challenges, scolds, and encourages his guests. Judge Judy, a sharp-tongued New Yorker garbed in the black robe of justice, presides over a television courtroom, ostensibly making legal rulings but in fact dispensing personal and relational advice, often making pointed comments about defendants' and plaintiffs' characters and lifestyles. Although one is male and the other female, their styles are remarkably similar. The stern father and scolding mother of TV land clearly tell inquirers, audiences, viewers, and the world in general what they should and should not do, say, be, or become.

What can we learn about communication ethics from watching these two exceptionally popular television personalities at work on the psyches of the American public? Before addressing these questions, I need to set the context in which these programs have flourished, that of televised talk shows, and provide the framework of communication ethics that will guide our inquiry. I then describe the two programs and their hosts and consider how their practices of advice-giving engage principles of ethical communication. Finally, I move beyond the programs to consider how these enactments of advice-giving might be applicable to everyday life relationships.

Advice in the Afternoon

Afternoon talk show programming is the venue in which these two programs were developed and have flourished. *Judge Judy* and *Dr. Phil* are just two shows available on any weekday afternoon; others include *The Maury Povitch Show*, *The Montel Williams Show*, *The Sally Jessy Raphael Show*, *The Jerry Springer Show*, *The Ricki Lake Show*, *The People's Court*, *Judge Brown*, *The Ellen DeGeneres Show*, *Oprah*, *Sharon Osbourne*.

Most scholars point to the *Phil Donahue Show* (1967; 1969–1996) as the grandfather of contemporary afternoon talk shows (Timberg 2002; Shattuc 1997). At their core, these programs are a blend of two very old traditions in America: advice-giving and entertainment. Jane Shattuc (1997) argues that "the talk show is as old as American broadcasting and borrows its basic characteristics from those of nineteenth century popular culture, such as tabloids, women's advice columns, and melodrama" (p. 3). Kathleen S. Lowney (1999) agrees, and believes that the modern television talk show is nothing more than an updated version of the "nineteenth century's carnivals and revivals":

> The talk show and the carnival both tempt us to watch portrayals of otherness. We see behaviors that are neither common nor publicly discussed suddenly exhibited for all to see.... And it is the talk show host, like the circus ringmaster of old, who identifies the guests' particular deviance for us from the outset, just in case those in the audience missed it.... Talk shows do not just entertain us—they are also a site for American revivalism, of a novel sort. They provide an "electronic tent" under which we can gather together and watch sinners confess, sometimes receiving absolution from the people whom they have hurt, and be reinstated into the moral community. The hosts are contemporary preachers, cajoling guests, studio audiences, and those of us at home to obey the normative order." (pp. 16–17)

While the roots of the American modern talk show are almost two centuries old, the tradition of advice-giving is much older:

> "Advice giving is the oldest racket in the civilized world," says E. Jean Carroll, whose sharptongued, wisecracking advice column in Elle magazine has spawned numerous books, TV appearances and a Web site. "The Old Testament is nothing but advice on how to live, how to eat and how to marry." According to Carroll, advice has always been a literary form, a narrative and a source of entertainment. "All advice givers are essentially performers and writers before they are problem solvers, and that's what makes them so popular," she says. (Paul 2003, n.p.)

But what defines the modern television talk show? Bernard M. Timberg (2002) notes, "Television talk emerges out of fifty years of television practice and the preceding three decades of radio. It is unscripted yet highly planned and invariably anchored by an announcer, host, or team of hosts. It is based on what sociologist Erving Goffman calls 'fresh talk': talk that appears to be spontaneous, no matter how planned or formatted it may actually be" (p. 3). Timberg goes on to note the "defining characteristics" of television talk shows: "Although hosts and shows change over time, the core principles remain the same. For fifty years, the television talk show has been host-centered and defined, forged in the present tense, spontaneous but highly structured, churned out within the strict formulas and measured segments of costly network time, and designed to air topics appealing to the widest possible audience" (pp. 5–6).

J. M. Shattuc (1997) agrees with Timberg (2002) that modern television talk shows are "united by their emphasis on informal or nonscripted conversation rather than the scripted delivery of the news" (p. 3). And in addition to the characteristics noted by Timberg, she adds important characteristics of syndication and time placement. Most of these shows are

> first-run programs financed and distributed by syndicators and put to-gether by independent producers.... Their independence from the net-works, high profits, low production costs, and daytime placement allow them a latitude in content that normally would be censored on network television. As a "degraded" form, they can bring to the fore politically and socially controversial issues rarely seen on network television.... They tend to be scheduled during midmorning and late afternoon as a transition from news programming to soap operas to the evening news. (p. 9)

Although we are surrounded by television talk shows as a normal ingredient of everyday media, the ubiquity of television talk shows has generated a fair share of controversy and criticism. Critics worry about the effect of these programs on viewers, particularly children. William Bennett, former national drug czar and secretary of education, called them "Trash TV" (Lowney 1999, p. 4). Donna Shalala, secretary of health and human services under the Clinton presidency, opened the first of at least three summits on talk shows, and challenged the industry "to use your influence more responsibly, so that we can help give all parents more stamina in their everyday reach to save our nation's children" (quoted in Lowney 1999, p. 5). Television talk shows have their defenders, however, who argue that their "democratic merits" are "a welcome change from the prime-time fantasies of perfection and happy endings" (Newcomb 2002, xi; see also Jagodozinki 2003). And despite their sometimes objectionable content, Lowney (1999) believes that most television talk shows "feature moral discourse": "Watching deviant persons suffer can make us rejoice at the life that we have while at the same time they can remind us of the need for a morality that binds people together" (p. 17).

Judge Judy and *Dr. Phil* carry on the tradition of populist "day-time dysfunction" (Kurtz 1996). Both shows are syndicated, feature a charismatic host, appear to be largely unscripted, and deal with current social issues of the day. Both provide consumers with implicit and explicit messages about what to believe and how to behave. In the next few pages I briefly describe each program and provide information on the hosts. My observations are based on several years of viewing both programs, but I work specifically with programming from November 2003 to January 2004. Throughout, the themes, styles, and practices selected for evaluation are consistent and predictable, as steady viewers will recognize.

Judge Judy

Judy Sheindlin, host of the popular show *Judge Judy*, served as a judge in New York City family court for a number of years. She is married to a former New York Supreme Court judge (who was "host" of *The People's Court* for its two-year run) and is a mother and grandmother. Judy was "discovered" in 1993 when she was featured in a *Los Angeles Times* story as well as on *60 Minutes*. Her show has been on the air since 1996, and in early 2003 her contract with Paramount was extended for four more years at a reported $25 million per year (Burkeman 2003). *Judge Judy* is "the top-ranked court show in syndication," and until the advent of *Dr. Phil*, it was often rated just behind *Oprah*. According to P. Albiniak (2003), "In many markets, Judy competes directly against *Oprah* and, in New York City, routinely wins at 4 p.m. The fact that Judy provides a strong 25–54 audience to lead into local news makes the show all the more valuable to stations" (n.p.). In addition to her success on *Judge Judy*, Ms. Sheindlin has written a number of best-selling books that showcase her values and dispense her advice, including: *Don't Pee on My Leg and Tell Me It's Raining* (1996), *Beauty Fades, Dumb Is Forever* (1999), and *Keep It Simple, Stupid* (2000).

Every weekday afternoon, viewers of *Judge Judy* see two back-to-back thirty-minute episodes, each consisting of two cases (although sometimes one case takes up the entire thirty minutes). Recent shows have highlighted custody of a dog, repayment of loans, return of property, and decisions of responsibility on property damage. Frequently, the cases heard before Judge Judy deal with peripheral issues of family relations and child custody.

Judge Judy's program offers audiences, according to her promotions, "justice with an attitude," a phrase that seems to strike neither the judge nor her audiences as oxymoronic. As the promos assure viewers, "the courtroom is real, the problems are real, the decisions are real"; that is, this is ostensibly the same treatment that would be accorded in a regular civil court proceeding, minus only the television cameras.[2]

Dr. Phil

Dr. Phillip C. McGraw got his big break in 1998, when he was hired by Oprah Winfrey to help her with a lawsuit initiated in 1996 by Texas cattlemen, who accused her of "causing great damage to the American beef industry" when she aired a show on the mad cow disease (Hollandsworth 2003, n.p.). After Winfrey prevailed in court, McGraw was a frequent guest on her show. While his advice initially struck Oprah's audience as too blunt, McGraw eventually won them over. Ratings on *Oprah* went up 26 percent when McGraw was on (Hollandsworth 2003). In 2002, McGraw launched his own show. Produced in Los Angeles, it is syndicated in 96 percent of the country (Peyser 2002) and "watched by approximately six million viewers nationwide" (Hollandsworth 2003, n.p.). Dr. Phil has become, as Hollandsworth (2003) notes, "one of the most talked-about celebrities in America. David Letterman cracks jokes about him almost every night. The tabloids have teams of reporters who follow him. The phrase 'I've been Dr. Philled'—a way of saying that someone has just been confronted about his screwy behavior—is part of the national lexicon" (n.p.).

On his website, www.drphil.com, McGraw admits that "traditional therapy was not [my] calling." He goes on to explain, "From the very beginning, it wasn't for me. I didn't have the patience for it." According to his website biography, Dr. Phil McGraw has "single-handedly galvanized millions of people to 'get real' about their own behavior and create a more positive life." Like Judge Judy, Dr. Phil is a successful author. His first three books (*Life Strategies*, *Relationship Rescue*, and *Self Matters*) have all been best-sellers, with

Self Matters the top-selling nonfiction book in 2002 (Hollandsworth 2003). Dr. Phil was reputedly paid $10 million for his latest book, *The Ultimate Weight Solution: The Seven Keys to Weight Loss Freedom* (Hollandsworth 2003), equal to the advance paid to former president Bill Clinton for his book (Beam 2003) and $2 million more than the advance paid to Hillary Clinton for her book, *Living History* (Gillespie 2003).

For an hour each weekday afternoon, Dr. Phil offers advice on "lifestyle" issues—that is, relationships, sex, parenting, addictions, money, careers. Each show highlights the "cases" of three to five different people, often revolving around a central theme (giving advice—being too honest, not being honest; girl bullies; self-esteem and plastic surgery; and so on). Every case starts with a short video segment that provides information about the case and ends with a question to Dr. Phil (for example, "Dr. Phil, I resolve to stop this shopping addition. Can you please help me?" or "Dr. Phil, how can I help my daughter choose the right friends so I'm not raising a future bully?"). Dr. Phil then engages the client in discussion in front of the studio audience. Few segments last more than ten to fifteen minutes. In the closing minutes of the show, Dr. Phil offers the viewing audience a few words of prescriptive wisdom. For example, at the end of a show on keeping resolutions, he notes, "It's important that you choose the right thing to resolve to do. You want to resolve to change issues; you don't want to resolve to change symptoms, or topics. Deal with the real issues and program yourself for success. It's all about lifestyle. You've got to change what you're doing to change what you're getting" (aired January 5, 2004). Sometimes he polls the studio audience about whether they think a client will be successful ("How about the gum chewer? Do you think he's going to get real, raise your hand."). To applause, he walks to his wife, Robin, who has been sitting in the audience, and together they walk off the set holding hands.

Similarities and Differences between the Two Programs

Certainly there are significant differences in a talk-formatted program hosted by a psychologist and a courtroom presided over by a judge. By training and personality, these two performers are vastly different. They have different realms of expertise, different goals, and different projected outcomes. The dysfunctional family or individual chosen to appear on *Dr. Phil* undoubtedly has different expectations than the feuding neighbors selected to appear in Judge Judy's courtroom. Audience expectations differ as well. We expect Dr. Phil to counsel and give relational advice, and Judge Judy to rule on the legal matters that bring litigants before her bench.

But despite differences, there are profound similarities. Both feature "real people, real problems" in the words of *Judge Judy's* promotion. In both programs, the host's pronouncements on what people—clients and litigants and by extension all others—should do and how they should do it are the centerpieces of the show. Both deliver their dictates in forceful language, reject ambiguity, insist on agreement, and solicit obedience. Judge Judy is as loud, aggressive, and "in-your-face" as Dr. Phil is, at times more so. Almost every article on Dr. Phil notes his "straight-talking" style. One of his fans summarizes Dr. Phil's appeal: "Dr. Phil, to me, is like somebody's conscience. He says the things that everybody wants to say, but doesn't dare. He's so brutally honest. I just love it" (Cass 2003). And in a "spat" between television judges, Judge Wapner, formerly of *The People's Court*, is reported as saying, "She is not portraying a judge as I view a judge should act. She's discourteous, and she's abrasive. She's not slightly insulting. She's insulting in capital letters." Not to be outdone, Judge Judy supposedly replied, "I refuse to engage in similar mud-slinging. I don't know where or by whom Judge Wapner was raised. But my parents taught me when you don't have something nice to say about someone, say nothing. Clearly, Judge Wapner was absent on the day that lesson was taught" (Judge Judy's $100M Windfall, n.p.).

What's Your Point?

Hopefully by now you—the readers—are saying, "Yes, but ..." or "Wait a minute, you're forgetting ..." or "But it's only entertainment ..." I am aware that I am slighting many factors that shape these programs: the selection of guests and issues, the scripting of dialogue, the time frame and formulas that structure action, the role of the studio audience—all are vitally important to the decision making of producers, the motives of the guests, and the shape of the final product.

For this short chapter, however, I want to bracket those concerns and address three questions regarding these two programs: First, looking at the programs themselves: Are principles of ethical communication, especially those related to advice-giving in relational communication, reinforced or violated? Second, realizing the potential of mediated representations to shape perceptions and behaviors, I move beyond the programs to consider a second question: Is the style of advice-giving enacted in these programs ethically appropriate if used in real-life situations, especially interpersonal relationships? This question does not seek a causal link between observation and action; rather it raises issues of what consumers might do with what they see, the ethicality of translating practices across domains, in this case from public entertainment to private relationships, without serious reflection on the differences between the domains. Third, I return to query the principles used to evaluate the ethics of advice-giving: Do the ethics of advice-giving in relationships discourage, or even prohibit, direct and blunt denunciation of behavior that is dangerous, dysfunctional, or destructive? Is there a societal need or justification for behavior that, given these principles, seems unethical?

Principles of Ethical Communication

The National Communication Association (NCA) recently developed a credo for communication ethics, distilling ethical principles from teaching and research across the discipline. Endorsed by the association, the credo describes ethical communication as that which "enhances human worth and dignity by fostering truthfulness, fairness, responsibility, personal integrity, and respect for self and others" and includes nine principles that ought to guide communication "within and across contexts, cultures, channels, and media." Although all nine principles are valuable, the following seem especially pertinent to the topic of interpersonal advice-giving: "We strive to understand and respect other communicators before evaluating and responding to their messages"; "We promote communication climates of caring and mutual understanding that respect the unique needs and characteristics of individual communication"; and "We condemn communication that degrades individuals and humanity through distortion, intolerance, intimidation, coercion, hatred, and violence" (Johannesen 2002, pp. 203–4).

Instructional materials reiterate these principles. Basic course textbooks, for example, emphasize empathic listening as essential to an individual's development and critical to establishing and maintaining healthy and positive relationships. When we listen to another, we communicate to that person that we value them; we are mindful of them. Julia Wood (2003) observes, "Mindfulness enhances communication in two ways. First, attending mindfully to others increases our understanding of how they feel and think about what they are saying. In addition, mindfulness can enhance others' communication. When we really listen to others, they engage us more fully, elaborate their ideas, and express themselves in greater depth" (p. 189). In addition to being mindful, effective listening requires that we suspend judgment and attempt to understand the other person's perspective (pp. 206–7). Thus, the ethical communicator is instructed to be a careful and nonjudgmental listener, to seek via that listening an accurate and empathic understanding of the other's perspective, and to convey a respect for the other as an equal participant in the communication situation.

Theorists and researchers in communication ethics support these principles as well. For example, most stress that communicators be respectful of others, that imposition of authority should be used only for the good of the other, not to maintain power at the other's expense. Communication should be dialogic rather than monologic. According to Richard L. Johannesen (2002), monologic communication is

> characterized in varying degrees by self-centeredness, deception, pretensions, display, appearance, artifice, using, profit, unapproachableness, seduction, domination, exploitation, and manipulation. Communicators manipulate others for their own selfish ends. They aim at power over people and view them as objects for enjoyment or as things through which to profit.… In monologue we are primarily concerned with what others think of us, with prestige and authority, with display of our own feelings, with display of power, and with molding others in our own image.… Other persons are viewed as "things" to be exploited solely for

the communicator's self-serving purpose; they are not taken seriously as persons. (p. 60)

In contrast, dialogic communicators engage the other, listen to the other, and refuse to employ power at the other's expense. Even in unequal role relationships, dialogue is both desired and possible. As Johannesen (2002), referencing Martin Buber, notes, "Dialogue to some degree is possible in virtually any realm of human interaction.... Many role-oriented relationships, such as student-teacher, doctor-patient, therapist-client, and parishioner-pastor, can be conducted authentically in partial mutuality with dialogic attitude between participants" (p. 64).

There is general agreement that ethical communication is open and dialogic, that each party listens to the other, respects the other, and avoids manipulation of the other. Communicators enter the communication situation with an open mind rather than with predetermined judgments, and refuse to label or stereotype the other via verbal or nonverbal behaviors. Communicators do not use power or authority to control the other. As is evident, these principles are not separate points in a "checklist" but an integrated attitude of ethical engagement in all types of situations—especially in interpersonal or relational situations.

Advice-Giving on *Dr. Phil* and *Judge Judy*

The first question focuses on the communication enacted by the hosts of these two programs: Are principles of ethical communication, especially those related to advice-giving in relational communication, reinforced or violated? To explore this question, I've selected several dialogues from the programs that feature typical exchanges between the hosts and guests.

Dr. Phil

The following exchange occurs between Dr. Phil and a woman who insists she is afraid to use or answer the phone in her home, although she has no problem answering the phone in her workplace:

Dr. Phil: But isn't that just kind of giving you permission to sit on the sidelines? It's just kind of like saying, "I don't have much to offer, so I don't have to play."

Client: Probably.

Dr. Phil: And I know that sounds like—that, well, that's really putting yourself down, but the truth is that it's also amazingly lazy.

Client: That's true.

Dr. Phil: The rest of us have to get out there and contribute and do and take what we have and try to contribute something, but you give yourself permission to take yourself out of the game.

Client: That's true.

(Stewart 2004, January 13)

Several "violations" are evident in this short exchange. While Dr. Phil seemingly asks questions, suggesting his willingness to hear the client, his questions are in reality monologic statements in the guise of dialogue. The client is channeled into one- or two-word agreements with his diagnosis. Clearly, Dr. Phil has already determined the appropriate answer and is seeking agreement with his judgment. This practice is typical of his interaction with clients. For example, on another program, "Ask Dr. Phil," when he questions a mother who after four years is still grieving over her only daughter leaving home for college, he asks, "Do you think that you can smother someone? Do you think you can overinvest in someone? Do you think you can, in fact, create the very thing you fear, which is driving her away from you and out of your life by smothering her and choking her with what you're calling love?" (Stewart 2004, January 13). What can a client say to this manipulation into agreement, to being labeled and stereotyped as an overprotective and neurotic mother and expected to concur?

In a show on making and keeping resolutions, "Resolutions Revisited," Dr. Phil works with Bobbie, who admits to being addicted to shopping and eBay. Keep in mind that Bobbie's addiction is over seven years old. Bobbie declared bankruptcy in 1997, when she was $22,000 in debt. Today she is $15,000 in debt. Dr. Phil reviews with her (and the audience) the five steps to creating a successful action plan and then says:

Dr. Phil: You need to set this up so you cannot cheat. You've got credit cards?

Bobbie: No, I don't.

Dr. Phil: How do you buy on eBay?

Bobbie: My husband's credit card.

Dr. Phil: Then you've got … then, I mean … (Turning to the audience.) Really, did they tell you all that I was stupid? (Laughter.) You have credit cards, correct?

Bobbie: Correct.

Dr. Phil: (Mimicking Bobbie.) "No, I don't." Then how're you buying on eBay? "I have credit cards; they're my husband's." You need to burn the bridges behind you. Get rid of the money, get rid of the credit cards. Create accountability where you can't do this. If you really want to change this, the resolution needs to be your self-esteem and the bridge you burn needs to be your ability to transgress against yourself and your husband. And if you just have this need to give to yourself? Give yourself exercise, give yourself attention; give yourself the things you really need. And if you truly want to fill that hole in your heart that makes this addiction possible, spend the next ninety days giving to other people. Get off your butt in front of that computer and get on your feet at a soup kitchen or at your church. Do something. The best way to get what you want is to give it away. (Stewart 2004, January 5)

Certainly here, as will be seen in Judge Judy as well, Dr. Phil has the role of an expert whose knowledge is intended to diagnose situations and prescribe remedies. However, such unequal degrees of power and knowledge ought not, communication ethics would say, to result in the arrogance of prefabricated judgments and manipulation of the other into accord with those judgments.

Not only does Dr. Phil violate the tenets of ethical communication, he violates those of therapy as well:

Psychotherapy isn't about the practitioner finding the right answer, but about guiding the patient to an answer and helping him deal with it appropriately…. "The problem with psychologists practicing advice-giving is that it's not the role of the psychologist to give advice," explains Sean Kenny, Ph.D., a psychotherapist based in Grand Rapids, Michigan. "As a therapist, I need to be humble enough to realize that I don't know you, what really makes you tick or what you should do with your life." (Paul 2003)

Judge Judy

In a typical dialogue from Judge Judy, we see the same violations of ethical communication, perhaps even more evident. In the exchange below, from "Parsons v. Arthur," the plaintiff claims that he's been harmed by an article written by a journalism student who wrote that the plaintiff smoked marijuana. The article resulted in a dispute between the plaintiff and the mother of his children over visitation rights. The legal case is obviously about harm done by possible libel, not about the children or visitation rights. Yet Judge Judy interjects the following comments:

> Judge Judy: How many children do you have with this girlfriend?
>
> Plaintiff: Three.
>
> Judge Judy: How old are they?
>
> Plaintiff: Five, four, and two.
>
> Judge Judy: Didn't feel like making a commitment to marriage?
>
> Plaintiff: No.
>
> Judge Judy: Or, don't you believe in marriage?
>
> Plaintiff: Not that I don't believe in it, it just wasn't the right person.
>
> Judge Judy: I understand that; I don't understand five, four, and two.
>
> Plaintiff: I was just young and made mistakes.
>
> Judge Judy: Just for my own information. I always just find this sort of interesting. You're not prepared to make the commitment because she wasn't the right person for you, but was the right person to have three children with.
>
> (Douthit 2004, January 8)

The exchange is typical of Judge Judy's communicative style. Like Dr. Phil, she asks questions intended to solicit the responses she desires and turn the conversation into a platform for her monologue on moral character.

Because litigants on *Judge Judy* are often dysfunctional, under-educated, or under- or unemployed, they become legitimate targets for the host's chastisement and the audience's disdain. The implicit message is that it is acceptable to treat those one believes to be socially or morally inferior with condescension at best and rudeness at worst. The audience apparently finds it entertaining to watch Judge Judy berate people she considers marginal or unworthy members of society.

In another example, from "Kamerman v. Beck," Judge Judy turns to the defendant and says, "If you live until you're a hundred, you're not going to be as smart as I am. That's just the way God crafted you" (Douthit 2004, January 8). In yet another exchange, in "Jones v. Eberhart," where one woman (the ex-girlfriend) accuses another woman (the current girlfriend) of torching her car, Judge Judy pronounces (after asking how many children the ex-girlfriend has by the ex-boyfriend):

> I don't know whether you torched her car or not. She doesn't have any proof that you torched her car. But I'm telling this to the two of you: The only thing that makes you look more foolish than devoting the best years of your life to a loser, who doesn't pay child support, who cheats on you, who doesn't work regularly, is to be angry at each other. What are you angry at each other for? It's stupid. It's stupid. He's the bad guy. Both of you are just dumb to hang around him. Don't you understand that a man who fathers two children he doesn't support is a loser? (Douthit 2004, January 9)

Like Dr. Phil but even more so, Judge Judy uses predetermined categories to label the problems of her litigants and apply stereotypes that resonate with her audience. She seems particularly fond of terms like "stupid" and "irresponsible" to characterize litigants' behavior.

In "Kamerman v. Beck," Judge Judy feels it appropriate to call someone a liar:

> Judge Judy: I don't believe a word you say.
>
> Older woman: Why not?
>
> Judge Judy: Because I don't believe a word you say.... I don't believe you, because that's my job, because I've been doing this job for a very long time, because you're his mother. I don't believe you. Do you understand?

Older woman: No.

Judge Judy: Well I'm sorry. I explained it as best as I can. Mull it over for a while. Maybe you'll get it. (Douthit 2004, January 8)

Because of her power and authority she considers it appropriate to be rude, to interrupt, and to accuse litigants of lying and manipulation. But litigants are expected to accept her rudeness and accusations meekly, deferring to her moral superiority. In no case are they allowed to answer back or defend themselves.

As with Dr. Phil, it is evident that Judge Judy violates the tenets of ethical communication as she fails to listen, to convey respect for others, labels and stereotypes, manipulates others, and uses them as a platform for her monologues on appropriate behavior.

Summary

Clearly there is a disconnect between what has been defined as ethical communication and the typical practices of these authority figures. Even infrequent listeners can very quickly predict where Judge Judy and Dr. Phil will go with their advice, moral dictates, and rulings. Those who read their books recognize the predetermined solutions that will be tailored to respond to virtually any problem. In fact, a steady viewer becomes suspicious that cases are carefully chosen to provide a foil for favorite issues that appeal to the hosts and viewing audiences. Certainly clients and litigants must know what they are signing on for when they agree to be on the show. Thus, they are not, or should not, be unaware that they will be used to further support the formulas that guide the program and enhance the images of the hosts as aggressive and blunt. Moreover, the demands of the television medium reinforce these tendencies, requiring the hosts to pronounce rather than listen, to simplify and "bottom-line" and quickly resolve problems rather than discover the complexities of each case.

As noted above, these programs are intended as entertainment, not as sober instruction in advice-giving. Thus, analysis of the programs is not in itself insightful; practices identified are predetermined choices of topic, style, and interaction by both producers and the hosts themselves, choices that translate into the best ratings for the shows and the advertisers whose revenue supports the shows. A more serious question is not what these entertainers do, but what consumers do with the behaviors they see enacted. Do these remain in a separate category called "unreal," or unconsciously cross boundaries into communicative behaviors in relational situations?

The Translation of Advice-Giving Styles into Everyday-Life Situations

The second question posed to these shows is whether the advice-giving styles enacted by Dr. Phil and Judge Judy should be emulated in other contexts: Is the style of advice-giving enacted in these programs ethically appropriate if used in real-life situations, especially in interpersonal relationships? Do relational expectations and assumptions in our culture allow for direct, blunt criticisms of the dysfunctional behaviors of others? Can we "Dr. Phil" our friend who is asking us to support his engaging in yet one more manipulative relationship? Should we "Judge Judy" our colleague, telling her that she is stupid for continuing to enable her husband's addictive behaviors? Would friendships be ruined and familial relationships strained by the style of talk we see daily on these and other programs? If we listen closely to Dr. Phil and Judge Judy, they often advise guests to deal with relational problems in the same manner; for example, "Just tell him to butt out," or "Tell her she is stupid." Thus, hosts encourage audiences to assume that the style enacted in the programs is one that is feasible for their relationships.

One approach to ethics, often called virtue ethics, suggests that rather than establishing and following rules or principles, a person should define and strive to be of good character. As James Q. Wilson (1993) explains, "When we describe people we admire, we do not often use the word 'moral.' Instead, we invoke the term 'character,' by which we mean both a distinctive combination of personal qualities by which someone is known (that is, a personality), and moral strength or integrity" (p. 240). And as he goes on to explain, good character is not a life lived according to a set of rules but a life lived in an appropriate balance of concerns (p. 243).

Principles are valuable guidelines, to be sure, but they cannot tell us precisely what we should do in a variety of contexts and situations. If we are a person of integrity, however, we can ask ourselves how that quality can best be exemplified in the given situation and act accordingly. A person of integrity will intuitively respond in an ethical manner because integrity has become part of her character and she would find it unthinkable to act in violation of that virtue. Wilson (1993) explains, "When, as inevitably happens, we confront circumstances that require us to choose among our moral senses or confuse us as to whether there is a moral dimension to the problem, the good guy, the nice person, engages in an inner dialogue about what is required of him" (p. 241).

Thus, we can learn ethical behavior by observing and emulating role models of virtuous behavior. Rosalind Hursthouse (1999) summarizes what she calls a "first premise" of virtue ethics: "An action is right if it is what a virtuous agent would characteristically (i.e., acting in character) do in the circumstances" (p. 28). Those who advocate teaching ethics through literature, for example, argue that as we see role models of integrity, responsibility, or truthfulness acting in their narrative situations, we learn what those virtues mean in a practical manner, in lived situations and relationships. Thus, "What would Jesus do?" or "What would my mother say?" or "How would my pastor respond?" are appropriate guidelines for determining ethical behavior by considering the probable actions of a role model whose moral character we respect.

Jason Kawal (2003) suggests two cautions to this approach: one must be sure the person being emulated is truly a moral exemplar, and one must inquire if the behavior being emulated is translatable to the new situation (p. 150). For example, what a virtuous law enforcement officer would do in a criminal situation might not be translatable to what one would do in a conflict among friends. Both the relationship of the participants and the nature of the situation are different.

So the question is whether or not these self-appointed relational experts, Dr. Phil and Judge Judy, are enacting virtues that could or should be emulated in our own relationships. (Keep in mind that we know only the moral character of the media-constructed and marketed personas, not the character of the real people.) While Dr. Phil and Judge Judy are certainly rude and self-serving by the principles of ethical communication outlined above, they also seem committed to campaigning for virtuous conduct. They continually rail against lying, cheating, laziness, and lack of relational/familial responsibility, and are very consistent in their articulation of these virtues and the problems caused by their guests' lack of character. They continually point out the necessity for moral evaluation of one's behavior and its effect on others. If we decide that Dr. Phil and Judge Judy can serve as moral exemplars (and we each may decide differently), the virtue approach suggests that we should be comfortable doing "as they would do" when confronted with similar human problems. If we have strong convictions about what others should or should not do, we should not hesitate to express those convictions as forcefully as do our role models.

If we do anoint Dr. Phil and Judge Judy as moral exemplars of advice-giving, we still have to attend to Kawal's (2003) second caution, whether or not their behaviors can be translated from their situation into real-life relational encounters. One immediate problem is that Dr. Phil and Judge Judy also reside atop the ladder of a social and intellectual hierarchy; they are experts in their respective fields, highly successful and well-paid professionals who, by virtue of their positions, are accorded respect. A second problem is that they are acting in situations deliberately constructed to showcase their moral and intellectual expertise, with guests chosen because of their willingness to submit to their authority. But if these experts were instead ordinary people—husbands, wives, mothers, fathers, siblings, friends—and those they engaged were their families or friends, would emulating Dr. Phil and Judge Judy's confrontational style lead to appreciation or anger, would relationships be strengthened or fractured? If the situation were a family meal, a friendly social hour, a colleague asking for advice over coffee, would the content and the manner of speaking be appropriate?

Those who have researched advice-giving in friendships would raise some objections to the Dr. Phil and Judge Judy treatment. Brant R. Burleson, Terrance L. Albrecht, and Irwin G. Sarason (1994) note that social support, of which advice-giving is one type, has a "moral foundation." That is, "supportive actions frequently display the highest expressions of the human spirit: altruism, charity, help, caring, rescuing, kindness, comfort, and love. Even 'supportive' actions stemming from nonaltruistic motives—those performed out of obligation or in an effort to foster dependency—have moral and ethical overtones" (p. xiv).

We must not forget that social support and advice-giving are provided within the context of a relationship. Offering advice is always about more than the content of the advice; it also communicates about the nature of a relationship, and as such has profound relational implications. Daena J. Goldsmith and Kristin Fitch (1997) find that in advice-giving "information is never *just* information" (p. 461). Inherent in giving and taking advice are three very powerful tensions. First, in relationships where friends see themselves as relative equals, advice is often viewed as "helpful and caring," while in other relationships advice is viewed as "butting in," implying that the recipient of the advice is "less worthy in some way than the giver" (pp. 461, 463). A second tension in advice-giving is one of support versus honesty. "Should an advice giver provide his or her *honest* opinion, even though it may disagree with the recipient's point of view, or should he or she be *supportive* by agreeing with the recipient's point of view?" (pp. 465–6). And finally, after the advice is given, what are the expectations that the recipient will actually follow the advice? If the advice recipient feels obligated to follow the advice, she risks losing her autonomy. On the other hand, if the advice recipient does not follow the advice offered, she may be viewed as disrespectful or ungrateful. As Goldsmith and Fitch point out, "In this third dilemma, we see how the meanings and implications of advice extend beyond the informational and emotional support it may provide for the advice recipient. Seeking advice and choosing whether to take advice involve enactments of *respect* (or disrespect) and *gratitude* (or ingratitude) for what the advice symbolizes about the relationship between adviser and advisee" (p. 470).

In sum, even if we can applaud Dr. Phil and Judge Judy's forthright "in-your-face" style of criticism, the hierarchical relationship (they are experts speaking to those who have less expertise) and the nature of their connection to the other (they are strangers and not friends or family) suggest that emulation of this style is fraught with potential for hurt feelings and misunderstanding.

Evaluating Communication Ethics Principles

But where does this leave us in our real-life situations? Don't some things need to be said, and isn't a friend someone who will tell us the truth, however unpleasant we may find it? The final question, then, reevaluates the ethical principles advocated by communication scholars: Do the ethics of advice-giving in relationships discourage or even prohibit direct and blunt denunciation of behavior that is dangerous, dysfunctional, or destructive? Dissonance is clear: in answering the first question, it is apparent that Dr. Phil and Judge Judy consistently violate agreed-upon standards of ethical communication in their advice-giving situations. Moreover, in answering the second question, it is equally apparent that enactment of their advice-giving styles in real-life relationships would violate what most people assume to be relational norms, the responsibility to be supportive of others' decisions, the desire for empathic and nonjudgmental listening.

It is necessary to now consider to what degree the principles, and thus the assumptions and expectations, of ethical communication might be flawed. If those principles prohibit us from challenging, on moral grounds, the behaviors of others, if being a friend or family member does not allow us to clearly speak out when someone is doing something wrong, or if we feel they are violating relational norms when they speak out against our behavior, then perhaps what we consider to be ethical communication is not really ethical after all.

"Civility" is an often-invoked ethical principle that tends to be equated with respectful language and empathic listening. Stephen J. Carter (1999), in a book aptly titled *Civility*, provides a different take on the concept. He argues that "civility does not require a suspension of moral judgment and must not make us reluctant to impose moral judgments on each other" (p. 213). Carter goes on to argue that, contrary to popular opinion, civility may actually require, rather than prohibit, the criticism of others:

> In fact, sometimes it is uncivil not to criticize others. One of the sacrifices that love of neighbor requires of us is the willingness to accept the anger and dislike that often result when we offer even constructive criticism of others. In the Jewish tradition, many scholars argue that correcting the

errors of others is an obligation. In the Christian tradition, Jesus preached love for others but still criticized people—often quite harshly—for their transgressions against God's law. (p. 217)

Obviously Dr. Phil and Judge Judy aren't civil if we use the commonsense understanding of the term, but might be called civil by Carter's definition. And if, as he suggests, it is uncivil to avoid engagement on moral issues, principles of ethical communication ought to reflect this need and encourage such conversations even if they might result in hurt feelings.

Although Carter (1999) argues that we have a responsibility to engage in moral discussions, he also insists that such discussions be characterized by respect for others: "We show respect for ourselves and others when we trouble ourselves to think carefully about what we say, rather than grabbing for the first expletive that comes to mind" (p. 282). If we are careful about our talk, we also must be careful to listen: "Civility requires that we listen to others with knowledge of the possibility that they are right and we are wrong" (p. 282). Certainly Carter would not recommend that we engage in such moral discussions lightly or without stopping to count the costs. If we confront a friend about inappropriate or dysfunctional behavior, that person may no longer want to be our friend. And if they confront us, we may retreat in anger and feel betrayed. But while we must count the costs of confrontation, he would argue, we also must consider the costs of failure to confront. And if we determine that despite the costs there is a need for more directness and confrontation in our relationships, then our principles of ethical communication ought to be revised to support that need. One additional principle from the NCA credo (Johannesen 2002, pp. 203–4) usually assumed to apply to public communication might be of help in reshaping our expectations in relational situations: "We are committed to the courageous expression of personal convictions in pursuit of fairness and justice." Certainly it requires courage to speak out in relational situations when we are expected to sympathize, and certainly such outspokenness, as Carter maintains, should be done in humility and with great care. But such courage should be among the virtues we define as inherent to ethical communicators.

Conclusion

This study of Dr. Phil and Judge Judy and their style of giving advice raises important issues for ethical communication. Perhaps we can agree that ethical communication precludes hasty and harsh judgments and knee-jerk rude responses. Certainly ethical communication involves listening to and respecting another's personhood. But should ethical communication discourage engagement on moral issues in personal, professional, and communal life? Can one listen respectfully and empathically and still be forceful in disagreement with what is being said? Should we point out self-serving justifications and inappropriate behaviors exhibited by those to whom we are listening? Can we be caring and open and at the same time refuse to be coerced into silent agreement because speaking out would seem rude? Do we have a moral responsibility as members of relationships, families, communities to confront dysfunctional behaviors?

Perhaps the popularity of *Dr. Phil* and *Judge Judy* and similar programs are indicative of a societal hunger for plain speaking about things that are important. Mediated popular culture seems to provide us with only two choices: either avoidance of moral debate out of respect for individual differences or moral debate engaged in anger, with rudeness, vehemence, and personal attack. The midpoint between the two extremes, engaging others in a respectful but forceful manner, with firm insistence on clarifying the moral dimensions of a problem, adamantly refusing to condone excuses, the courage to state our convictions clearly—such would not make for good entertainment (or mediated politics) but might make for a better quality of relationships from interpersonal to global. Thus, while it may not be desirable to declare Dr. Phil and Judge Judy role models of ethical advice-giving, they do provide valuable examples, rich in potential for reflection on our own and others' conduct and ripe for discussion about possible flaws in our understandings of ethical communication.

Notes

1. I use italics to refer to the programs, *Dr. Phil* and *Judge Judy*; roman to refer to the media personalities, Dr. Phil and Judge Judy; and their given names, Phil McGraw and Judy Sheindlin, to refer to the real people.
2. As Mike Farrell (2000) of the California State Commission on Judicial Performance notes, the organization exists "to protect the public from exactly the kind of thoughtless, mean-spirited and destructive behavior that pours forth from the 'courtrooms' of our television every day ... the rude, contentious and flagrantly biased histrionics that are the hallmarks of these shows are in direct contradiction to the standards mandated in the Code of Judicial Ethics" (n.p.).

References

Albiniak, P. (2003). Judy has bench strength. *Broadcasting and Cable* 133(17): 15. Retrieved November 18, 2003, from InfoTrac Expanded Academic ASAP database at St. Cloud State University: http://web6.infotrac.galegroup.com. itw/infomark/1/1/1/purl=rc6_EAIM.

Beam, Alex (2003). Alex Beam; From NASA to BU, and still seeing stars. *Boston Globe*, July 5. Retrieved April 30, 2004, from LexisNexis Academic Universe database at St. Cloud State University: http://web.lexis-nexis.com/universe.

Burke, K. (1974). *Philosophy of literary form: Studies in symbolic action*, 3rd ed. Berkeley: University of California Press.

Burkeman, O. (2003, January 3). Move over Oprah. *The Guardian (London)*. Retrieved April 30, 2004, from LexisNexis Academic Universe database at St. Cloud State University: http://web.lexis-nexis.com/universe.

Burleson, B. R., T. L. Albrecht, & I. G. Sarason (eds.). (1994). *Communication of social support: Messages, interactions, relationships, and community*. Thousand Oaks, CA: Sage.

Carter, S. J. (1999). *Civility*. New York: Perennial.

Cass, D. (2003). Dr. Phil is a softie. *Slate*, October 2. Retrieved November 28, 2003, from LexisNexis Academic Universe database at St. Cloud State University: http://web.lexis-nexis.com/universe.

Douthit, R. (executive producer and director). (2004). *Judge Judy*, January 8, January 9. Los Angeles: Big Ticket Television (Paramount/Viacom Co.).

Farrell, M. (2000). There's disorder in the court—and television stands accused. *Human Rights Watch California*. Retrieved April 28, 2004, from www.hrwcalifornia.org/Mike%20Farrell/tveditorial.htm.

Gillespie, M. (2003). Hillary Clinton remains polarizing figure. *Gallup Organization*, June 6. Retrieved April 30, 2004, from LexisNexis Academic Universe database at St. Cloud State University: http://web.lexis-nexis.com/universe.

Goldsmith, D. J., & K. Fitch. (1997). The normative context of advice as social support. *Human Communication Research* 23: 454–76.

Hollandsworth, S. (2003). Love thy self-help. *Texas Monthly*, September. Retrieved November 28, 2003, from LexisNexis Academic Universe database at St. Cloud State University: http://web.lexis-nexis.com/universe.

Hursthouse, R. (1999). *On virtue ethics*. New York: Oxford University Press.

Jagodozinki, Jan. (2003). The perversity of (real)ity TV: A symptom of our times. *Journal for the Psychoanalysis of Culture and Society* 8: 320–31. Retrieved November 29, 2003, from InfoTrac Expanded Academic ASAP database at St. Cloud State University: http://web6.infotrac.galegroup.com.itw/infomark/1/1/1/purl=rc6_EAIM.

Johannesen, R. L. (2002). *Ethics in human communication*, 5th ed. Prospect Heights, IL: Waveland.

Judge Judy's $100M windfall. (2002). *New York Post*, December 31. Retrieved April 30, 2004, from LexisNexis Academic Universe database at St. Cloud State University: http://web.lexis-nexis.com/universe.

Kawal, J. (2003). Should we do what Buffy would do? In J. South (ed.), *Buffy the vampire slayer and philosophy: Fear and trembling in Sunnydale* (pp. 149–59). Chicago: Open Court Press.

Kurtz, H. (1996). *Hot air: All talk, all the time*. New York: Basic Books.

Lowney, K. S. (1999). *Baring our souls: TV talk shows and the religion of recovery*. New York: Aldine de Gruyter.

Newcomb, H. (2002). Introduction. In B. Timberg, *Television talk: A history of the TV talk show* (pp. ix–xv). Austin: University of Texas Press.

Paul, Pamela. (2003). Dear reader, get a life: Today's talk show therapists and edgy advice columnists are bolder, and possibly more effective, than genteel advisers of newspapers past (Bully Pulpit). *Psychology Today* 36(4): 56–63. Retrieved July 28, 2003, from InfoTrac Expanded Academic ASAP database at St. Cloud State University: http://web6.infotrac.galegroup.com.itw/infomark/1/1/1/purl=rc6_HRCA.

Peyser, M. (2002). Paging Doctor Phil. *Newsweek*, September 2. Retrieved November 28, 2003, from LexisNexis Academic Universe database at St. Cloud State University: http://web.lexis-nexis.com/universe.

Shattuc, J. M. (1997). *The talking cure: TV talk shows and women*. New York: Routledge.

Stewart, C. P. (executive producer). (2004). *Dr. Phil*, January 5, 13. Los Angeles: Harpo Production Inc. (Paramount).

Timberg, B. M. (2002). *Television talk: A history of the TV talk show*. Austin: University of Texas Press.

Wilson, J. Q. (1993). *The moral sense*. New York: Free Press.

Wood, Julia. (2003). *Communication in our lives*, 3rd ed. Belmont, CA: Wadsworth/Thomson Learning.

CONTRIBUTORS ━━━━━━━━━━━━━━━━━━

Jeffery L. Bineham (Ph.D., Purdue University, 1986) is a professor of rhetoric in the Department of Communication Studies at St. Cloud State University, Minnesota. He teaches classes in rhetorical theory and criticism, communication ethics, and argumentation. His research interests are in the rhetorical dimensions of popular culture, especially in relation to religious and political discourse, and in the philosophy of rhetoric. His work has appeared in *Philosophy and Rhetoric, Communication Monographs, Communication Education, Communication Studies, Western Journal of Communication, Southern Communication Journal, Journal of Communication and Religion*, and *Communication Reports*.

Greg Carlson (M.A., California State University Dominguez Hills, 1997) is currently a doctoral student at North Dakota State University and an Instructor in the Communication Studies and Theatre Art Department, Concordia College, Moorhead, Minnesota. His teaching and research interests are in Film and Cinema Studies, Film Production, Television Production, Telecommunication, and History of Film and Literature.

Jon A. Hess (Ph.D., University of Minnesota, 1996) is an associate professor in the Department of Communication at the University of Missouri-Columbia. His research interests focus on

communication in personal relationships. Of particular interest are issues of closeness and distance in relationships, as well
as ethical issues in interpersonal communication. His research
has been published in journals such as *Human Communication
Research* and *Journal of Social and Personal Relationships* as well
as being publicized in major newspapers and magazines. He is
currently a member of the editorial board of *Journal of Social and
Personal Relationships*.

Phyllis M. Japp (Ph.D., University of Nebraska, 1986) is an associate professor in the Department of Communication Studies at
the University of Nebraska-Lincoln, where she teaches contemporary rhetorical theory and criticism, cultural studies, health
communication, and communication ethics. She has authored a
number of essays, most utilizing narrative theory and focusing
on public and mediated discourses. She is co-editor of a recent
book on environmental communication and popular culture
and of a forthcoming book on narrative and health communication. She has served on the editorial boards of a number of
communication studies journals.

Debra K. Japp (Ph.D., University of Nebraska, 1989) is a professor of Communication Studies at St. Cloud State University
(Minnesota) and the Academic Affairs Coordinator for the Inter
Faculty Organization, the faculty union for the Minnesota state
universities. She teaches courses in persuasion and rhetorical
criticism. Her research interests include media and popular culture, gender communication and political communication.

Jennifer McGee (Ph.D., University of Minnesota, 1998) is an
assistant professor at Aichi Shukutoku University in Nagoya,
Japan, teaching media studies and rhetorical theory. Her research interests include computer-mediated communication
and media fandom.

Mark Meister (Ph.D., University of Nebraska, 1997) is an associate
professor in the Department of Communication at North Da-

kota State University. His primary area of scholarly interest is how politics, popular culture, religion, and international development symbolically manifest nature. He has published articles in such venues as the *Quarterly Journal of Speech, Environmental History, Communication Studies, Communication Research, Mass Communication and Society, Communication Quarterly, Communication Studies, American Indian Quarterly, Environmental Communication Yearbook,* and *Critical Studies in Media Communication.*

Dan T. Molden (Ph.D., University of Minnesota, 1998) is an assistant professor of Communication at Aichi Shukutoku University in Nagoya, Japan. He teaches courses in argumentation theory and rhetorical theory. His research interests include the rhetoric of community shaping (specifically as it applies to the World War II internment camps in the United States) and intercultural argument.

Joy Piazza (M.A., University of Colorado at Denver, 2000) is a doctoral student in the Department of Communication at the University of Missouri-Columbia. Joy conducts research in the areas of
communication ethics, film and television criticism, political communication, and organizational communication. She has taught courses on communication ethics, women's studies, rhetorical communication, public speaking, and mass media.

Diana L. Rehling (Ph.D., University of Nebraska, 1998) is an associate professor in Communication Studies at St. Cloud State University in St. Cloud, Minnesota. Her primary research interest is in the intersection of interpersonal and family communication and public discourse. She teaches in the areas of communication theory, small group communication, and listening.

Jeffrey St. John (Ph.D., University of Washington, 2000) is an assistant professor in the School of Communication Studies at Ohio University. He teaches courses in communication theory, legal and political communication, public deliberation, and free speech. His research interests include legal and public argument, public sphere studies, and communication theory.

Scott Titsworth (Ph.D., University of Nebraska, 1999) is an assistant professor and Basic Course Director in the School of Interpersonal Communication at Ohio University. In addition to directing the basic course, Scott teaches courses in communication theory and research methodology. His research interests focus on issues of instructional communication, communication pedagogy, and popular culture criticism.

Paula S. Tompkins (Ph.D., University of Minnesota, 1987) is Professor of Communication Studies at St. Cloud State University, Minnesota. Paula teaches courses in communication ethics, freedom of speech, apology, and communication. Her research interests include communication ethics, apology, and communication and technology.

INDEX

Toby Miller
General Editor

Popular Culture and Everyday Life is the new place for critical books in cultural studies. The series stresses multiple theoretical, political, and methodological approaches to commodity culture and lived experience by borrowing from sociological, anthropological, and textual disciplines. Each volume develops a critical understanding of a key topic in the area through a combination of thorough literature review, original research, and a student-reader orientation. The series consists of three types of books: single-authored monographs, readers of existing classic essays, and new companion volumes of papers on central topics. Fields to be covered include: fashion, sport, shopping, therapy, religion, food and drink, youth, music, cultural policy, popular literature, performance, education, queer theory, race, gender, and class.

For additional information about this series or for the submission of manuscripts, please contact:

Toby Miller
Department of Cinema Studies
New York University
721 Broadway, Room 600
New York, New York 10003

To order other books in this series, please contact our Customer Service Department:

(800) 770-LANG (within the U.S.)
(212) 647-7706 (outside the U.S.)
(212) 647-7707 FAX

Or browse online by series: